What people are saying about this parenting guide …

Nurturing with Love and Wisdom, Disciplining with Peace and Respect

"This is an excellent, informative and useful book for parents and professionals who work with parents. The writing is accessible and the format is very user friendly. The wisdom and useful examples provide tools and skills that reflect the peace, respect, nurturing and love promised by the title. **One of the best parenting books I've read,** as a Licensed Marriage and Family Therapist; this book is very relevant to the challenging cultural issues children and their parents face in today's world."

~ *Linda Slauson*

"I absolutely love this book and would recommend it to any parent! It has lots of great parenting strategies."

~ *Tiffany Hughes*

"This is the book I have been waiting for! **Diane's thoughtful book is now my 'go to' when I am having a parenting dilemma** or just need a bit of support to reinforce my parenting values. Since purchasing this book, I have used many of Diane's techniques of active listening and conflict resolution to help my children navigate difficult situations with a true sense of love, compassion and responsibility. My family has benefited from my renewed calm that this book has helped me grow and maintain. Diane has beautifully infused her many years of experience as a school psychologist and Living Values educator into this parenting guide. It is full of practical ideas for parents to try when they are facing discipline issues or when trying to help their children navigate this increasingly complex, and often negative, world. I found the section on handling technology specifically useful and my children and I have had very purposeful and meaningful conversations about the benefits and drawbacks of technology use in our lives since reading this section. **I no longer need to be a mommy witch who forbids my child from playing violent or inhumane games on our iPad. This book gave me tools to talk with my son** about the objectionable content I was seeing in many video games in a way he could really appreciate. My son has now learned to only choose games that reflect the values of our family on his own. Even at six years old, he has now learned to be thoughtful about the way violent games normalize cruelty and he is wary of it. If creating a values-based atmosphere in your home is important to you — a place where love, peace, honesty and kindness are cornerstones — then this is the guide book for you."   ~ *Natasha Panzer*

"This guide to parenting is imminently readable and combines philosophical issues (values to live by and how to give love, affection and attention effectively) with practical advice, not only for parents but for teachers, counselors and family therapists. This approach is unique and features tried and true approaches of recent decades (e.g. active listening, positive discipline, logical consequences) as well as advice for dealing with the current troubling increase in violence in the media, video games and the modern issue of cyber bullying. Early in the guide, play is emphasized as a facilitator of joy in the parent and the simple gift of the parent's genuine enjoyment develops the sense of worth and self in the child. There are many specific examples gleaned from Diane Tillman's vast and varied experiences to help the reader learn and apply new interventions. There are plenty of suggestions for dealing with disrespect, problems with siblings, the "I hate you" syndrome, refusing to do homework and household chores, and many more. But **this guide is more than a how-to book, it is a source of inspiration and hope for a more loving and fulfilling relationship with your child."**
          ~ *Sue Cosgrove*

Nurturing with Love and Wisdom, Disciplining with Peace and Respect

... A mindful guide to parenting

Diane G. Tillman

To receive posts on parenting through Facebook from Diane G. Tillman, "like" **www.facebook.com/NurturingwithLoveandWisdom**

Excerpts are taken from *Living Values Parent Groups: A Facilitator Guide* and *LVEP Educator Training Guide*, written by Diane Tillman, with the permission of the publisher, Health Communications, Inc. and with the permission of the Association of Living Values Education International (ALIVE). Excerpts are also taken from *Living Values Activities for Street Children Ages 3–6* and *Living Values Activities for Street Children Ages 11–14*, also written by Diane Tillman.

For more information about Living Values Education: www.livingvalues.net.

Cover design by David Warrick Jones.
Cover photograph of aromatherapy bowls by Yastremska (Bigstock).
Illustrations in Chapter 30 by Joanne Corcoran.
Back-cover photograph of the author by Ary Woodbridge.

Love, peace and respect
rekindle the beauty and strength
of what each of us holds at our core.

~ Contents ~

A Note from the Author

I worked with thousands of parents during two decades as a school psychologist, and had the privilege of guiding a few others outside of my job, sometimes sitting on the steps outside my front door as I responded to a neighbor calling out, "Hey Diane, have a minute?" The minute would turn into many more.

With each parent, I always began by listening closely, to hear the concern and learn what was going well and poorly. I listened, knowing we would discover and explore together which keys were needed to resolve the current dilemma and move forward — to restore balance and harmony to the relationship.

I resigned from my job as a school psychologist in June of 1996 to embark on an international values-education project. I began to write Living Values Activities for toddlers, school-aged children and young adults. Then there were activities for refugee children affected by war and a guide for parent group facilitators. Living Values Education (LVE) grew into a comprehensive values-education approach. Students need many different skills if they are to be able to love values, commit to them, and have the social skills, cognitive discernment and understanding to carry those values with them into their lives. LVE provides methods and activities for educators and caregivers to actively engage and allow young people the opportunity to explore, experience and express twelve universal values.

As the project grew and other educators and psychologists wanted to help train educators around the world to implement Living Values Education, I was asked to write a training guide. Years later, I was still writing. A colleague was deeply concerned about street children and wanted a resource for children three years of age and older living on the streets of South Africa. An LVE colleague in Asia wanted activities for young adults in need of drug rehabilitation, and another wanted a resource for young offenders. Books for at-risk youth and green values were next, the latter completed in time for the United Nations Conference on Sustainable Development, Rio +20, in June of 2012.

Fifteen values-education books later, I have circled the globe many times, teaching and facilitating a process for adults to explore how they can teach children about peace, respect, love, tolerance, cooperation and honesty and develop a values-based atmosphere where values are readily acquired. In addition to some fascinating experiences culturally, I have had the opportunity to really think about why disrespect, corruption and violence are increasing in countries around the world, and how we can optimize helping young people to explore and develop values while building the social and emotional skills to live them.

For years, parents and colleagues have suggested I write a book on parenting. Requests for a parenting book only increased as I became more involved in values education. Parenting is a topic dear to my heart as I love and value children immensely and feel parenting is one of the most important jobs in the world. Each child is unique, a sacred trust — to love, to nurture, to guide, to help be responsible and to keep safe. Children come into the world with their own sense of being and personality. Some grow up easily with love and a little guidance, rarely needing correction. Others challenge parents to understand their needs and cope with their behavior.

This book is more personal than anything I have written before, for it brings together what I have learned over the years as an educational psychologist, a values educator, a lecturer and workshop facilitator on personal development, and a meditator. I have included stories about my experiences to illustrate some of the concepts. I hope you will enjoy reading this book and that you and your family will benefit from exploring, experimenting and playing with these practical ideas. May it make parenting easier, more mindful and enjoyable — and kindle even more balance, love, peace and fulfillment in your life and that of your family.

All good wishes,

Diane

How to Use This Book

Short versions of three chapters on values

Just like children, adults have different learning styles. Some are like artists who enjoy creating and expressing when learning, and others are like professors who want to delve into theory. Some adults like to design bridges while others enjoy building them. I have created a brief version of three chapters on values for those of you with similar learning styles to artists and bridge builders. Feel free to read the short version and go onto the practical parenting chapters. You can always revisit the longer version.

A book and a resource

The second through fifth sections of this book, *Nurturing with Love and Wisdom, Disciplining with Peace and Respect, Healthy Foods for the Mind and Body* and *Taking Care of You*, contain vital building blocks for a positive, nurturing family life that allow children to naturally grow up with the values you model. I hope you will use these sections as a resource, to refer to again and again as you experiment with ideas, attitudes and skills for your parental tool kit and as situations and questions arise. Reflecting and trying out these ideas as you see how your child responds will allow you to make them your own. The sections on *Practicalities in Everyday Life* and *Prevention and Intervention* offer guidelines and activities on a variety of subjects important in today's world. Please do read the chapters on helping children deal with bullying and preventing sexual abuse and drug use. Other topics may also catch your eye.

Section One

Values
in Today's World

~ 1 ~

The Importance of Values

The short version of this chapter!

What two values do you think would change the world if *everyone* lived them? Reflect for a moment…. Peace and respect? Honesty and compassion? Love and courage? Each person may have a different answer, but each one of you is right. If everyone in the world lived just two values, all the time, the world would change completely. Living just two universal values consistently would create values-based homes, schools, organizations, communities and countries around the world.

Our world is in crisis, environmentally, socially and economically. While global turmoil manifests at the physical level, it is really a crisis of values, for the origin is within the hearts and minds of men and women. Values are the essence of who we are as human beings. They powerfully impact what we create in our lives and the world. Living the values of peace, love, respect, honesty, kindness and compassion makes us happy — and creates a world of peace and respect for our children.

The regular version of the chapter

Our world is in crisis, environmentally, socially and economically. To name a few concerns many people hold: Global climate change is endangering the Earth and her oceans. Unkindness and bullying are rampant in many schools and businesses; suicide rates of 11- to 14-year olds are increasing; terrorism and war create fear, havoc and senseless death in many countries; the lack of potable water for one-fifth of the globe's population creates hardship and poor health. The global economy is fragile with many families in distress because of high unemployment rates or low wages.

This crisis has been created by people. While global turmoil manifests at the physical level, it is really a crisis of values, for the origin is within the hearts and minds of men and women. As the constitution of UNESCO so aptly states: "Since wars begin in the minds of men, it is in the minds of men that the defenses of peace must be constructed."

What universal values could have prevented the current set of global problems? Some of the answers are easy. Many pundits point to greed as the cause of economic meltdowns. Honesty and regard for others as well as for the common good would have made a dramatic difference — and they still can. What values would prevent war? Compassion and respect for every person and culture seem obvious, as does peace and cooperation. What values would you add? Each problem of the world can be analyzed for contributing factors, the anti-values at the root of each factor, and the values that would solve the problem.

Imagine all people using the values of kindness, respect and integrity in their daily interactions with their family, friends and at their place of business. What difference would that make in communities and in international relations? What difference would a culture of peace, kindness and respect make in schools and neighborhoods, if every student were empowered to love these values and had the social and emotional skills to live them?

How can we revitalize values in our family, schools, places of work and communities — indeed, in the world? As the late Nelson Mandela said,

"Education is the most powerful weapon you can use to change the world." Education begins in the home.

Values are the essence of who we are as human beings. They powerfully impact what we create in our lives and the world. When we live our values we rekindle the beauty and strength of what each of us holds at our core. Living the values of peace, love, respect, honesty, kindness and compassion would not only create a safe world for all, it would create happiness. As Aristotle noted in his original taxonomy of emotions, happiness is not an emotion, but a result of virtue.

Living values with our family awakens beauty in human interactions. It opens doors to reflection, dialogue, understanding and growth through which loving, safe, respectful spaces are created; spaces in which each individual is understood, valued and enjoyed. It creates a common language of values to help us more easily navigate the challenges of life. What we teach our children becomes woven in the fabric of our family and the larger community. What values do you want to weave into the fabric of life with your family?

~ 2 ~

Young People Used to Acquire Values Easily —
What Happened?

The short version of this chapter!

The parental challenge of helping children and youth acquire and hold positive values is no longer as simple as it was decades ago when being a good role model and relating moral stories was often sufficient. Most children spend less time with their parents than decades ago and are affected by violence in films and videos, and advertisements and peer pressure to own certain things and look a certain way. There is also the influence of negative role models who are admired for their crassness or violence. The vast majority of preteens and teens spend more time with video games and their peers through texting, phones and social media sites than they do with their parents. One lapse of judgment by a tween or teen can have disastrous social consequences through social media sites.

Is it time to change to a culture of values — a culture of peace, love, respect, honesty, kindness and compassion — for the sake of our children, ourselves, all children and our world? We created it, we can change it. Each one of us is important in this process. However, as the world is the way it is, we must simultaneously protect our children and educate them about negative factors. Values are a powerful tool to help us do so.

The regular version of the chapter

The parental challenge of helping children and youth acquire and hold positive values is no longer as simple as it was decades ago when being a good role model and relating moral stories was often sufficient. Several changes in societies around the world have contributed to the decline in acquiring positive values, and the increase in the propensity to admire and be willing to engage in the opposite.

Violence in the media

In the last 30 years, the level of violence in movies and video games has grown tremendously. The glorification of violence, gratuitous violence, cruelty and meanness has desensitized youth to the effect of such actions. It appears to have opened a gateway to the acceptance of disrespect, meanness and revenge as common ways of being. Access to violent media was limited decades ago. There were few violent shows on television, no video games and no DVDs. Most young people spent very little time in front of violent media. Now people can access demeaning video games, videos and movies 24/7.

Less time with parents

In times past, most mothers did not work outside the home and fathers were home for dinner in many countries around the world. The evening meal was family time, a time to talk about the day and inadvertently share cultural mores and values. In today's world, many families do not sit down and share a meal together even a couple of times a week. Watching television or playing video games has replaced conversation and story time for many families. There are greater numbers of single-parent families, increasing the tasks one adult must do to care for her or his children. Some parents bring work home from the office or are accessible through their cell phones. With all of this, and more, one research study from Great Britain found mothers spend an average of eleven minutes a day talking to their children. Fathers averaged seven minutes a day. Eleven minutes communicating with one parent or eighteen minutes relating with both, versus hours with video games, social media and movies? Children need time with their parents — time to feel the joy of being and belonging, time to feel valued and loved, time to learn to be responsible and time to learn about values.

Materialism and greed

With greater prosperity for the general population in many developed countries after World War II, the benefits and glories of materialism were increasingly communicated to the world. The desire to have more and better possessions became a driving force for increasing numbers of people. Gradually, sensibility and commonplace respect for honesty was replaced with wanting to "get ahead" and greed. In time, the perspective of "Why shouldn't I have what they have?" changed to "They cheat, why shouldn't I?"

Ads today blatantly link your worth to wearing a particular brand or fragrance, owning expensive cars and drinking certain labels. Unfortunately, many people buy into the propaganda of believing their worth can be measured by the things which they possess, their wealth or how they look. They seem unaware of their own innate worth and dignity as human beings — and of the innate worth of others. The acquisition of this materialistic mindset by families, role models and advertisers has had devastating effects on youth. Tragically, some young people have even killed to possess a popular item in an effort to gain respect from their peers.

Negative role models

Young people see others their age and older, in real life and in films, display meanness, bullying, selfishness, arrogance and violence. Negative behavior is frequently rewarded with admiration and status. Real life unkindness, disrespect and bullying are accepted by some as the new normal. While attempts to help are now more frequent through character education and anti-bullying programs, bullying and cyberbullying continue. In an effort to avoid the culture of meanness and to belong, many young people are overly attached to their phones and social media, concerned about not missing out — yet often missing out on social interactions with people in the same room.

The sexual content portrayed on television, in music videos and in ads, by teens, young adults and grown adults, has steadily increased over the years. These also serve as negative role models. I know a mother who took her children to a developing country during the summers. She felt that without the social pressures in her country to look and act a certain way her children would be able to play and act like children again for a few months. Children are having "shorter childhoods" in many countries, that is, fewer years of innocent play as the desire to look and be "hot" is steeping down to a younger and younger age. As young people engage in behaviors which they are not ready for emotionally or developmentally, their anxiety increases and natural happiness declines.

Ratio of parent to peer contact and drawbacks of social media sites

With ever-increasing usage of cell phones and social media websites, the ratio of parent to child versus peer to child contact continues to decline even in the preteen years. The influence of peers has grown tremendously. Silly or stupid mistakes in judgment, such as a mean or threatening comment, can be incredibly amplified on social media sites. Years ago, a comment may have been spoken to one person. Now, with a few strokes of a keyboard, it is broadcast to hundreds or thousands, sometimes with horrible consequences for the sender, and target.

Lack of education leads to vulnerability and exploitation

On an even more serious note, the lack of education in countries where corruption and violence are rife is robbing children of their childhood as well as literacy. Little or no education and lack of opportunity deprive hundreds of millions of children of achieving their potential, and make them more vulnerable to exploitation. The vast majority do not have parents to protect them, either because they are orphans, abandoned, or their parents have been so impacted by their own lack of education and opportunity that they do not have sufficient awareness or the wherewithal to protect and guide. Many become child laborers or street children. Others become pawns in illicit, dangerous and harmful activities, be it becoming victims of sex trafficking, child soldiers, part of the drug trade or recruits of violent extremists. As Nelson Mandela noted: "There can be no keener revelation of a society's soul than the way in which it treats its children."

A time for change — a tool for change

I have been devastated many times, as I am sure you have, reading about child soldiers or learning about the killing of children and teens by their peers in schools, movie theaters and neighborhoods, and the suicides of preteens because of cyberbullying. I feel it is time to change from a culture of violence to a culture of peace, from a culture of meanness to a culture of kindness — for the sake of our children, ourselves, all children, and our world.

We created it, we can change it. Each one of us is important in this process. However, as the world is the way it is, we must simultaneously protect our children and educate them about negative factors. Values are a powerful tool to help us do so.

Section Two

Nurturing
with Love and Wisdom

~ 3 ~

The Importance of Play and Us Time

You probably bought this book because you're a loving Mom or Dad and want to learn even more about parenting. As the last chapter got a bit serious, let's do the importance of play and Us Time before another chapter on values. Please enjoy reading this chapter and playing and being with your children. Then you'll be doing something fun, nurturing, bonding and wonderful every day. You may then even want to read the next chapter on values!

Play is the work of the child

Play is a time for a child to have the freedom to express the self and experience joy. A time when children can feel "full of themselves," it is said play is the work of the child. During play, children work out their emotions, and if there have been traumatic experiences, play can help the healing process. Play is a time of learning and growing cognitively, emotionally, socially, spiritually and physically.

Children whose parents play with them as infants and toddlers usually begin to play alone spontaneously when the parents are otherwise occupied. Children whose parents play with them usually play with other children easily. It is important to include time to play at all ages — for your children, and for you.

Once I counseled an eight-year-old girl who had poor social skills. Her mother asked me a year later if I could also counsel her younger sister. I saw the younger girl for a couple of sessions, talked to the teacher to confirm my perception, and then told the parent the little girl did not need counseling, she just needed to play more with others. I asked the mother if she and her husband played with their children. "No," was the response. She shared she did not know how to play!

Both she and her husband were raised in a developing country and worked on the streets selling gum when they were little. One parent had only a year of primary schooling; the other parent had two years. The whole family was a lot happier when they learned how to play — and the social skills of both girls blossomed.

Playing and Us Time adds joy — and protects

As a parent, playing with your children sustains a loving bond and adds to the joy of the relationship. Too often the world of adults makes us hurried and harried, and playtime with children can be seen as a nonessential. I would like to suggest that play is essential. It is a time to enjoy being mindful . . . in the present moment as you are attentive to your child and allow peace, love or contentment to flow through your mind. It is important to your joy and fulfillment as a parent, your relationship with the child and his or her feeling of belonging. It lets children know they are important to us. It creates and sustains a quality relationship of love, happiness and closeness. It is a time for sharing and a time together without pressure. It also provides a daily opportunity for them to voice any questions or concerns in an easy way.

Us Time helps children stay safe in this world as they grow older — for it is a close relationship with their caregivers that allows them to come to us should there be a need. Their love for us and their pride at our pride in them helps them resist the tempting "wrongs" of the world.

From sadness to smiles and play a refugee camp

In 1998, I visited a refugee camp in Thailand along the Myanmar border with Rachel Flowers, a friend who was the Living Values Education (LVE) Coordinator in Thailand at the time. We returned to spend twelve days at the camp the following year at the request of the head teacher and Karen officials in Chiang Mai, living in a small hut on stilts constructed only of bamboo and leaves. I was struck by the feelings of hopelessness the adults expressed, their deadened gaze, and the lack of play exhibited by the children. We did not see any toys, other than one volleyball. This prized item was used only by older teens and young adults. It was kept on the steps of another bamboo hut on stilts, nearest the flat space for playing volleyball. The younger children would stand for hours and watch them, or us. During the twelve days we were there, I never saw any younger child engage in play. The children looked sad, and it was difficult to obtain a smile. I was appalled.

I made yearly visits to that particular camp from 1998 to 2002. Rachel had initially persuaded me to accompany her to the camps as she and one of the Karen leaders in Chiang Mae felt the teachers and children would benefit from the LVE lessons for children affected by war. In addition to conducting nine days of training in 1999, we brought in several hundred toys — little rattan balls and mosaics, clay, plastic bowling pins and balls, badminton sets, volleyballs, soccer balls, and sets of chess and checkers. A jeep drove up the riverbed to bring in crayons and paper for the children and youth to draw with during their LVE lessons. They drew pictures about their experiences. Many of them had run for their lives when their villages were attacked in Myanmar. In the lessons, the children were told they were naturally valuable and lovable. The teachers learned to listen to them patiently and lovingly when they shared — and taught them they were Peace Stars. There were lessons weekly on peace, feeling peaceful, conflict resolution, respect and love.

One of the highlights of my life was driving into the camp after the program had been implemented for two years. The houses on the steep hillsides of the jungle looked the same. There was still a stream running down the middle of the narrow valley which the truck drove up. There were a few pigs under some of the houses. The Karen people still wore worn t-shirts with their more traditional sarongs. But the difference was remarkable.

There were smiling faces and children playing. A little boy about eight years old sat and waved as he held a toddler in his lap. A minute later, I observed a group of boys laughing and running, playing ball with a wad of plastic secured by rubber bands. The bat was a large plastic flip-flop. There were three little girls sitting under the overhang of a hut, smiling and laughing as they played a game with small rocks in the dirt. Two little boys were playing with a tiny toy wagon they had made with bamboo. The children were playing, and engaged in spontaneous and creative play. The expressions were those of happiness. The animated expressions, the caring and the laughter were music to my soul.

The teachers told us that the children and young adults in the Living Values Education classes, from six years of age to 20, would tell their peers when they saw them fighting, "You don't need to fight. You can solve your problems. Would you like us to help?" And, they would spontaneously use their conflict-resolution skills.

The teachers told us their hearts used to be hard and had become soft. A male teacher shared, "I used to hit the children, now I guide their hand." He gestured, indicating how he guided a hand as he taught a child how to write. In the process of working through some of their trauma during the nine-day training, the teachers had begun to heal. Their willingness and courage to change, their understanding of the importance of stopping the violence and creating relationships of trust and caring, were invaluable in giving the children what they needed.

One mother came to a teacher and told him her eight-year-old daughter was a good example to her. She asked the teacher if he could teach her how to be a Peace Star. A couple of the teachers met with groups of parents, sharing the skills they had learned.

The students received nurturing positive messages about who they were, tools to fill the self with peace, love and respect, activities to explore and express their emotions, and explanations of why things had happened and how things could be different. Trust and caring grew in relationships with their peers and teachers, and their world became more understandable as they learned about the effects of violence versus peace. Resiliency was restored. In this instance, there was initially so much violence, trauma and sadness that the play had disappeared. It re-emerged in the healing process — and became part of the healing process.

Play is often used in therapy with young children. I would even use it with older children. Play allows a space to simply enjoy a person for who he is. The therapist allows the child to lead and may choose to introduce other nurturing elements. It is affirming to children, and adults, to be enjoyed for who they are. Trust and closeness in relationships grow as children feel valued and learn essential social and emotional skills in a natural way.

Play with infants and toddlers

Enjoy being and playing with your baby. As most parents will agree, children of this age require an inordinate amount of attention. Time to cuddle, hold, play, attune and attend to the child is invaluable. Simply being with the baby, smiling, talking, making noises, doing little exercises and rolling on the floor is wonderful when we are relaxed. Infants need to be touched; they thrive with love, cuddling and play. Without loving touch they do not thrive and can actually die.

I remember an experience a friend shared. His baby had called him "Dada" for months, but did not call his wife "Momma". My friend knew his wife, "Renee," loved the baby very much and took good care of her. She even made her own baby food. One weekend, he watched the interaction between the baby and his wife and said, "Renee, I think I know what's happening. You don't *play* with the baby."

"What do you mean," she asked, "by play?"

"You know," he responded, "sit down on the floor and play, interact . . . make eye contact . . . do things and get a reaction . . . enjoy." He added, "I'll take you out to any restaurant you want if you play with Jennie every day for a week."

Renee started playing with her daughter the same day. By the end of the week, she was calling her Momma. I am sure that was far more rewarding than the fancy dinner.

There are many terrific toys for babies and toddlers. There are dangling objects of bright colors to attract the attention of infants, objects to push and pull, and dolls, puppets and educational toys that say words and make animal noises and letter sounds. The stimulation and information is important for cognitive, physiological and language development. However, it is the emotional interchange in playing with people who are light and loving that is invaluable. Choose safe, peace-giving toys, toys that are fun and allow your infant or toddler to experience their creativity. Play peek-a-boo. Play with puppets. Have the puppets hug and kiss the child. Perhaps spend a few quiet, peaceful moments together with a star puppet or with God.

There are thousands of wonderful books for babies and toddlers. Read to them daily. It's a good time to hold them in your lap, strengthening your bond while simultaneously developing their interest in books, building their vocabulary and receptive language skills and helping them learn to focus. Make your voice dramatic at times to hold their attention. Let them flit off to the next task when they are ready. Read them nursery tales and rhymes. Sometimes name the letter names and sounds when you are reading. Spell a word to them occasionally, even when they are 18-months old. Don't expect a response. Let them learn how they learn best at this age, absorbing like sponges. Bring out the crayons and paper at an early age. Paint peace and love with finger paints.

Talk to your children. Name their eyes, nose and mouth as infants, and make up games where you name their ears, hair and knees, etc., as toddlers. Use the primary color names as you name the colors on their clothes and toys. A child of average ability needs to hear his first color word 2000 times. 1000 repetitions are required to learn the second color word, 500 for the third, 250 for the fourth and 125 for the fifth. It is about 60 repetitions for the sixth color word and 40 or less for the remaining color words. When you are talking, infants and toddlers are automatically learning the sounds of your language, mimicking those sounds, learning words and the structure of the language.

Make up songs and sing to them. Include music in their day. Allow them a little play flute or other musical toys. Play them peaceful music and joyous music. Dance together. Perhaps there is the opportunity to learn to swim. Go outdoors and play. Look for worms and slug bugs. Teach them to touch the worms gently. Dig in the sand and make waterways and castles. Point out clouds in the sky and new leaves on the trees.

Enter into their world. Play at their level and pace. Join the world of pretend. When they pretend to give you a bite of food, pretend to give them a bite. Play with clay and blocks, with dolls and trucks, and be silly. Make a tent inside on a cold day by throwing a blanket over a few chairs. Simply be — accepting, reflecting, laughing.

As your toddler grows, allow him or her to dress up in costumes and make up plays and songs. Let them experiment with exercise and music. Take them to parks, the woods and nearby lakes or beaches to explore the wonder of nature.

Many parents find opportunities for their toddler to play with other children if they do not have brothers or sisters. If you are playing with your children, your child will naturally develop the social skills to play with other children. You might need to give a few directions occasionally to help them be gentle or to learn to share. If they have difficulty with certain social skills, positively model and reinforce those during Us Time.

Toddlers engage in repetitive play. They put things in buckets, take them out, and put them in again. They will roll the ball the same way over and over. It is not only that they are exploring how things work, they are developing mastery physically, and emotionally growing feelings of competency. It is important to let the child lead when they are playing. Have fun engaging in what they create. Be imaginative along with them. Talk to the toy animals they present to you in different voices as you take one up in response. Perhaps act out rowing down a river as you rock together in a rocking chair or hold them on the floor in your lap. Perhaps pretend the toy dinosaurs are hungry and like to gobble up palm trees. Laugh and be silly together.

When a child structures a game and is enjoying it, do not come along and make it so hard that he is not successful. Some parents err in trying to instruct the child during times of play. To hear, "That isn't the way you do it," in a stern tone is a downer to the delight of play. Let them shine and be in a state of creativity and happiness.

I remember once visiting a friend who was taking care of her two-and a-half-year-old granddaughter. The little girl was rolling a ball down the coffee table, engaging in a task she found enjoyable and fun, especially with her grandmother and me supplying a few "ohs" and "wows". But when her father came 20 minutes later to pick her up, within five minutes she was crying. He had changed the game she had created to a much more difficult task. He was disappointed she was not able to do it, and was instructing her, "No, *this* is how you do it." He had made the task too difficult and was clearly communicating his displeasure.

Her father was trying to be a good parent by teaching her how to do something more difficult. I sometimes see wonderful parents who dearly love their children overly instruct and direct them during play time. It can quickly degenerate into a time of frustration and tears. Yes, it is important for children to learn skills — and they may learn to roll the ball down the table just the way you want a couple of weeks later — but will they want to? Will they have a feeling of competency and enjoy learning?

We let children know they are competent or incompetent through our voice tones, facial expressions and reactions. The feeling of being enjoyed and successful — and having trust in us as the giver of love — is invaluable for the child. From this the child learns he or she is valuable, capable and good. Shame harms. Love and enjoyment nurtures.

Play with five- to nine-year olds

It's sometimes hard to find time in this busy world for play and values activities. After all, there are all the necessary tasks of a household and things that need doing in the outside world. And then there is homework with the kids, arranging for their school-related needs, etc., etc. You might want to reflect for a few moments.

- ❖ Why do I love my children?
- ❖ What times with them are most enjoyable?
- ❖ What times are the most uplifting?
- ❖ What do I want to do more of with them?
- ❖ In 20 years, what will I be really pleased about that I did with them?

Find some time every day to play with your children. That precious time is when relationships are enjoyed and the feelings of love grow. The full attention children receive during Us Time tells them they are valued and valuable.

Reflect for a few moments . . .

- ❖ What would be fun for both you and your child to do?
- ❖ What did you love to do when you were his or her age?
- ❖ What do you wish you had been able to do with your parent(s)?

There may be a few feelings of loss in answering the last question. But reflection of the past allows us to create more powerfully the future we want — for ourselves and our children. Love is the most powerful emotion on this planet.

❖ What do you want to do with your children when they are older?

All children want and need love. If they are not getting a sufficient amount of their parent's time or attention, they will misbehave or engage in an excessive behavior in an effort to draw their attention. Acknowledgement that one exists is better than nothing.

I remember a mother who came in to see me about the incessant talking of her eight-year-old daughter. The parent told me her child talked to her most of the time. She would even stand in the kitchen and talk as her mother cooked. I asked: "Do you ever listen?"

The mother looked at me surprised, paused as she looked down for a few moments, and then said, "No."

I asked her if she would spend 15 minutes of Us Time every day with her daughter, simply giving her complete attention, listening to her carefully and enjoying her. She said "Yes."

We talked about how the child might want to talk sometimes and choose to play at other times. Whatever it was they did together, the purpose was to give her full loving attention. If the child was talking incessantly at another time, the mother was to ask with a smile, before she was annoyed, "Can you tell me about that at Us Time?"

When I saw the mother the following week, she told me the talking had decreased 80 percent — and that she was enjoying the time listening to and playing with her child.

Play games you enjoyed at the same age or would have liked to have played. Play pretend games, play with balls and dolls or simply play while enjoying your children. Introduce them to the common games of your culture — perhaps cards and board games or circle dances.

Teach children things in such a way that it is interesting and pleasurable to learn. Share your interests. Perhaps they want to learn to knit, crochet or weave. Perhaps they would like to do beadwork, make friendship bracelets or work with clay. Do they enjoy making puppets and creating plays? Go on hikes together and explore nature at the local parks or in the hills, desert or mountains. Tell them the names of the trees. Look for animal tracks. Find books on trees, plants and animals. Read stories about the culture and habits of indigenous peoples and their crafts. Perhaps make up poems while you explore. Are you interested in astronomy? Look at the stars together and read about how the stars were named. Teach them to swim or play catch. Explore the tide pools. Read about animals and the coral and kelp forests under the water.

Make time every day to simply play or have Us Time with your child, even if it is for 15 or 20 minutes. Us Time can be a time of just listening with your full attention. Also, as you are engaged in daily routines, enjoy interacting with your children. For instance, converse when you go to the store and when they help in the kitchen.

Don't get competitive! Win and lose . . .

When you are playing checkers, chess, cards or board games, don't get competitive, but model graceful winning and losing. Congratulate children when they win. Offer specific affirmations, such as "You got a couple of triple jumps this time!" or "Good game. You played well," when you win — or lose. These are important social skills.

In playing with hundreds of kids, I found winning one-third of the time was about the right balance. If the adult wins all the time, they will be discouraged and won't want to play those games with you. If they win all the time, they will lose respect for you and your intellectual ability! If they win more than half of the time they will feel successful and will begin to enjoy a challenge.

Play and Us Time with 10- to 18-year olds

As children grow older, interaction with their peers becomes more important. This does not mean parents are less important. You are their most ardent admirer and supporter. They need you to be there for them, to love, comfort, reassure, support, model values, guide, create opportunities for them to be responsible and set limits and consequences, as needed. Us Time continues to be essential.

Reflect for a few moments . . .

- ❖ Why do I love my children?
- ❖ What times with them are most enjoyable?
- ❖ What times are the most uplifting?
- ❖ What do I want to do more of with them?
- ❖ In 20 years, what will I be really pleased about that I did with them?

You have probably read the story frequently shared by email of a CEO who was told by an employee how much he was admired and appreciated. This was part of the employee's class project to share with three people how important they were in his life. As part of the project, the employee was to ask those people to pass it on to three others. The CEO chose his son as one, and when he went home that night he shared with his teenage son how much he loved and admired him. The son began to cry, sharing after the sobs subsided that he had been planning to kill himself that night. He didn't think his father cared about him.

Providing for the family is essential, but young people need our loving attention and positive words to know they are important to us — to know they are treasured.

Reflect for a few moments . . .

❖ What would be fun for both you and your child to do?

❖ What did you love to do when you were his or her age?

❖ What do you wish you had been able to do with your parent(s)?

Finding quality time every day to be with your tweens and teens is important for your relationship. Sometimes their schedule may be full with academics, sports and other activities. If so, give them five to ten minutes of your *full attention*, chatting with them about their day, stopping what you are doing to really be there. If it is ten minutes before they go to sleep, wonderful. But if time is this short most days, make sure you have at least an hour together a couple of times a week. It is said a 13-year old needs as much attention as a five-year old. With peer pressure what it is today, a key safety factor is a good relationship between parent and child. If the communication channels are open and the feelings of love and closeness are there, some of the turbulence of teenage years can be avoided. Additionally, when the child is in conflict, he or she is more likely to come to you for love and advice.

Find something both you and your child like doing together that you can do for a longer period of time every few days or for a couple of hours once a week. Is there a sport or an art activity they enjoy? Can you walk, jog or workout together? Find something they are interested in that you can talk about or do together. If they don't seem to have an interest, help them discover one. Perhaps you are both interested in cooking, ecology, astrology, caring for rescued animals or volunteering to feed the homeless. Perhaps you are both interested in building miniature planes or biking. Perhaps join a green group and plant trees in your community or go hiking together. By consistently giving them the regard and love involved in Us Time, they will feel better about themselves, and navigate the teenage years more easily and safely.

~ 4 ~

My Values

Values affect our lives every moment. They are a guiding force in all we do and pursue. When our values are in congruence with our actions, we are in harmony. But what are values — and how did and do we develop them? Please take a few minutes to reflect as you read the following lines.

- ❖ Think of a person who influenced your life in a positive way.... What values or qualities did you see in the person that made a difference for you? ...... If everyone in the world demonstrated those values or qualities in their actions, would the world be different?

- ❖ Please think of the songs you love. What values are reflected through the words and music of those songs?

- ❖ Think of your favorite books, poems and quotes. What values or qualities are in them? Are there certain books or passages you read again and again? What values or qualities in them do you love?

- ❖ What images are important to you? Think of your favorite scenes and images. Perhaps they are scenes of nature, family photographs or works of art. What values and feelings are elicited by these?

- ❖ Please spend a few minutes and think of three especially positive or fulfilling moments in your life. What feelings were you experiencing? What values were you demonstrating in those moments?

❖ Think of what you enjoy most about being a parent. What values are you demonstrating in the moments you treasure?

All the values and qualities you wrote down are yours. These values are a few of the many you hold inside yourself.

Now, please take a few minutes to reflect on the values that are most important to you in your life. Please write down at least six values, those that you use to make decisions, those that are most important and those you would like to experience in your life all of the time. What are the values that make life worth living? What are the values that make you happy? You may have a list of six, seven or eight — perhaps eleven! Please write your values below.

❖ What are values? Please write down your definition.

In my travels conducting LVE workshops, I often ask people to define values. Many beautiful definitions have been received. I will share a few.

★ Values are innate qualities in the self that function as principles in my life, guiding my thoughts, words and actions.

★ Values are inner treasures which give meaning and purpose to life.

★ Values are consciously chosen principles which you live that develop strength and character.

- ⭐ Values are basic beliefs that are your foundation for life and behavior.

- ⭐ Values are a harmonic of life, an interactive sharing, touching our inner being. The lifeline of our existence as humanity, bringing meaning and contentment to life.

- ⭐ Values are what make you think and act in a particular way in different situations. They are that which give you the strength and pride to go on with your life and to face anything in life.

- ⭐ Values are inner qualities that emerge naturally within one to propel us into action, and motivate and inspire us to change in a positive way.

- ⭐ When values are incorporated in our daily lives dealing with others and ourselves, they bring love, true satisfaction, accomplishments and feelings of joy.

We share a common vision — and universal values

I was involved in a project many years ago, in the late 1980s, called Global Cooperation for a Better World. A project created by the Brahma Kumaris as part of a peace project with the United Nations, many people volunteered to gather small groups of people around the world to ask them to visualize a better world and ask how they would feel in that world. After the visualization, each member of the group shared about their feelings, and what they thought relationships and the environment would be like in that better world. They were then asked to think of one thing they could do in the present to make part of the visualization a reality.

I did this with girl scouts in Long Beach, California, professionals and religious leaders in Orange County and children in rural schools in Costa Rica.

Thousands of small groups of people from four years of age to 90, of all religions and of many different cultures and socio-economic backgrounds, gathered in 129 countries to do this. What was amazing was how similar the responses were. Everyone wanted to be peaceful and happy, have love and harmony in relationships and peace in the world. And you?

It seems human beings share universal values. Is the problem with today's world that we are not living our values? One premise of Living Values Education is that if we do live our values, we will create a better world for all.

Learning about values begins early

We learn about values as children from our parents, extended family and peers. We learn what values and qualities we treasure, and sometimes we realize we like the opposite of what we observe and experience. Children naturally love to be loved, they value kindness and people keeping promises, they don't like meanness and screaming. They want their parents to see who they are and listen, to play with them and hug them. We learn to value friendship. Sometimes we learn about the importance of honesty when people are honest. Sometimes we learn about the importance of honesty when people lie. We continue to learn about and develop values as we get older.

Reflect for a few moments . . .

❖ What values do you want to permeate your home?

❖ What values do you think are important for our world?

❖ What values do you think will help your children be happy, productive people?

❖ What do you think helps create children create those values — and the social and emotional behaviors which go with them?

~ 5 ~

Love, Affection and Attention

For young children, the love, affection and attention of their mother and father is life's greatest treasure. Without love and affection, infants fail to thrive; some die. Young people of all ages want, and need, the love and attention of their parents and caregivers. Whose love and attention did you want and enjoy as a child? Remember a time as a child when you received special love and attention....

As human beings, our basic need is to be loved. The need for love and acknowledgement is central to our daily existence, as children and adults. Love can be given in many ways. For infants and children, love is given through the vibrations of closeness, cuddling, hugging, holding, affection, playing and rough-housing — and the thousands and thousands of acts of taking care, feeding, listening, encouraging, soothing, protecting, laughing together, story-telling and guiding. Affection is given differently in different relationships as we grow older and play different roles. The attention we want remains much the same. We all enjoy the full attention — the genuine, interested and respectful attention of others — as children, as teens and as adults. Love, affection and attention are acknowledgement of our value and worth as human beings.

As adults we work harder and are more thoughtful and creative in workplaces where we feel loved, respected or appreciated. It is harder to focus when we feel others do not like us or when we are criticized frequently.

The energy of love and appreciation helps us be in our flow of light, respect and happiness, with the self and with others. In today's work environment, many adults must learn to manage without love and respect, for many people have forgotten the value of others and love things and their own importance more. They are really searching for love, but mistakenly think if they have more possessions and prestige, they will be loved and feel loved. As adults, most of us can manage without love and respect when the work environment is cold, but it takes more effort to function well. Some adults manage well as they know how to give love to the self. Others have supportive networks. Children cannot manage well without love, affection and attention from their parents and caregivers. This essential energy and care is needed for infants to survive and for young people to thrive.

What do you most enjoy about your children? Spend a few moments reflecting. Enjoy thinking about the ways you show love to your child. What would you like to do more of?

It is the love and respect between us that nurtures and binds. It is the love and respect between us that elicits natural cooperation and happiness. Part of respect is guiding and helping children to develop respect for others and responsibility.

Working with many parents over two decades allowed me to see patterns. Most parents I worked with fell into one of two camps. Some were terrific nurturers. They were loving and kind, great listeners and enjoyed their children. But, they were weak on discipline. Some of their children took advantage of them, not picking up their toys, not doing chores, asking for things constantly, whining, arguing and not complying with requests and directions. They did not take responsibility. Some had temper tantrums when they didn't get their way. Some spoke rudely and were bossy with their parents.

Other parents had discipline down, but were weak in giving love, listening and enjoying their children. Their children might also be having temper tantrums or not doing their chores, but there was often a lot of fighting between siblings or behavior problems at school. Some were defiant. Some sought the love of their parents and would whine incessantly in an effort to get contact. I was very concerned when children didn't care how much they were punished and would not comply. They were very angry and had closed off emotionally. With those parents, after we explored the importance of play, listening and time to be together, I would gently share: "When there is love, there is cooperation." We would work together till there was positive change.

A tiny percentage of parents I've seen were not able to offer nurturing love nor discipline because of their own inner turmoil. Their children were usually downcast and sad, some would try to care for their parent. I would start by listening until we could come up with one or two simple things they could do daily to nurture their children, such as gathering the children together and reading them a story.

I didn't usually have sessions with parents who were great at both, simply because they didn't need to see me! They had the balance of nurturing and discipline.

In this section and the next, you will see two main themes, nurturing with love and wisdom and disciplining with peace and respect. You may feel you want to learn more about one topic than other, but please read both. Children know all of our buttons, for they do want their way, but our job is to love and guide so they can venture forth with respect, confidence and purpose — and as the radiant, loving, responsible, joyous beings we know they are.

~ 6 ~

Appreciation and Building Positive Behaviors

In the field of contingency management or behavior modification, the term "positive reinforcer" is used to indicate something which increases the frequency of a behavior when applied. In early experiments, researchers found animals would repeat certain behaviors more often if they were given the positive reinforcer of food. I am not a behaviorist, but find some of the concepts of this branch of psychology to be useful. Even as a university student, I tended to think in a humanistic way.

Positive reinforcement — root beer or loving attention?

When I was at UCLA, I took a class from Professor Lovas. During the class, we were all asked to design and conduct a behavior-modification experiment to benefit children who were profoundly developmentally disabled. Two other students and I went to Lanterman Hospital, now called Lanterman Developmental Center, once a week to work with youngsters. The other two students used squirts of root beer to teach two young teens to put on their t-shirts correctly. (Root beer is similar to a cola drink.) The 14-year-old boy I was asked to work with lightly hit people frequently, 200 times an hour. He was said to have an intelligence quotient of seven. I was told he spoke four words. I only ever heard two. I felt he wanted loving attention.

For my "experiment," I would take this young teen for walks around the grounds. I would simply enjoy his company, talk to him and we would swing on the swings. We would smile and laugh. When he would lightly hit me, I would immediately say "No," firmly and turn away from him for a few seconds. Then I would turn in his direction again and continue walking and talking with him. We both had a pleasant time just being. Within six sessions the hitting was reduced from 200 hits an hour to two or less. During our last session there were two light touches. This young man was getting the caring attention and friendly company for which he had been reaching out.

A smile, laughter and an appreciative glance are always with us — always available for us to give. The same is not true for a squirt of root beer!

The dilemmas of praise

Praise is usually a positive reinforcer for children. If your praise acts as a positive reinforcer, then by definition it means the behavior you are praising will increase. Is this always true? If so, terrific! However, does your praise always work or is he worse after receiving praise? Is she constantly dependent upon and needing praise or is she irritated at your praise? Or, has he become too full of himself? Does he have an attitude of "Oh, I know I did it right," after being praised? If so, continue reading!

You can tell if your praise or affirmation is working as a positive reinforcer by watching to see if the behavior being praised increases. If the behavior does not increase, that praise was not a positive reinforcer.

Not all praise is equal. If instead of looking pleased, does your teen look sour when given verbal praise? Did your preteen find the praise embarrassing when spoken in front of his peers? Did the child not believe she deserved the praise as she felt it was not true? Perhaps you said something was great and she didn't think it was very good.

A few children occasionally get worse immediately after praise if the praise is excessive. For example, a boy with the habit of hitting younger siblings may revert to hitting when praised excessively when he stops hitting for 30 minutes. So why does he immediately hit again? One possibility is he is so accustomed to getting frequent negative feedback that the positive feedback is anxiety provoking. Another possibility is the praise is so overboard he feels angry, knowing he doesn't deserve the praise yet hurt and resentful that he receives so little.

Another problem with praise is praising children too much. Children can become overly dependent on praise, or if the praise is excessive and not merited, they may develop an inflated view of themselves. Conversely, their self-esteem can decrease over time if they feel it is not deserved.

Guidelines for effective acknowledging, affirming and "praise"

I would like to share a few simple guidelines for acknowledging, affirming and praising. These allow your "praise" to avoid the above pitfalls while adding to the beauty of human interactions and helping children build the responsible and respectful behaviors needed for happiness and a productive life.

1) Be Genuine

Whether acknowledging, affirming, appreciating or praising, be genuine. The person receiving the acknowledgement or praise will know if it is sincere — or not sincere. Having delight in a person, appreciative eye contact and respect are indicators of sincerity, easily perceived by two-year olds, teens or adults.

The heart responses to an appreciative genuine remark or look. As love is a basic need of human beings, genuine love, affection, attention, appreciation and respect serve as easy and natural positive reinforcers. The energy of these feelings flows from you to the other person, confirming the value of the other person and the relationship.

Some adults rely too much on words, thinking if their words are positive, it is a positive reinforcer. Have you ever heard a person say positive words in a slightly peeved or annoyed voice? It can serve as a punisher. I remember a teacher who used to say to half of her class as she glanced at the other half with irritation, "I like the way *this* side of the room is being quiet." Her negative emotional tone increased tension and anxiety in the classroom. The noise level went up very soon afterwards in response. "Wonderful job," in a sarcastic tone, from a parent or employer, acts as a punisher.

2) Age-appropriate delivery — socially appropriate for the person

The manner of delivery, of course, needs to be different for different ages. Gushing is well received by many two- to four-year-old girls, if they already know you and love you. Boys eight and older tend to prefer praise delivered in a matter-of-fact manner, most of the time — although some mothers are still allowed to gush a little. Some teenagers are like soft-boiled eggs, hard on the outside, soft on the inside. If they are tough on the outside, and their history is of receiving little appreciation, attention or praise, a thumbs-up signal may be the most they can tolerate while in the company of their peers. A few quiet words spoken privately and in a matter-of-fact manner can be well received. Some may not seem to notice your praise and simply shrug in response, but you know the acknowledgement or affirmation was heard and appreciated when the positive behavior increases, when they start hanging around you more and when the hard facade fades.

3) *Positive or appreciative affirmations and "specific praise"*

What would life be like without any positive affirmations or praise? When you are dressed up for a special event and ask your partner how you look, what do you want to hear? If he or she gives you an active listening response and says, "So you want to know how you look," or describes what is happening, "You have on your new outfit," how do you feel? Your partner is in trouble! "Gorgeous" or another equally affirming response is a thousand times better.

There are many appreciative or affirming responses which feel good and create a caring atmosphere at home or the workplace. They don't need to be used all the time, but are a nice part of everyday life. Some of these words are: good, nice one, gorgeous, brilliant, well done and terrific.

Often the word "good" is put in front of what you want the child or adult to notice or know you appreciate, such as "good thinking," "good figuring it out," and "good catch". This quick affirmation of a person's effort or behavior with an appreciative glance or smile signals the importance of a task and adds positive energy to the relationship.

"Good girl" or "good boy" may sound similar, but is not recommended as a quick affirmation or as praise. It comes too close to labeling a child rather than affirming a behavior. To positively build a behavior, use words which focus on the behavior. If you are going to label a child, do it carefully and with wisdom, such as "I know you are good. God made every child naturally good."

Sometimes children, and adults, do not believe the praise they are receiving is genuine, even when it is. This usually relates to their level of self-esteem. If children have received praise for a particular behavior or for other similar behaviors, and have fairly good self-esteem, they are likely to believe the praise. "Great job!" works well for them. However, children and adults who have not received much praise in their lives, especially for the kind of task they are doing, are not likely to believe the same praise. *Specific* praise gets around this difficulty and is also an excellent form of feedback.

A couple of times when I went into a classroom while working as a school psychologist, I would conduct my own little experiments with praise. If I gave general praise, the results were not uniformly positive. Some children tried harder and others did not. However, when I gave specific praise, all the children appeared to believe what was said to them. It was fun to observe their brightened countenance, increased efforts and the improved outcome.

"Specific praise" is simply describing what is occurring or what has occurred. For example, as I went around one classroom a seven-year old looked at his handwriting paper as I pointed to the letter he had written and said in a positive tone of voice, "The back of that 'b' is really straight and there's a space between these words." He could confirm what I said was true. The back of the b was straight. His liking of the positive tone of voice and validation was seen with neater printing on the next line. As I went around the room, saying something specific in an affirming tone of voice to each child who was working, every single one of the children applied themselves, and each child's handwriting improved. The specific description, delivered with interest in the person and their work, in a positive tone of voice, had acted as a positive reinforcer.

Did you notice that the comment to the boy did not contain any "praise" words, such as great, terrific or well-done? While those are wonderful words we like to hear, a child with poor self-esteem is unlikely to believe they apply to him. Descriptive words delivered in an affirming voice tone are believed as they are verified by their own observation. This then acts as a positive reinforcer. Believable "specific praise" delivered in a mater-of-fact voice, or a simple thumbs up sign, is much more effective and real to a struggling teen than superlatives.

A description can be more appreciated by a four-year old or an adult than a word of praise. Imagine a four-year-old girl with a just-done painting. The parent says with a smile and loving eye contact, pointing to the things he is describing: "Wow, you made purple circles and green lines that go up and down — and this looks like a yellow and orange flower!" This is much preferred over a hurried glance and a "Very good," without loving eye contact. The love and attention is what is wanted, and there's usually more of that with a longer description. With a description they know we are paying attention. From your boss, wouldn't you rather hear about five specific things she really likes about what you are doing rather than receiving one word?

Specific praise is also a teaching tool. You are letting the child know what is important about his behavior. With specific praise you can increase the desired behavior while simultaneously sharing detailed information about the critical elements in a task. For example, delivered in a pleased tone of voice:

- ★ You remembered to use please.
- ★ You buckled your car seat all by yourself!
- ★ Wow, you pulled those sheets all the way up and the bedspread, too.

- ⭐ You remembered to put all your things by the door for tomorrow — great!
- ⭐ You came in by yourself, without me having to call. That was a big help.
- ⭐ What a clean counter-top.
- ⭐ It took a lot of thinking to come up with such a respectful solution.
- ⭐ I appreciate you putting down your iPad the second Aunt Lena arrived, without even a glance from me.
- ⭐ Thanks for running out so quickly to help me bring in the groceries. It was a double hug.
- ⭐ Your hard work on the essay really got you the grade.

From a team leader or committee chair, which of the following would you prefer? "Good job," or "Your comments are practical and help us focus on what needs doing. I appreciate you being here."

Giving specific descriptive praise also gives us the opportunity to positively reinforce a behavior important for the development of the child. It can be instructional, as we are informing the child of the steps of a task. The child can use that information later to affirm his competency in accomplishing a task. Hence, it is part of teaching how to self-praise or have positive self-affirmation. For example, if you have been using specific praise to reinforce a child for setting the table, the child will know all the elements important for the task. So, when the child asks, "Did I do a good job?" You can indicate "yes" with a smiling look and say in words, "You tell me. What did you do well?" The child is now a step farther on the road of developing intrinsic motivation.

Reflect for a few moments . . .

❖ What does your child do well?

❖ What does he or she do consistently without being reminded?

❖ Have these areas received your acknowledgement, appreciation or praise?

❖ What kind of praise does your child like to receive from you?

❖ How do you let your child know what you appreciate?

❖ Do you enjoy sharing positive affirmations with your child? Is this one way you express your love?

❖ Are there certain qualities your child has that you would like to affirm?

❖ Is there a behavior you think your child needs to develop?

❖ How can you nurture that?

4) *When you are helping the child develop a new positive behavior, praise it immediately. Decrease attention to the behavior once it is established.*

When you want to reinforce a new behavior, provide immediate positive feedback. Reinforcement may be given through a word of praise, specific words of description, a few words of appreciation or nonverbal acknowledgment, that is, a thumbs-up sign, a smile or another positive facial expression or gesture. It is then more likely to be viewed as an important behavior by the child, and repeated more frequently.

As a new behavior, skill or attitude is established, begin to reduce the frequency of praise or affirmation. Occasionally, positively reinforce the continuing effort, such as "I appreciate you remembering to _____." When it becomes a habit, you will no longer need to draw the child's attention to that, but you may have something else you would like to see him develop. For example, you might use specific praise when a child is learning to use a fork correctly. It would be inappropriate to do so when the child is older and has mastered the skill.

As you reduce attention to the new behavior, resume the normal positive flow of conversation and relationship. A constant daily diet of praise is unnecessary and tends to leave people dependent on it, always needing more. However, appreciative thoughts and glances, loving looks and smiles are at the core of human relationships. They are an outstanding diet which nurtures our spirit and ability to be positive, productive beings.

As you know from the story about the 14-year-old boy living at Lanterman, positive reinforcers can be tangible. Two of his mates received squirts of root beer. Other tangible reinforcers are candy, raisins or stickers. I have rarely used tangible reinforcers as I feel it is always a good idea to go as high up on the ladder of human social interaction as possible. Tangible reinforcers can create dependency on rewards for good behavior. It is healthier emotionally for a child to receive love, affection and attention for developing new skills and responsibilities. Treats and special desserts are then not used as bribes and rewards which are bargained for and argued about. Instead they are simply part of the pleasure of family life, part of celebrating special occasions or accomplishments — of the children and the parents!

However, a tangible reward is useful *if* praise and attention are not getting the desired behavior. For example, once I was asked to evaluate a five-year-old child who was doing poorly in kindergarten. He did not know the names of any colors and could not count three objects. I approached him initially as I did other kindergarteners, turning on the music box in my office and inviting him to draw at the round table. He did not want to do anything with me or for me. After a while, I walked him back to his classroom. The next day, I brought raisins and almonds with me and tried again. When I asked him to sit down, I put a few raisins and almonds on a napkin on his side of the table when he sat, taking them from a pile on a napkin on my side of the table. "Thank you," I said. I put more on his napkin when he took the pencil I offered. He immediately understood and was soon working hard for those raisins and almonds.

What surprised me was he did not eat one raisin or almond. I put all of them in a little bag at the end of our session. When I walked him back to the classroom, I told his teacher they were his. I mentioned I was surprised he didn't eat any during our time together. She said, "His family is very poor. They migrated here a few months ago. I'm sure he's saving them to take home to share." After three sessions, he was happy to work for positive attention only. It was not necessary to dole out raisins and almonds during the session. The bag of raisins and almonds at the end of the session was simply a tiny gift.

5) Qualities

Telling children about their good qualities is a gift. They will remember what qualities, virtues or values you tell them they have. As these qualities become part of their self-perception, they can also serve as measures with which to evaluate their own behavior.

Do you remember what your parents told you about yourself when you were little? Perhaps they said you had pretty hair, or were responsible, smart or sweet. We remember those positive remarks as children and have faith that they are true as we are told those qualities over time. And for those who had parents who labeled them negatively? It takes years of effort to not believe the old labels.

Of course, children should never be labeled with negative traits, such as dumb, clumsy, lazy, sloppy or mean. It would be shaming and harmful to say, "Bad boy," or "Bad girl." If you need to give them constructive feedback or a correction because you don't like what they are doing, talk to them about their behavior. Several beneficial ways of doing that are in the discipline section.

Build the vocabulary and knowledge of different qualities with young children by naming your own positive feelings when you are experiencing them. For example, as you sit quietly outdoors on a pretty day, you might share, "The sky is so blue today and the wind is softly moving the leaves of the tree. It's so peaceful." "Daddy loves you so much. You are his loving, precious jewel." "Moving the table was so easy with all of you helping. A few cooperative helpers was just what I needed."

Do not *only* comment on physical appearance, such as telling the child, "You are cute," or "What a darling outfit." While it is good to know one is pretty or attractive, there is far more to us as human beings than our bodies and appearance. Notice more often your child's positive qualities and ways of being.

- ❖ Was he loving with a sibling, kind to a friend, considerate or compassionate, was he able to handle a conflict peacefully?
- ❖ Is she curious, creative and persistent? Does she have an interest in creating a better world?
- ❖ Does he stop and consider things carefully, is he responsible and gentle with animals?

As you value and notice their qualities, you are teaching them about what is important in life. A wonderful practice is to give specific descriptive praise and occasionally pair it with a quality, virtue or value. If you do this even a few times a month, it will help your child see their own qualities, and the self, in a positive light. It helps children understand what that quality or value means, as well as reinforcing positive behavior and adding to their sense of self-respect.

A few examples . . .

- ⭐ I liked the way you helped Todd. You were patient and kind.
- ⭐ You listened to Steve when he really needed you to listen. That was being a caring friend.
- ⭐ You used words instead of your fists. That was being a peacemaker.
- ⭐ You didn't hit when he called you a name. You stayed in your self-respect and power. Good for you!
- ⭐ Thank you for putting away your things so quickly. That was real cooperation.
- ⭐ I like the way you thought about it and were able to stop and say "Arms are for hugging, not for shoving." You chose peace.
- ⭐ It was kind of you to reach out to Amanda when she was upset. That was sweet and loving.

6) One achievable step at a time

When helping a child build a new behavior, think about the next step, not the final goal. If you want a child to be a good cook, start with making something simple in the kitchen and having a good time, not by setting out a recipe for an elaborate dessert. If you want a child to make his bed well, start by showing the child the beginning steps and praising the child for pulling up the sheet and the cover. Practice communication skills to help children do well with conflict resolution and co-creating harmony. Make each new behavior achievable and the child will not only feel like a success, the child will be successful.

Part of making new behaviors achievable is to clearly and positively state what you wish to be done. For example, to a two-year old: "Hold the glass carefully," rather than "Don't drop the glass." "Come home right after school," rather than "Don't be late." "Pull the sheet up to the top, all the way across," rather than "Don't leave the sheet rumpled." "Stay in your self-respect and use your peace words," rather than "Don't say bad words." Clear positive messages, optimistic messages, fill the subconscious with a higher percentage of positive messages, hence they help children have a sunnier outlook on life. "With a bit of work, you'll learn it easily," is more positive than a message about certain failure without more effort.

Enjoy family life and being with your children. If you want them to grow into a new attitude or skill, model that yourself. Do not try to build ten new behaviors at once! Pick out one or two behaviors that are important at the time. When a new behavior is learned, then perhaps look at another behavior that needs help. Think about which positive behavior will best substitute for a particular negative behavior, provide the opportunity for the child to do the positive behavior and reinforce it. But mostly, live life, enjoy your children and be positive with what comes up. Appreciate and affirm the beauty you see in your children.

7) "Praise" always leaves a positive feeling — No spoilers or comparisons

Ensure the praise you give is full of positive feeling and leaves a positive feeling with the other person. Do not end praise with a "spoiler". For example, to your partner: "Honey, you did a great job cleaning the garage. It looks so organized." Does the feeling change if you add the following sentences? "I don't know why you don't keep the garage like that all the time. It's always such a mess! I get so tired of tripping over things, why …" Oops, that was a spoiler! Or, when one partner says to the other, "What a delicious meal. Why don't you make something like that more often?" Or, when the parent says to the child, "It was fun working with you today. You concentrated and finished your homework quickly." Great! Now for the spoiler: "If you'd only do that all the time, it wouldn't be such a hassle to get the homework done every day. I get so sick and tired of you complaining about your homework." Or, there is the feeling-worse-with-every-second comparison: "Harold manages to keep their garage neat." "Your sister always has a dessert after dinner." "I don't have to work with your brother like this. I don't even have to remind him to do his homework."

The praise began well, but when the comments turn negative and the voice tone becomes exasperated, the positive feelings the receiver may have experienced can quickly change to feelings of frustration, irritation or an attitude of "Why try?" Spoilers and comparisons too often work as an invitation to a bitter exchange — or bitter feelings. In contrast, specific praise, acknowledgment or affirmation leaves you both with a pleased, happy feeling. There's more energy to grow in a positive direction.

Please stop and relax for just a few moments … and think of three things you appreciate about each person living with you. And three things you love about yourself.

~ 7 ~

Active Listening

Listening to our children, partner, friends and co-workers — anyone — is a gift. It is a gift of time and love. Often the listener does not realize the importance of her or his gift of listening at a time of need, until a time comes when he or she needs to be listened to and someone listens with respect, love and kindness.

Parents can feel helpless and fearful for their children when their children feel bad about peer problems at school or when they are upset with themselves, friends, coaches, teachers or something that happened. Many caregivers instantly dispense advice. Some parents become upset with teens when they are upset at someone and complaining or venting in a loud voice at home. They inadvertently slam the door shut on communication when they get angry in response.

Think about a time when you were really upset about something, began to share the tale and the "listener" immediately started giving you suggestions or shut you off. How did you feel? Chances are you didn't feel understood, valued or better. You may have even felt worse. How do you feel when an understanding friend quietly listens to you with love and sincere interest?

A person who listens with loving interest and respect helps us process our emotions. When another accepts our emotions, it has the effect of giving us permission to accept our own emotions. We are then more empowered to process or resolve the issue.

In the same way, actively listening to children allows them to accept and own their emotions. When emotions are accepted, they gradually reduce in intensity. For example, a child who is really upset about something will usually begin to calm down with one, two or three active-listening responses. A teen will frequently move from anger to talking about feelings of hurt with one to four sincere active-listening responses. They are then more empowered to process their emotions or resolve the issue.

A runner

I remember standing outside my office at school one day, when I observed a seven-year-old boy rapidly running toward the front of the school. A young long-legged teacher was running after "Sean," her long hair streaming behind her. "Diane," she yelled, "stop him! He's a runner!" I managed to run across the courtyard quickly enough to grab his arm before he was out the gate. He pulled hard against me, struggling to get away. Observing his anguished face, I bent down so my face was at his level and said seriously and respectfully, "You're really upset."

"Yeah," he replied. He completely stopped struggling. His eyes clung to mine.

"What happened?" I asked quietly.

"Someone took my pencil." He was now on the verge of tears.

"Oh…. Shall we go back to class and solve the problem?"

"Okay."

He had been heard, and a respectful caring offer had been made to help solve the problem. He was ready to go back to class. His teacher told me later that the day before Sean was involved in a long yelling match with one of the school authority figures. I imagine their interaction could have taken a few minutes rather than two hours if she had been willing to respect his emotions and listen.

At the same school, I remember sitting around a table one day with three students who were in a special education class. Their fairly new teacher had brought them in as she was so frustrated. They had been fighting on the playground and had brought the argument into the classroom. This was before my days of teaching conflict resolution to teachers, so I sat them around my table and began to actively listen. They continued in their usual mode for a while, blaming and accusing, denying they had done anything wrong. One student kept saying, "*I'm* not going to say *I'm* sorry!"

As I just continued to listen, it was as if they all became amazed at the same moment. They stopped and were silent for a moment — and looked at me as if they really saw me. They changed their tone of voice and began telling me what really happened. My guess is they realized I was not going to blame, criticize or get angry. I continued to actively listen and then we went respectfully through the steps of conflict resolution. They soon came up with a constructive alternative behavior for the next recess.

When we blame and get angry, others simply react with their already existing anger. If we do not blame and get angry, they have the opportunity to be still and see themselves.

Listening to anger and hearing the fear — Anger as a secondary emotion

Active listening, that is, verbally reflecting back the emotions or the content of what is being said, is helpful with young people and adults when they are upset. One afternoon in a school in a gang area, just before school let out, I heard a man yelling in the office. I entered to see a large man confronting the school secretary. I don't like people yelling at or intimidating others, so I reached up and tapped him on his shoulder. As he swung toward me, I looked him in the eye and said seriously and respectfully, "You're really concerned about something."

He stopped yelling and looked at me. "Yeah," he said.

"I can help you solve the problem if you'll come with me." He quietly followed me as I led him to my office.

This was not frightening to do as I knew something that seems to be a secret in our world. It is not a secret, but people forget. That is, the emotions of hurt, fear, shame or feeling unsafe are beneath anger. They are primary emotions. The anger comes afterwards; it is a secondary emotion.

I did not hesitate to interact with this father as I knew he wouldn't be there unless he was really concerned about his child. I was in a position to help and knew he wanted help, so it was easy to listen. When people are not heard, or do not feel they will be heard, they will fight to try to protect themselves or those they love. Actively listening with respect allowed him to feel valued and understood enough to reveal his fear and concern. It is then that the process of working on a solution begins.

Sometimes people, especially children and teens, think they are the only ones who ever felt a certain way. Consequently, they may feel embarrassed or shamed, believing they are odd, different or defective. Expressing emotions that may have been hidden allows them to let go of some or all of the shame when they are listened to with love and respect, especially when your understanding and acceptance affirms their emotions as a normal response to a difficult situation.

An aside: In my experience, almost all people are willing to let go of overt anger fairly easily if they feel respected and understood. Adults with borderline personality disorders or people with serious mental illness can be exceptions when unwell. However, a balance of consistent kindness and firmness over time works well even with very difficult personalities.

What is active listening?

Active listening is reflecting back the *content* and/or *emotions* which the other person is communicating, without sounding like a parrot. It requires taking the time to be present and really listen with an accepting respectful attitude. The listener does not interrupt nor are questions asked, except for clarification. It does require practice. Listen with your heart.

Examples of active listening . . .

Child happily hopping up and down: "I can't wait, I can't wait." Parent with a smile: "You're really excited about going."

Child with a smile, snuggling a plush toy in bed. Parent: "You're really content." Or, "You love to snuggle with your bear."

Child coming into the house with a frown after a day at school. Parent: "It looks like you're concerned about something."

Child with a frown: "What a lousy day." Parent: "It looks like you had a tough one."

Child crying and pointing to a bloody toe. Parent: "Ouch, it looks like you really hurt your toe."

Child crying: "Sarah said I was ugly." Parent: "Your feelings got really hurt when she said that."

Child looking angry and dejected at the same time: "I'm never going to play with Henry again." Parent: "You're really upset with Henry right now."

Child: "I'm never going to talk to Maria again." Parent: "You're feeling really angry at Maria right now."

Child looking sad: "Ashley didn't even say hello to me today." Parent: "It looks like that was hard and you're feeling sad."

Why does being listened to allow us to accept and "own" our emotions?

When someone listens to us with respect, a feeling of being respected, understood and valued is created. It helps us accept the emotions we are experiencing. When we reject and struggle with our own emotions, it is as though we are rejecting the self. As we understand and accept our emotions, we are empowered to accept the self. This influx of positive energy in the mind, and the relief of accepting the self, interferes with the downward spiral and loss of energy from negative thoughts and emotions.

Avoid blockers and stoppers

Many people are tempted to offer a solution when someone is upset rather than listening. Usually people do this as they wish to help; they want the other person to be out of pain. What else do people do? Below is a list of common responses. Sometimes "blockers and stoppers" begin to close the door of communication. At other times, they slam the door shut.

- Giving Solutions: "I know what you should do. First _____."
This may have the effect of the receiver feeling unworthy or not valued, as the other is not taking the time to really hear. The person may feel less accepting of his emotions, or more inadequate as

being given a solution can imply one is not handling things properly.

- Diminishing: "Don't be silly. That isn't important."
  The other person is trying to help, but the response indicates the talker's emotions are not important or valid. This can generate emotions of not being seen, feeling hopeless or a response of anger.

- Distracting: "Think of something else. Don't think about this."
  The "helper" does not wish the person to feel bad. However, not talking about what you wish to talk about can make one feel something is wrong or shameful with feeling a certain way.

- Moralizing: "One day you will learn. My mother always used to say, _____. Why I remember one time when _____. And what I learned from this was _____. Now what you need to learn is _____." This may be appreciated by a few, but can elicit eye-rolling and avoidance from tweens and teens. Adults may feel patronized and also avoid further sharing.

- Sympathizing: "You poor thing. Bad things always happen to you." Sympathy of this kind can be disempowering. Supportive compassion or empathy is more readily perceived and received with attentive active listening.

The following negative responses act as punishers. With these responses, the receiver can feel wrong to have certain emotions and hence may feel inadequate, misunderstood, hurt or angry.

- Judging "You are wrong to feel this way."
  "You always overreact."

- Accusing "Why do you always feel bad? What's the matter with you?"

- Admonishing "How many times have I told you not to do that? You should never _____."

- Blaming "You are always creating a mess." "You caused this by _____."

More active listening examples . . .

Child coming into the house with a frown after a day at school. Parent: "It looks like you had a tough day." Child, looking dejected: "Yeah. Sally teased me and Sarah was mean. I didn't know what to do and my face just got all red." Parent: "So you were embarrassed and didn't know what to do when they were mean." Child: "Yeah. Tam came up and helped a little." Parent nods, listening with full attention. Child: "She said they shouldn't be mean." Parent: "So, Tam tried to help." Child: "Yeah. Tam is a good friend. And Sally and Sarah are usually nice." Parent: "They're not usually mean." Child: "No." Hangs head a little. "I guess I was mean to them yesterday." Parent: "Oh." Child: "Sometimes I get really grumpy inside." Parent: "So, you weren't nice to them when you were grumpy." Child: "Yeah." Child reaches out and hugs Mom. "Thanks, Mom. Sometimes you have a grumpy girl."

Mom, recognizing her child's emotions have settled and she isn't as upset, stops active listening. A validating response is given first: "We all get grumpy sometimes. Is there something else you can do when you're grumpy that would help make you feel better?" The question lets the child know the parent thinks she is capable of coming up with a solution and points out a sensible direction. Child: "I'll think on it." Mom, with a smile: "Okay, my loving star." The mother has ended with a positive affirmation of one of her child's qualities.

Teen coming home after soccer practice, looking really angry and talking loudly: "I quit! That's it! That stupid coach is a clown. I'd like to see him play!" Parent doesn't act disgusted with the teen's anger nor send him to his room, but actively listens: "You're really upset." Teen: "Yeah. Where do they get these coaches anyway?" Parent nods, showing he is listening. Teen: "Ya' know, Dad, I really practiced my side-step kick, but criticize, criticize, criticize, that's all he could do." Parent: "So you really worked this week on your kick and he criticized you a lot." Teen: "Yeah. I guess he was like that with everyone today." Parent nods. Teen: "I guess he wants us to really get it down. But I wish he wouldn't yell." Parent: "You don't like it when he's so negative." Teen: "Yeah. I think he thinks we'll try harder, but it doesn't work for me."

Parent, recognizing his son's emotions have settled, stops active listening. "What value would you use if you were the coach?" This question does a couple of things: it implies the negative situation will not last forever and it values the teen, trusting he will figure out a value that would be helpful.

Teen: "Respect, I think. It helps to treat people like decent human beings."

Parent: "Yes, I know respect certainly feels better to me." This is agreement —a validating, emotionally-supportive response.

After active listening

You don't need to actively listen forever when a child has a problem, just listen until the emotions of being upset subside. You will notice in the above examples that the parents are not taking sides or blaming. The parents are reflecting back what the child is saying and/or feeling in order to help the children process their emotions and think about the situation.

When the child has moved into feeling more settled, perhaps tell the child you're glad he shared, make an encouraging comment, engage in some problem solving if you think it is appropriate and might be accepted, or simply ask about what value he thinks would be good to use in the situation. After this, some situations may call for help with problem solving. Help children build their capacity to problem solve. However, if the situation is dangerous, parental intervention is called for.

Please note: While active listening is also very helpful to adults, some adults have powerful, persistent negative thoughts and false beliefs, so they can easily swing back into being upset. Hence, it can take much longer for an adult to settle.

After actively listening, consider doing one of the following . . .
1) Give a gesture of caring and closure.

This might be a touch on the shoulder, a hug or a smile and a comment, such as "I'm glad you shared."

2) *Give a validating response.*

Active listening is compassionate and understanding, but it is *not* agreement. For example, when counseling physical abusers, I listen as they share their story and the emotions they were experiencing. However, I then intervene, using other methods to develop their empathy, be in tune with their underlying emotions/dynamics and learn to control their anger. It is never right to hurt a child.

In contrast, a validating response is agreeing. After listening to a person who has felt unseen or is perhaps in grief after a tragedy, an agreeing response is validating, that is, it is verifying their experience as "right". Examples: "I feel upset too when people treat me that way." "Yes, war is awful." "Yes, it is really hard when people are so mean."

3) *Encourage, give hope or confirm one or two positive qualities or values.*

Examples: "You're working so hard to help. You have a lot of love." "It's tough now, but it sounds like the hardest part is over." "You are a real gem. Your good efforts will be seen." "I appreciate your sweetness and determination."

4) *Reassure, give love and carry on.*

Often adults need to carry on with other activities. It is not always possible to stay nearby when children are upset, especially when a child is upset because we are leaving. A reassuring response from the adult is appropriate and helps the child feel loved and valued. When children are upset, I begin with an active-listening response.

I remember a time at my niece's home when Grace-Ellen was about four. We had had a wonderful time playing. She became upset when I was leaving, crying and saying, "I don't want you to go. I don't want you to go." "You don't want me to go," I replied, an active-listening response. My "I-message" to her: "I'd love to play with you more, but I need to go. I'll see you in two weeks. How about I give you five extra kisses to hold you until I see you again? Do you think five extra kisses will hold you or will you need more?" She smiled through her tears and said with a nod, "Five." She promptly received her five kisses, and a couple more. A happy wave followed me through the door.

Another example: Child, starting to cry: "I don't want you to go." Parent: "You want me to stay at home with you." Child nods. Parent: "I know you feel sad sometimes when I have to go out (second active-listening response), but I'll keep you in my heart and give you extra kisses tonight when I get home (assurance of love and coming back), and a big hug now. (Parent leaves after hug.)

Sometimes when a loved adult is leaving, there is a feeling of the love going away. Giving a promise about when you will return, and giving more love, often fills the need.

Please note: It would not be wise to stay home when the child cries and begs you to stay as this would teach the child that crying and begging are useful social skills to get the parent to do what he wants. The first time, the parent may feel important and loved, the tenth time the parent is likely to feel manipulated, trapped and resentful.

5) Help them understand — explain emotions or situations.

Often children do not understand how emotions work, so it is helpful for them to receive an explanation.

One day when I was visiting a relative, one of my favorite four-year olds was looking quite upset. He was sitting on the couch, staring into space. He had just gotten in trouble for hitting his younger sister. He stared at me seriously when I made my active-listening comment of "You look upset." He then announced, "I'm a bad person."

I said, "You're not a bad person, but you feel bad after you hurt your sister."

"I wanted to hurt her," he said.

"Oh." I thought for a moment. "Sometimes people get angry and want to hurt. But, we're naturally good inside, so after we hurt someone we feel bad. But, that doesn't mean you're a bad person. When you feel bad after you hurt someone, it means you really are a good person."

"Oh," he said. I was pleased to see the look of relief on his face. It would have been a terrible belief to hold.

It is important to explain things to young people in an age-appropriate manner. For example, when a toddler moves to another town and misses her caregiver, it is important to explain that the caregiver still loves her but can't come to the new town because she needs to stay with her husband and children. Of course, in such a circumstance it is important to explain before and after the event and whenever there are questions. One might also want to help the transition with the giving and receiving of a gift and a few phone calls.

6) Help them move out of victim mode by reflecting on the value or behavior they would like to see.

An example: A young child crying over being called a name, "She called me ugly." Parent: "It really hurt your feelings when she called you a name." Child: "She was mean." Parent nods, indicating listening. Parent: "You don't like it when she is mean." Child: "No." Parent, stopping active listening and beginning to start a possible solution: "How would you like her to act?" Child: "Nice." Parent: "Yes, it would be good if she didn't call you names and was nice. What would you like to tell her? Child: "Be nice and don't call me names?" Parent: "Wow, it would be great to tell her that. Pretend she's standing over here and tell her." "Good telling her."

Other responses which can help the child move out of victim mode by reflecting on the value: "What value do you think would have helped in this situation?" Affirm their response. "What would he have done differently if he had used the value of _____?" "What wouldn't have happened?" "How do you think you would feel if you used the value of _____?" "What are some of the things you could do if you stayed in that value?" "Good thinking!"

7) Offer a different perspective — help them reframe the problem.

Once I conducted an LVE training for street educators in Indonesia. A few of the street educators had been street children themselves. One of them really got into his emotions during an active-listening demonstration and shared how bad he felt when rejected by a girlfriend. After actively listening, I reframed the situation he had related: "I know you cared very much for her and wanted to marry her, but you're actually fortunate she left before you got married and had children. You want to marry someone who can really see your beautiful qualities." His smile indicated that the reframing had hit the mark.

8) Help the child think about solving the problem.

1. Empower the young person to solve the problem.

"What do you think you can do about it?"

2. If the above question does not generate a sensible solution, move on to helping her think about who or what could help. Ask: "Who do you think could help with this?" or "What do you think might help?"

3. If the child has still not come up with a sensible solution, give an idea about a sensible direction to take. "What can you do to <u>stay safe</u>?

4. When all else fails: Give a direct suggestion about how to solve the problem.

9) Give correction.

We'll do this one in the section on disciplining with peace and respect.

~ 8 ~

Allowances and Opportunities to Be Responsible

I remember a boy who was going to a neighbor's house to care for their cats while they were away. He was so proud of the money he earned and happily told the neighbors what he was going to buy with it. His enthusiasm to come over and work was completely dampened when his wealthy father said, "Oh, you want one of those. I'll get it for you."

The parents of the child were trying their best to be good parents. They wanted their child to have everything he wanted. However, a child needs to feel capable and useful. He was proud about earning money to pay for something he wanted. His sense of self seemed to deflate with his motivation.

It is important for children to have some chores or responsibilities, even at a young age. It helps them learn how to do things, physically and intellectually, and they acquire social and emotional skills in the process. As they engage in mastering tasks, they feel useful and capable.

In the book, *The Secret Garden*, Martha shares with young Mary about her sickly cousin, Colin: "Eh! Poor lad! He's been spoiled till salt won't save him. Mother says as th' two worst things as can happen to a child is never to have his own way — or always to have it. She doesn't know which is th' worst."

Allow your children to do regular chores and have responsibilities. It is important for the child to feel like, and be, a contributing member of the family. They may go through a short period of complaining and whining about regular chores, but it is well worth the effort. Your reward, in time, will be responsible cooperation, and seeing your child develop new skills and feelings of competency.

Allowance or no allowance?

I'm in favor of a weekly allowance for children. A weekly allowance allows the child to understand the relationship between work and money and provides an opportunity for the child to explore choices, manage impulses and become familiar with the benefits of long-term gratification as she manages money. If providing an allowance is not possible in your situation because there is no extra money, don't be concerned about it, but please don't leave aside regular chores. Each child can be responsible and help the family.

An allowance can act as motivator. Some children easily remember to do their chores and carry them through without complaint. Others do not. If your child is having difficulty remembering, then a chart or list of chores can be a good visual aid. When you start an allowance, you may wish to start with just a couple of chores. Preteens can make their own list. If the child is young, you can make a chart together, using pictures for each task. Enjoy making it; make it pretty and colorful. Then instead of verbally reminding the child about each task, lightly say, "Chores?" and point to the chart with a smile. One word and a smile is a million times better than a frown and 100 words, especially if the words are about chores!

Children helping is a natural part of daily life. As toddlers they can help put away their toys. As they grow they can help set and clear the table, butter the toast, etc. Look at your family life and see when and where they can help. Dishes need doing and trash cans need emptying. Could they help with the garden or with the animals? Perhaps your preteen likes cooking and could make a salad or vegetables a couple times a week for dinner. If they are older, perhaps they are ready to make the entire dinner if you work together to plan it out. What other needs are there? Are the older children doing their laundry? As you positively help them build skills, their confidence will grow.

An allowance serves as a logical consequence. If the chores are done, the allowance is given automatically. If the chores are only partly done, then only part of the allowance is given. For example, if the child only remembers to feed the dog and take out the trash five out of seven days, then most but not all of the allowance is given. As always recommended in this book, dispense the consequence in a sensible, matter-of-fact manner, rather than in a punitive, shaming manner with a moralizing finish. The latter will only generate less of an inclination to do chores while a cheery, "Pretty good, five days without any reminders!" will encourage.

For your own sanity, you may wish to put sensible guidelines around certain chores to consider them to be done properly. For example, the dog needs to be fed before dinner and the dishes need to be washed after dinner. You may wish to set up a bonus on the allowance, that is, an extra 50 cents or pence when all the chores are done properly without reminders.

Children also need time to play, explore and do their homework. Please don't give too many chores unless it is really necessary because of a difficult family situation.

Managing money — Begging for the latest thing

In most societies there are holidays or special dates, such as birthdays, when children receive gifts. As advertisements geared toward young people have proliferated over the years, many children have developed the habit of asking for what they see advertised or what some of their friends have. A child earning an allowance creates an opportunity for the parent to have a practical response, other than no, to yet another request to buy something which is not needed.

Possible responses might be: "That's really nice. Sometimes it's hard to choose what you want to spend your money on," or "Do you have enough money for that?" Perhaps: "Sometimes things grab our attention. Maybe take a little time to think about what you want to spend your money on." If they are persistent and don't have enough of their own money, you might ask, "Do you think you might want to put that on your birthday wish list?"

If a tween or teen wants a ludicrously expensive pair of jeans, you might sit down and talk about it. Occasionally, you may wish to bring up the topic of needs versus desires, or even how advertisers try to convince people they will be liked more or receive admiration if they own or use certain brands. Question: "Is it true that you will be more valuable if you have that or is the company just trying to make more money?" "Who do you really like? Think about so-and-so…. Why do you like him?" …... "So you like her because of her qualities, not because of what she wears."

But return to the request with a sensible reply: "Yes, I think it would be okay to get another pair of jeans. Normally we spend X amount. I'm willing to provide that amount of money. But, if you want a really expensive pair of jeans, you will need to come up with the money greater than X." If she wants to earn extra money for this purpose, together discuss something useful and productive for her to do that is okay with you. For example, you might be comfortable with her babysitting for certain neighbors, tutoring younger children or doing some extra chores over a period of time.

If the child doesn't want to work for the extra money and doesn't have the money saved, but is still asking for the item, perhaps it can go on the birthday wish list. Are you tempted to give in to the begging for an item that is not needed? Do you feel guilty about not getting the child what he or she wants? Perhaps work through it by knowing it is important for people, both children and adults, to be able to resist impulses and delay gratification. Love and detachment is a beautiful balance – love the child and detach from the whining. Toward birthday time, perhaps you can query to see if the pair of jeans is still the most important thing on the list.

~ 9 ~

Each Child Is Unique

Once a woman who came to see me wanted to know, "Why are my four children so different?" She continued, "They have the same parents, they have all lived their lives in the same home and we have treated them the same way. Why are they so different?"

I answered her query with psychological theory and talked about the effect of birth order. We continued talking for the rest of the hour about a few problems she wanted help with, but as she was leaving she turned to me again with a perplexed look and said, "But I wish I knew why they are so different."

I looked at her and decided to tell her what I really thought — even though it was a spiritual answer rather than a psychological one. "They're all different souls."

"OH!" she replied with a surprised look. "Of course!" She left with a happy smile.

Each child is unique, a sacred trust. To love, to value, to nourish, to guide and to keep safe. Parents are the protectors as they provide a safe, nurturing nest from which children can explore and be creative, discovering who they are and developing the skills and capacity to venture out in the world, with respect, confidence and purpose. Children are not blank slates, but come into the world with their own sense of being and personality. Some grow up easily with love and a little guidance, rarely needing correction. Others challenge us to understand their needs and cope with their behavior.

I think each child has something to teach us. Some teach us how to love unconditionally, some teach the importance of patience, others the importance of compassion and controlling our anger and some teach us the importance of sweetness or keeping our promises. Life has lessons for us all.

Why is your child in your life? What beauty has each of your children brought into your life that you would not have experienced without them? What are you learning from them? If things are difficult at times, for there are those times for all, which value, virtue or quality would help you deal with the challenge? Bring that value or quality into your mind and imagine the possibilities. Use the strength of that value or quality to help make the possibilities a reality.

Section Three

Disciplining
with Peace and Respect

~ 10 ~

Punishment — To Cane or Not to Cane

Once I was interviewed in Singapore by a reporter who wanted to know if I thought parents should cane children or not. As you may have guessed, I said, "No." I talked about why I thought violence was harmful in relationships.

Violence violates. Violence destroys the feelings of trust and safety that are so vital in healthy relations. When parents are violent with children, fear and hurt are created. With repeated violence over time, children develop a deep sense of inadequacy and shame. Those who grow up being treated violently usually either stay with the emotions of hurt, fear and inadequacy, or those emotions fester into resentment and rage in an attempt to have some sense of identity and control. Unfortunately, these tendencies interfere with being happy and having healthy relationships.

The reporter asked if my father had ever caned me. I said, "No, he never hit me. The most punishment I ever received from him was a fifteen-minute talk." I shared a story about a girlfriend and me walking into town, only a few blocks away, when I was eleven. We stopped at the Greyhound Bus Depot and got something to drink. When my Dad found out, he came into my room and told me he was upset. He explained that I should not go to the Greyhound Bus Depot without him or my Mom as there could be dangerous people there and he wanted me to be safe. I understood and never did it again.

I really enjoyed being with my father. As children, he would play with us, swinging us around and teaching us to build little wooden trains in the garage. My earliest memory was sitting on his shoulders with my hands holding onto his forehead. He taught us things, took us camping and to the beach . . . and he always treated me with respect. One of the ways he taught me about responsibility was asking if I would like to do extra chores, and then paying me by the hour. I became his bookkeeper, an hour a week, at 13.

Fifteen years before my father died, he asked me if I would go on vacation with him and my mother. For the next 14 years, I would fly out to wherever they were for a couple of weeks and we would enjoy the beauty of the nearest national park. We loved hiking and rafting, simply talking and being in nature. I miss him still.

I looked at the reporter and asked if her father had ever caned her. She looked down initially, and then told me, "He had canes in every room in the house. We all got canned almost every day."

"What are canes made of?" I asked.

"Bamboo. He would buy them by the bundle."

"How do you feel about your father now?" I asked.

She looked uncomfortable. "Well," she answered hesitantly, "I feel okay about him now."

I think she had to work through a few things earlier in her life to even be able to share that okay.

I imagine her father loved her. He was probably enacting what his parents did, thinking it was best. But, I am sure that now he would love to have more than an okay.

Punishment looks effective . . . for a little while

Punishment often seems effective as the results are immediate. The parent yells or hits and the child immediately stops doing the offending behavior. Of course, the child may begin to do the behavior again once the parent is out of sight. So has the child really learned more than simply not doing the behavior when the parent is within sight?

When a child is punished for doing something minor, the suppression of the negative behavior usually lasts no longer than three days — although for many children it is much briefer. However, after the period of suppression the negative behavior usually becomes worse. Why? The punitive action toward the child negatively affects the parent-child relationship.

The common emotional reactions to punishment are fear, hurt and/or feelings of inadequacy. These can quickly change into resentment, anger and a desire to retaliate. If the adult communicates, verbally or nonverbally, that the child rather than the behavior is bad, the child develops shame. Many children, in their anger, repeat the offending behavior on purpose. Their revenge is often getting the parent upset.

The parent may get more upset, frustrated and/or angry at the child's worse behavior and perhaps at his or her own feelings of inadequacy with the lack of control. The parent may punish more in an effort to gain control, unwittingly entering into a power game. Unfortunately, there is then further damage to the relationship. The child may feel abandoned emotionally and react by becoming depressed, oppositional (completely defiant and rebellious) or withdrawing from the relationship. In the latter instance the child usually voices not caring about any of the punishments /consequences the parent is handing out. The latter behaviors are, of course, cause for concern.

Parental love is the treasure

For young children, the love and affection of their mother and father is life's greatest treasure. Withdrawal of a parent's love is devastating to children, even later in life.

Some children misbehave if they cannot get the parent's love and attention. If they still cannot get the attention, they ratchet up their misbehavior. After all, even anger from the parent is emotional contact; it is acknowledgement they exist. Without love, without attention, without emotional acknowledgement and connection, they feel as if they are nothing.

Negative attention harms

When children are subjected to verbal negativity, be it in tone or harsh words, their sense of trust and wonder is violated, the feeling of safety evaporates and their joy of being is crushed. Few emerge unscathed from childhood, for harsh negative attention, punishment or abuse can come not only from parents and caregivers but from adults in different roles of authority and from peer bullies.

Children on the receiving end of frequent negativity who have a tendency to feel disheartened can become fragile. They become timid and almost desperately try to please others in an effort to avoid the harshness of anger and violence. When they become parents, they often try to do the opposite of what their parents did. They may be too passive at times, not recognizing their own rights and fearful of setting appropriate boundaries. But in extreme situations, the negative behaviors their parents modeled can erupt for a few moments. A lot of healing needs to be done as they become adults and learn they do not need to be victimized any longer. It is beautiful to see their depth of compassion and love as they heal and learn to fly again.

Other children who receive frequent negativity, gradually bury their hurt and fear with anger and learn to imitate the actions of their parents, adopting the belief that this is the way to be in order to not be hurt, in order to be powerful. Research demonstrates that children who are hit by adults are more aggressive than their peers by the age of five. They try to control others in order to feel in control. They tend toward arrogance, can be mean and do not honor the rights of others. As they grow older, some use the same tone of voice to their parents that they received. It is difficult for them to want to change as they are afraid of the fear and hurt inside and do not know how to manage the anger. But, they too can heal in a beautiful way if they have the fortune of relationships with people who are loving, kind and healthy, people who can set boundaries while seeing and understanding the pain of another.

Twenty seconds of negativity from an adult increases the child's negative behavior!

Almost all parents want to be good parents. They want to treat their children with love. However, it is easy to get caught up in giving negativity despite the best of intentions, sometimes out of frustration, sometimes out of tiredness and sometimes simply because one doesn't know what else to do. The aim of the occasional-negativity-giving parent is to stop the child from continuing a particular behavior, to control the child's negative, frustrating or dangerous behavior and get it to go away.

Research shows, however, that when an adult gives more than 20 seconds of negative attention, such as scolding or shouting, the child's negative behavior increases after a short time. By heightening the dynamics of frustration, blame, anger, hurt, resentment and alienation in the adult-child relationship, the child's overall negative behavior grows.

One hour a week of play — and half of the negative behavior went away

As a young educational psychologist, I enjoyed reading a book by Robert Eimers and Robert Aitchison on the importance of play in the parent-child relationship. They noted research in which there was a 50 percent decrease in children's problem behaviors when their parents played with them three times a week for twenty minutes, for three weeks.

In three short weeks, half of the problem behaviors simply ceased when the parents played with them one hour a week! There were no other interventions on the part of the parents. If they had added speaking peacefully and respectfully, listening, using encouraging words and noticing the children's positive qualities, thinking time and logical consequences, what would the percentage have dropped to? What do you think would happen to the whole family if the parents were to enjoy being mindful and nurture themselves, each other, and the children more? Consistent love and respect have many fruits. Happiness and deep trust are only two.

What kind of relationships do you want?

I remember a child who told me about spilling a glass of milk at home. His parent screamed at him and then made him lick it up from the floor. There is a world of difference when the adult "in control" is demeaning, or respectful and kind.

When small children drop something, it is an opportunity to help them learn to clean and to show them how to hold the object properly. Could it also be a moment to realize that mistakes are opportunities to learn? That one does not need to become angry at the self or others when "things happen"? Could the unexpected become a time to laugh and cooperate together? A kind and positive attitude does not fly into blame.

When the "big person" does not go into blame, the "small person" does not need to feel shame. A task can be learned more easily when our dignity is intact.

True discipline . . . leading the way?

The root word of discipline in Latin is to educate. The root of educate is educe, "to draw from within." Another word associated with the word discipline is disciple. A disciple follows the master. Would the model of real discipline be a parent who peacefully and respectfully leads his or her children to discover and develop their natural beauty . . . qualities . . . and values . . . to be the gift they are meant to be to the world?

~ 11 ~

The Real Timeout — Thinking Time

Timeout is a method often taught to parents and teachers to deal with children when they are misbehaving. In timeout, usually the child is directed to sit alone for a short time or go to another room for a certain amount of time. Originally drawn from the theory of contingency management, also known as behavior modification, timeout is not considered punishment but a withdrawal of positive reinforcement. We were told timeout would be effective if the child liked the environment and did not want to be excluded from it. Conversely, if the child did not want to be in the environment from which she was being excluded, timeout would not be effective. The positive reinforcement might be the parent's love, the task being enjoyed or the attention of a friend or teacher.

The principal reason for implementing timeout? When done properly, it stops the negative behavior in a non-punishing manner, eliminating the need for punishment and all its negative ramifications. This fits in well with a values-based approach. If we want to create a positive, loving healthy environment, we need to get out of the cycle of blame, inadequacy and shame, fear, hurt, resentment, anger, alienation and retaliation. When timeout is used in an angry or shaming manner, it acts as a punisher rather than a removal from the positive.

My understanding of how to do a "thinking-time timeout" has grown as I have worked with Living Values Education over the years. Creating peace tents, talking to children about the purpose of family and offering peace bears as thinking-time companions makes a real difference in children's receptivity to being timed out. It also improves the quality of their response after thinking time as well as their desire to "grow" the positive behavior. Before I share about that, I would like to share a couple of stories about using timeout in extreme situations, simply to illustrate how effective it can be and how it can be adapted for individuals in different circumstances.

An extreme situation

When I had been a school psychologist for just a few years, I worked with a wonderful special education teacher of developmentally disabled children, with IQs of 30 to 50. She called me one day when I was at another school to ask me to immediately come and help her. I quickly drove over and learned she had a new 11-year-old student. He was a foster child and had very little language. His misbehavior was frequent and violent. When I arrived he was picking up a typewriter. He threw it on the floor and then went to a bulletin board and began tearing down the papers. The teacher told me he had torn out some of the hair of one of the other students. We tried timing him out in a chair, but he stood up, picked up the chair and threw it toward us. We cleared out the teacher's small glass-paneled office, adjoining the classroom. She obtained a blue padded mat for the floor the next day. When "Tom" would do something inappropriate, we calmly, firmly and respectfully named what he was doing, for example, saying "No throwing, Tom. Timeout." One of us would take his hand and lead him to her office from which he could watch the activity in the classroom. Once he was in the office, we would close the glass-paneled door and stand there, looking away from him and holding the door shut. He would scream and pound on the door.

The first time I led him into the office for a timeout, he screamed for a very long three minutes. As soon as he stopped, I counted just two seconds, opened the door and said, "Good being quiet, Tom. Now go sit down." I remember the first time I pointed to his chair. He went and sat down on top of another student and began pulling her hair. "No sitting on people, Tom. Timeout." I led him back to the office and repeated the procedure, making sure I led him directly to his own chair the next time. This went on for a few days, but the screaming quickly reduced from three minutes, to two, to one, to a few seconds. Within several days, when led to the office he simply stood — without screaming or banging on the door. Then we gradually increased the time he was quiet before opening the door and directing him to his chair. Initially we opened the door after two seconds of quiet, then it was five, ten, fifteen, then twenty seconds and longer. After a couple of weeks, the teacher put her furniture back in the office and rolled up the blue mat next to a classroom wall. Tom would quietly stand by it for three minutes when timed out.

The beauty of this change was once the behavior was controlled, he began to learn. His teacher paired saying a word with sign language and a picture. Soon his vocabulary grew and he could talk in four-word phrases and communicate. He quickly became a cooperative pleasant student who enjoyed interacting with the adults and other students.

The boy with 1000 fights

Another timeout story is about a boy who had 1000 fights before coming to our school as a fifth grader. An intelligent, good-looking lad with an easily-triggered temper and a history of abandonment, hurt and anger, we did not allow "Jason" to start school until our team met with his father and step-mother. We came up with an array of positive consequences should he control his behavior. The parents were helpful in agreeing to carry through with a couple of negative consequences, if needed. Our hope was the positives would be powerful enough to work alone. We talked of a new beginning with peers if he was fight-free. There was a promise of weekly counseling with me, lunch with me if his first three weeks were fight-free and the opportunity to be a peer mediator. An important part of the plan was the option to timeout himself.

I asked, "Does your chest get tight when you're getting upset and feel like fighting?" With Jason's "Yes," I continued: "You have the opportunity for a new beginning here, where you can make friends and do well in school. You're smart and good looking. If you don't have any fights, perhaps "Mr. Chase" will let you be a conflict resolution mediator in three months." Mr. Chase nodded. "Would you like to have the privilege of timing yourself out when you start to get upset? Jason looked interested. "Great," I said. "Just signal the teacher, and when he nods, you can go outside and cool yourself down for five minutes. That means you can stand by the door and cool yourself down. It does not mean you knock on the door, call out to kids passing by or go play basketball. It means you stand by the door. Then when you feel you're ready to go into the classroom and be able to accomplish what you want to accomplish, then you can go back in. You would decide when you want a timeout. Would you like that privilege?" Jason nodded, and we were on our way to the rest of the school year — without a single fight.

Thinking-time timeouts — Without the anger

When an effective timeout is established, there is no need to give punishers. It allows us as caregivers to stop using negative methods with a child. If the adult is beginning to get upset, timeout also creates a few minutes to regain the peace and respect we are consciously choosing. Without the "need" to be negative, our focus can be on enjoying the self and each other as we live life.

A thinking-time timeout can be used with children as young as 18-months. The timeout period can range from part of a minute up to 15 minutes. Longer than 15 minutes is ineffective.

Timeout is much easier to set up and carry out once the adult truly understands it can be done without anger — and is best to do without anger. I often see people use timeout only when they are feeling angry. It is as though the adult is not comfortable setting a limit, boundary or consequence without feeling justified by his or her own frustration.

It is good, and essential, for parents to give appropriate limits and guidelines to their children. Doing this without anger has many benefits. First, we can stay peaceful. A second benefit is we don't have to wait so long to stop the misbehavior! When we timeout in a firm, kind and matter-of-fact way, we avoid the downward spiral of feelings of frustration, blame and anger on our part and feelings of inadequacy and shame, resentment, alienation and retaliation on the part of the child. Without these emotions the child can look more clearly at his own behavior, increasing the likelihood of positive change.

A talk about family — Introducing thinking time

In the family, plan to introduce a thinking-time timeout when you are feeling calm and loving. You might want to say something like the following to your child, adapting it to your own beliefs, style and the age of the child: "Families are for giving happiness and love to each other, and growing up strong and kind and healthy." Ask: "What do you think families are for?" "How do you give love and happiness?"

Continue: "In our family, we are good at giving love and happiness to each other lots of the time, but sometimes we forget and give sorrow." You may wish to ask, actively listening or acknowledging after each question: "How do we give happiness?" "How do we give sorrow?" "What kind of giving sorrow hurts someone else's feelings?"

Continue: "So, when a person gives sorrow, it's important to think about what we can do instead. So, from now, when someone is giving sorrow, your Dad/Mom and I will _____." Tell the children the signal you will be using. It might be holding up your hand, pointing, making a peace sign or saying "Thinking time." "That means I would like you to go to _____ and sit for __ minutes to think about what you could do or say to give happiness instead of sorrow."

For young children — Select a peace bear and a thinking place

Have you ever seen a two-year old tantrum when they are timed out? This often happens if the child is introduced to timeout in a stern manner and sent to another room to sit alone. It makes sense if you know that the scariest thing for a two-year old is losing the parent. If the parent is angry, and the child has to go to another room and stay alone, the child may fear he is losing the parent — or the love of the parent. Hence, it is doubly important to introduce thinking time in a positive way to two-year olds.

When you introduce thinking time to a toddler, in addition to the above, choose a plush animal "to help you think" and a place to have thinking time. Ask: "Which one of your animals will help you think about a way to give happiness instead of sorrow? Your brown bear or your kangaroo or . . . ?" Regarding the place, ask: "Where would you like to sit with your bear for thinking time?" Go with the child to get the chosen plush toy and then walk to the thinking place. The place can be in the same room as you, but let it be a specific chair or cushion.

Explain in a sweet but slightly firm manner: "If I notice you are giving sorrow, then I will ask you to think about how to give happiness by giving you this signal. I want you to sit here with your bear. Your bear can help you calm down and feel full of love again — and your bear can help you think about what would be good to do instead. Then I'll ask you what you thought of to do instead." Practice doing a thinking time when they are feeling good. Lead the child gently by the hand to the place, have her sit for a little while with the plush animal. Perhaps say, "Wow, you sat so quietly. Did your bear tell you a special way to give happiness?"

Most three-year olds will be able to go to their special thinking-time place independently and some four-year olds are quite comfortable having thinking time in another room. If they are weepy or hesitant, allow them to be in the same room. Generally, once the procedure is established, increase the time to two minutes for a two-year old and three minutes for a three- to five-year old. When you are starting timeout with a toddler, 20 seconds is fine for the first few times.

With an 18-month old, it is an opportunity to stop a negative behavior quickly and/or help the child calm down. Go with him to his plush toy waiting on a special pillow or chair. Perhaps say, "Listen to what your peace bear has to say for a moment." After ten seconds, actively listen to the emotions you observe or in a few words describe the behavior you saw, such as "No pulling the puppy's tail. The puppy only likes loving touches, just like you." "Can you think of a good way to touch the puppy?" . . . "Show me on my arm." "That was a nice touch. I think the puppy would like that very much." Gradually increase the time from ten seconds to 30 seconds.

Ask what they learned — or what they think would give more happiness

For a toddler or young child using a favorite plush toy as a thinking-time partner, you may wish to ask: "What does your Peace Bear think would be a good idea to do next time?" Listen respectfully. A 20-month old might give just a one or two-word response. Replies might be: "Well, that's a good idea." "It sounds like that would work." "It sounds like that would help." Or even, "Oops, I think you and the Peace Bear still need to do some thinking. It sounds like you thought that when you were still angry. Did your feelings get hurt?" Actively listen with love and respect and acknowledge the feelings shared. Problem solve together, for example: "What do you think would help?" You might help them think about how others might feel with such queries as: "How do you think _____ would feel if you did that?" "How would you feel if someone did that?"

If the child cannot come up with an appropriate positive thought, feeling or behavior to try, suggest one. You might try something like: "I was thinking too while you were sitting with your bear. One thing I thought of was _____." However, always let the child suggest one or two things first. Always end with love and warmth. If they are little, you might think about how long they can do the new positive behavior and add, "Do you think you can do that till snack time?"

The insights and wonderful alternatives two- and three-year olds can produce are remarkable! Give the child a hug or a special smile when you see the new behavior.

Peace tents for toddlers and up!

One of the things we suggest doing in LVE is making Peace Tents in classrooms or common rooms. Once when I was in South Africa at a residence for street children, we made a Peace Tent out of see-through material attached to the ceiling with an opening in front. The children had drawn pictures of a peaceful world after a visualization and a colleague from France had them practice filling themselves with peace as they all laid down on the floor in a circle with their feet together. The children loved visiting the Peace Tent and we would see a few quietly sitting there whenever we passed by.

In the Peace Unit of the *Living Values Activities* books there is a visualization of a peaceful world and an activity or two on filling yourself with peace. You can download the Peace Unit from livingvalues.net free of charge. Children can draw pictures of what makes them feel peaceful or objects from their peaceful world visualization and decorate the Peace Tent. Perhaps your children would like to make a Peace Tent in their room or maybe you would like to create a peace place in the family room. A Peace Tent can be small and simple. Gather see-through material together at one end, secure it with a ribbon or string, attach that end to the ceiling and let the other end drape on the floor. Create an opening in front.

You might wish to do the "Filling Yourself with Peace" Quietly Being Exercise in the tent. Perhaps the children would like to have a pillow or two on the floor. The Quietly Being Exercises and values songs for children three through seven years old are also available on the livingvalues.net website if you wish to play them. You might want to make up your own. Imagine huge bubbles and have fun creating a flow of peace, love and comfort. After a few months of listening to the commentaries, perhaps the children would like to make up their own.

Be consistent, give the consequence

Six- and seven-year olds have it down! "I don't need thinking time, Mom," they call out, "I know what to do!" They tell you this after they have been engaged in teasing a sibling or breaking a house rule and you have told them to go to thinking time. Simply reply in a matter-of-fact way: "Too late, thinking time," and point to their special place for the allotted time. Please note:

> Don't continue the conversation at that time as it would positively reinforce their tendency to argue with you and get out of a consequence.

> You are providing an opportunity for the child to break away from the energy and momentum of teasing or misbehavior and have a few minutes away from the attraction.

> Allow the full time once the child is timing out easily, that is, two minutes for a two-year old and three minutes for a three- to five-year old. Five minutes for six- to ten-year olds is fine.

If they choose to stay longer in their Peace Tent because they want to, allow them to do so. You may even wish to join them there to ask what they learned or think they should do instead — or to be peaceful with them! Remember, this is not punitive, so enjoy being with the child. Perhaps something is going on and you can provide a listening heart.

Thinking time with teens

One of my favorite LVE teachers in South Africa is a small, short woman. Her teenage students often towered over her. She established a Peace Corner in her classroom with a small sofa. The students had decorated the corner with pictures about times when they felt peaceful. In LVE, students are introduced to the concept that it's when we are having a difficult time and don't feel okay that we get grumpy or are disruptive. When we are feeling okay, it's much easier to do well. When this teacher would notice one of her students becoming upset, she would simply walk up with her CD player, look up at the student and say, "Would you like to borrow my CD player for a while?" The students knew this was her way of telling them they had the opportunity to do a thinking time and pull themselves back together. She told me they always accepted the offer and would come back to the classroom routine when they were okay again. The teen would decide when to leave the sofa and come back to his desk. Some would sit in the Peace Corner for five minutes and others ten.

Is thinking time appropriate for your teenager? With many teens it is not necessary. However, if the teen is being negative with younger siblings, it can be a useful tool. Thinking time will stop the negativity temporarily. However, it is your attitude and the talk afterwards that is even more important.

If a teenager is starting to be rude, you may want to affectionately say, "You seem a little upset, would you like to take a few minutes to cool down?" Or, if your teenager is getting into a verbal argument with you, it is a good time to have a thinking time for both of you. You may want to say somewhat firmly, "Let's both take thinking time for ten." Including both of you is a respectful way to initiate thinking time. I have excluded myself when children are arguing and I'm tired, saying, "I'd like the two of you to go into the family room or outside for a while, I need some Me Time." As the attention of a positive adult is the sought-after commodity, removing yourself from their company is removing the positive reinforcer, hence this also acts as a timeout.

If you are thinking of establishing thinking time with your teen, perhaps reflect on the bigger picture by yourself or with your partner. Are you having family time together? Are you having at least three uninterrupted dinners a week together? Are you getting some Us Time with your child daily? Perhaps there is an old ritual they would like to reactivate. How is your relationship with your teen? If you feel they are getting sufficient loving relationship time, but are going through a period of negativity with their siblings, and you've talked together with insufficient results, thinking time might be a good idea.

When establishing thinking time with your teen, do the introductory talk noted previously. After discussing the purpose of the family, and the need to give happiness instead of sorrow, you may wish to expand the discussion and ask if there is anything they would like to share and if there is something they would like from you and your partner.

Then discuss the details and the purpose of thinking time. The purpose is to "center" again, to get into a state of peace, respect and sensibility where you look at the importance of giving happiness and not giving sorrow, and have enough self-respect to come up with a positive solution. When we feel good about ourselves, and recognize the love our family has for us, and we for them, it is much easier to come up with a way of interacting that gives happiness. You may wish to ask, "What would help you center? Once you're centered it's a lot easier to think of a way to handle the situation that gives happiness."

Thinking time is not a time for playing video games or texting other people — it is time to be with yourself. You may wish to ask, "How much time would you like for thinking time?" Discuss your reality, such as "Sometimes we both get upset with each other. When that happens, it helps me to have a bit more time than you usually need. It takes me about ___ minutes to calm down and be loving and receptive again. I really want to be in a loving space with you when we talk because it's only with love and respect that we solve things in a good way. I'll call you when I'm ready. If you're okay in ten minutes, then it's okay with me if you do something else while you're waiting for me."

As noted in earlier sections, it is important to timeout the child before you are upset. Try to do it even before you are annoyed — when you first notice the inappropriate behavior which merits timeout. Thinking time should depend on their behavior, not on your mood. If you do it calmly, it will work well.

Talking after thinking time with teens

After thinking time, help the teen create an alternative behavior. Then, you can respectfully ask, "Were you able to think of a way to give happiness? What could you have done instead of hitting your brother?" Or, "Were you able to think of a way to do that differently?" Positively remark on the teen's alternative.

Your attitude is important. You are not just discussing a possible alternative behavior. You are being an example of communicating when there is a challenging situation or a conflict. Be prepared to listen with love and respect to whatever the child has to say. When we listen with respect, the teen can share his feelings. When we accept those feelings, the teen is better able to generate the self-acceptance that will allow him to come up with a sensible and positive solution.

If your child comes up with a negative solution, reflect. What is happening? Is there hurt, resentment or anger? Detach a little. Sit back and be accepting, be the listener. Know the most important thing you can do is be a safe haven for your child. Listening and being accepting helps keep your child safe. Listen until your teen's emotions subside. Actively listen. Then ask if there is anything you can do to help.

You may wish to reread the section on active listening and explore the alternatives given "After active listening." But always, if this has been an emotional or serious conversation, let your child know you are glad he shared and that you love him — and will work with him till the situation is better.

The frequency of timeouts will decrease over time as you help your children explore how to give happiness — and acknowledge their positive efforts. But, don't hesitate to use it occasionally if there's a need.

~ 12 ~

Do Your Children Only Listen When You Shout?

Parents often rush, telling children what to do as they quickly pass through a room and go on. After three requests, or five, seven or ten, with no response, parents are frustrated. It is then that many parents find themselves speaking a lot louder than they wish. The complaint: "Why do my children *only* listen when I shout at them?"

When a child begins kindergarten, it's easy to tell if the parent is a screamer because when you ask the child to do something, he completely ignores you. It is as though you don't exist. You then know he believes he doesn't need to pay attention to an adult unless the adult has a certain "tone". Yes, that screaming or threatening tone.

I establish friendly eye contact with the child and ask in a light way, "Do you know what I want you to do?" If the child does, I smile and say, "Great. I want you to do that." If the child does, wonderful. If not, I tell him again and then lead him by the hand to do what is requested. Very quickly, the child learns he needs to pay attention to this adult even when she is speaking in her quiet voice!

Children watch us and know our habits. They know if we will remind them of something as we are going through the room, not bothering to check to see if it has been done. It is much more fun to continue playing. Yet, they remain alert to the parent's voice tone and know when they had better start complying. They know at which tone a threat is likely to become a reality. "Okay, okay, I'll do it, I'll do it!" they shout.

The next time you want the child to do something, pause, get within a couple of feet, look at him with friendly eye contact, and say what you want done. When the task is done, make a positive remark or thank the child for doing it so quickly.

If your young child does not respond, then do the above again, that is, pause, get within a couple of feet of your child, look at him with friendly eye contact, and say what you want done. Gently lead the child to the task. If the child gives you a hard time, calmly call a thinking time. After thinking time, and a little chat, he can complete the task.

If the child is older, also be more aware and let her know in a light and friendly way that you are paying attention. Add I-messages occasionally if you are feeling a little pressured. For example, "I'm feeling a little stressed as I like having everything cleaned up before company comes. I would appreciate you doing this now." Or, "I would like you to chop the vegetables now. If they're chopped now, dinner will be on time." Or, simply, "Honey, I'm running late, could you do that for me right now?"

Children soon figure out you are paying attention to what you say to them. All the above is simply establishing that you do mean what you say when you are speaking in a normal tone of voice. As a rule, think about what you realistically want a child to do, communicate that clearly and positively, and follow up. As they improve in follow-through, gradually decrease positively affirming every time. A smile, a "Thanks, buddy!" or a remark about how responsible they are being serves as a loving acknowledgement of their cooperation.

Don't micro-manage older children and partners ...

In general, the prior is appropriate for small children who are not paying attention to the directions of their parent. You are helping your child learn to pay attention to you and obey when you are speaking in a regular tone of voice. This is important for your stress level, their safety and peace in the household.

With older children or adult partners, the above is appropriate when you need something right away. For example, perhaps you are stressed because you need to leave for work or the airport. However, with older children and partners, it is best not to micro-manage. Always give the least amount of direction needed which allows things to function well. Constant requests are a drain on a relationship. People need "space". They need freedom to carry through their responsibilities in their own way. By the time children are older and partners are partners there is usually a normal routine, and daily and weekly responsibilities are established. They know what needs doing. A patient, appreciative attitude adds harmony to daily life.

If an older child is not doing what is needed in the family, that is a different matter. It may be time to put requests on hold for three weeks. Instead, reflect, be appreciative of who she is, listen, spend some Us Time and enjoy family time together. Actually, the same is true for a housemate, friend or partner! Rebuild the relationship for a few weeks and then have a dialogue. Share your feelings and ask for help with what you need, with love. Cooperation follows love.

Years ago I lived with a delightful friend who was a bit untidy. Clean, but untidy. We got on very well until I hit a point in my life when I began to ask her frequently to pick things up, not leave things around, etc. It took me a little time to realize my nagging was damaging our relationship. I returned to my normal positive, non-nagging behavior, knowing I needed to rebuild the relationship. After three weeks, when things were good between us again, I shared, "It's really demanding at work right now and I'm feeling stressed. When things are untidy around the house, I feel like my life isn't in control and I get even more stressed. Could we keep the house tidy — except maybe for one room? Would that be okay with you?" She instantly said "Yes," and I asked her if she would like to choose which room would be the untidy room. She did a fabulous job of honoring my request. It was never a problem again.

~ 13 ~

Are They Pestering You? — Think Before Saying No

I remember being in the living room one morning with my partner and his two children. One of the girls was at him to do something after he had already said, "No." "Please, Dad? Can I? I really want to. Can I please? But why not? How come? Just for now? Can I?" I quietly minded my own business, but silently counted the number of times she asked as he continued to say "No." 28. 29. 30. She kept at him. He finally became exasperated at 40 and gave in. A loving father and a brilliant scientist, he was somehow oblivious to what was happening.

Sometimes when children ask to do something, parents quickly say "No." The response may be automatic when one is busy. Often we just want to finish what we are doing rather than stopping to do what the child or youth is requesting. But frequently the parent feels guilty later when the child continues to ask, thinking, "Well, why can't she help with the _____? It would be good for her."

When a child has asked to do something he really wants to do, sometimes dealing with the reaction to the request being denied takes more time than it would have to fulfill the request! Some parents give in to the child's request at that time, simply to try to stop the whining, begging, crying or shouting. However, when the parent gives in after saying "No," the child has learned that asking repetitively or acting up works. Some children ask to do something even more than 40 times after the initial no. The parents who change their mind after being asked so many times, are letting the child know nagging works. It builds the tendency to ask even more times the next time!

If you want your children to listen to your no's, think first. Ask yourself: Would it be good for him?" "Would it be good for her?" "Would it be good for us?" If you think it would be beneficial and you can't do it then, think about when you can do it. If you know it is good for the child, it is hard not to feel guilty later. Often it is this feeling of guilt that has us change our mind later. So, if it is good for the child, and you can cope with doing what is being asked for in a kind and nurturing manner, say "Yes."

If you feel it is good for the child and do not have the time right then, or do not want to cope with it at that moment, think about when you will have time. Can you do it in 30 minutes or after dinner? Would tomorrow be better or next week? Let them know when you can do it and keep your commitment. A light approach usually works well: "A great idea. Let's do that after dinner . . . after you clean up your toys . . . after I've had a nap, I'm really pooped right now." Then stick with what you say.

That aforementioned loving father learned to pause and reflect before answering. He was soon sticking to a no or saying, "I think that's a good idea. Shall we do that this afternoon?" Soon the girls were only asking twice.

If your answer is no, stick to it

If it is not good for the child, say "No." If you have thought about it, and your answer is no, stick to it. Children listen well to parents who say what they mean, stick to what they say, and do what they say. They don't keep asking that parent the same question over and over. They only ask once or twice. Say what you mean and do what you say.

It may take two minutes longer to let a child stir the cookie batter if he or she wants to, but it helps the child develop age-appropriate skills and experience the competency and pleasure of cooperative helping. The latter is essential if you want children who wish to help in their teenage years.

Sometimes it is important to explain why the answer is no. I remember a 13-year-old girl who really wanted to go out with a 22-year-old man. I sat with her father to help him think about how he could explain his reasons for the no in such a way that the teen could understand the decision came from love, and concern for her safety and wellbeing.

With tweens and teens, seemingly small decisions can have a large impact. Take time to understand how they feel and why they think it is important. Ask them about their reasons and listen to what they say. Become educated about the situation. For example, students who engage in sports usually have higher academic scores and are less sexually active than their peers. Some sports are safer than others. What are the habits of the social group connected with that activity in your area? Why do they want to be part of the swim team, the football team, be a cheerleader, be on the debate team, go to the tide pools with friends, ride a motorcycle or play paintball? Is it good for them? Do they have their heart set on it? Why? Are there better alternatives that would be acceptable to them? Really listen, dialogue, explore. Take time to think before giving a yes or no. If you feel it is important to deny permission, after listening and conversing, explain your decision so your child can understand it comes from love. Take time to generate an alternative together … or agree to think about possibilities over the next few days.

~ 14 ~

Positive Alternatives, Modeling and Choices

A simple yet often effective way to stop a negative, unsafe or troublesome behavior is to help a child substitute a positive behavior in its place. Not all, but certainly many behaviors can be changed by simply suggesting a positive alternative, modeling the desired behavior or skill or giving the child a choice.

Positive alternatives

Suggesting a positive alternative is especially effective with toddlers when they are acting in a troublesome way. I remember a time when my niece and her 16-month-old son and I were waiting in a lobby. The first few times the elevator chime sounded and people got on or off the elevator, Pierce ran across the carpet onto the marble floor toward the elevator. Monica ran after him the first couple of times and then suggested an alternative: "Wave hello," "Wave goodbye." Soon Pierce was quite content waving to the people coming and going from the elevator and his mother did not need to run after him every two minutes.

Positive alternatives can be used in a variety of circumstances and ways. Occasionally when playing with four or five-year-old boys, they would begin to bomb things with their blocks, Legos or toy planes. I would pick up a similar object and engage in play, but pretend there was a fire. My plane would drop water on the fire. I would call out, "Oh, the fire is still there! I'm going to scoop up more water from the ocean. Wwwwwuuuuu, okay, all full! Take that you fire! It's almost out." Without fail, soon the child was engaged in helping with his water drops.

One of my favorite social skills taught in the LVE activities is called "benevolent assertion". Before LVE, I used it when counseling students who frequently fought at school. With a short fuse and only two ready alternatives in their social tool kit, name calling and fighting, they were often in trouble. We would discuss what happens when people reply aggressively to being called a name and what happens when people respond passively. They never wanted to just walk away as they felt they might be perceived as a coward. Then we would discuss assertive responses.

One assertive response is "I don't like you to call me names, I want you to stop." That is okay for younger children, but sometimes wasn't cool enough for older students. We talked about assertive yet benevolent responses. I would give them an example of something to say to a discriminatory remark: "It wouldn't be such an interesting world if we were all clones." We would then put on our thinking caps to think of other responses for their situation.

A benevolent-assertive statement does not agree with what the offender has said, but is not offensive. I would role play with the student. First, I would ask him to call me a name or say the offending statement and I would give an assertive response. Then I would call the student a name or say the offending statement until he could handle giving me the benevolent-assertive response while staying in self-respect. I remember one young man with a long history of fights who avoided a fight during a basketball game by holding up his arm to the other student's arm and asking, "Why are we fighting? We're the same color." A civil instead of an angry response was enough to stop the downward spiral.

Sometimes we need time to think about what a positive substitute behavior might be. You may want to generate alternatives with the child. Perhaps you could ask in a peaceful or respectful tone, "What could you do instead that would _____ (help, keep you safe)?" Often the child/teen will be able to come up with a positive alternative. If not, perhaps suggest, "Let's think on it a bit more," and bring up the topic later in the day or later in the week.

Modeling the desired behavior

Modeling the desired behavior is a great way to demonstrate a positive alternative. For example, when a toddler asks for something inappropriately, perhaps in a demanding tone of voice, quietly model how you would like her to ask. "Mommy, juice please," or "Daddy, may I have some juice please?" depending on the level of language development. No need to scold, just say what you want her to say in the tone of voice you want to hear. With a teenager, instead of modeling you might lightly say, "Could you use your sweet/kind/real-you tone of voice when you say that?"

There are many wonderful things to model, be it our love for nature, for animals, for sunlight on trees, for peace or for the world as our family. Our way of giving love and communicating with ourselves and others are clearly on display. You are modeling a mindful way of being.

Choices

Two-year olds are an absolute delight, most of the time. They enthrall us with their sweetness, innocence and curiosity. Their wonderful questions can get us thinking, and their desire to explore the elements of nature and learn about animals allows us to re-experience the wonder and intricate beauty of small objects and tiny beings in nature. Yet this age has frequently been called "the terrible two's" as it is at two, or a bit before, that most children begin to explore their sense of self and autonomy. All of the sudden, they want to make decisions. It is important for them to do so.

Giving a child choices is a win-win for parent and child. The parent benefits by avoiding a squabble or tantrum while being able to name safe choices which are convenient. The child benefits by feeling some separateness and independence in a positive atmosphere, rather than feeling frustrated. The child benefits by thinking about alternatives, beginning to make decisions consciously and learning about consequences that go with different choices.

Giving choices doesn't stop with two-year olds. Giving choices continues throughout life with people of all ages. It is one of the thinking steps in setting appropriate boundaries.

Remember to make sure you are okay with the choices you offer — and that they are safe. Do give choices that are possible! Have you ever offered a guest something to drink that you didn't have in the house?!

As with anything else, the delivery is important. A caring, respectful tone is terrific.

A few examples . . .

- ★ Would you like some apple juice or orange juice?
- ★ Would you like to wear the blue shirt or the orange shirt?
- ★ Would you like to walk or take your scooter?
- ★ Do you want to choose which color you want now, or would you like to think about it?
- ★ Do you want to set the table or help with the dishes?

☆ Would you rather watch your little sister now or help with dinner later so you can play now?

Giving a choice is a good option when children misbehave in public. The choice for a misbehaving three-year old who is already accustom to timeout might be: "Would you like to sit and eat your meal quietly or go to the car/outside and have thinking time?" To give this choice, one caregiver must be willing to leave the restaurant for the required time. As at home, say this before you are upset, let the child be in silence for two to five minutes and then ask if he can think of what he needs to do instead.

It is always a good idea to prepare the child for a new place, such as going to a nice restaurant or going to see the dentist or doctor. For example: "Eating there takes longer than at home and I want you to be on your best behavior. What does that mean?" "That's right. Good thinking of so many quiet ways to be." Perhaps ask: "Would you like to bring some colors or something else to play with quietly?"

As we are all human, it is also a good idea to prepare for our needs. For example, we get grumpy sometimes when we are hungry or tired and so do the children. It is wise to give young children something to eat just before they must tag along with us to go shopping. If you are grocery shopping, it will then be easier for them to tolerate your no to an all-sugar diet! You may wish to allow them a choice between two cereals you select. "I want _____!" A possible parental reply: *"I love my girl to be healthy.* You may choose between _____ and _____. Which one would you like?"

The words in italics, "I love my girl to be healthy," is not part of the choice, it is a sentence giving meaning to the choice you are about to give. In the statements below, the first sentence is italicized. These sentences connect meaning to the choice or give clear information about a limit.

> ★ *Grandma's trying to sleep and so it helps if we are quiet.* Would you like to talk quietly or go outside and play?

> ★ *How shall we thank Tasha?* Shall we draw her a picture or pick her some flowers?

> ★ *We have 30 minutes for electronic time today.* Would you like to watch _____ or play _____ video game?

> ★ *Mommy can't carry you right now.* Would you like to walk or be in your stroller?

Often there are reasons behind our decisions. If the reason is one which is age-appropriate for a child to hear, it helps them understand others have needs or informs them about important social behaviors. With "Mommy can't carry you right now," you are modeling that it is okay to state your needs. With "Grandma's trying to sleep and so it helps if we are quiet," you are modeling sensitivity to the needs of another. You are modeling appropriate appreciative behavior with "How shall we thank Tasha?"

~ 15 ~

Doing Tasks They'd Rather Avoid — Grandma's Rule

I remember a mother who came to school to see me about her son. She told me he had been having a problem getting to school on time.

"For how long?" I asked.

"For three years," she replied.

She said she had tried everything. She had tried getting him up earlier and earlier. She laid out his clothes the night before. The morning cartoons had been taken away long ago. When questioned, she told me more about the child. He had friends at school and did well academically. So after a while we returned to the getting-to-school-on-time dilemma.

"What does he like to do in the morning?" I asked.

"Eat."

"Great," I replied, "that makes it simple. Tell him that when he has finished dressing for school and has all of the things he needs for school at the front door, he can have breakfast. Explain that you will be taking breakfast off the table at 7:50, as it is important for him to get to school on time."

"But what if he misses breakfast?" she asked, appalled.

"He may miss it for a day or two. I doubt he will choose to miss it any longer. But, this will only work if you don't nag him in the morning."

"You mean like remind him?"

"Yes. How many times do you remind him in the morning to get up, get dressed, etc.?"

Looking slightly downcast, the mother said, "A hundred?"

"I think we could call that nagging."

Grandma's Rule has a simple format: *When you _____, then you can _____.* The unpreferred activity is stated first and then the preferred activity. While a mother may revert to a cross tone of voice to say, "If you don't eat those peas, you can't have dessert," our theoretical Grandma would sweetly say, "When you eat your peas, then you can have dessert." Or, "As soon as those things are picked up, then you can _____."

If the child whines and asks, "But, can't I play the video game now?" or "Can't I go to Maria's now?" quietly stick to what you said, repeating in a calm, light, reasonable tone of voice, "As soon as you take out the trash, you can play the video game." Or, "As soon as you pick up the toys in the family room, you can go to Maria's." State the unpreferred activity before the preferred activity.

When adults act from a peaceful, sensible place, children hear the message better. A logical and fair message sounds logical and fair when stated in a calm voice. With Grandma's Rule, you are helping your child carry through a necessary chore or life skill. You are helping your child be responsible and create good habits.

No nagging

Have you ever been nagged? Think of a time you were nagged. ......
Did it increase your feeling of resistance? Like people of all ages, children often perceive negativity when nagged or scolded. Consequently, they feel more resistant to complying with the request and are more likely to pout, be sullen

or act more resistant. Nagging changes the dynamics. It becomes the parent's need rather than the child's responsibility.

When I saw the mother with the child who was chronically late to school the next week, she told me he only missed one breakfast. He had been to school on time every day since we spoke. And, she had stopped nagging. Congratulations, Mom!

- 16 -

Logical Consequences —
Allowing Children to Take Responsibility

Logical consequences are a terrific tool for the parental tool kit. A cousin of Grandma's Rule, logical consequences can be positive or negative, but they are always related to the behavior the child is learning. Logical consequences help children learn how life works. When applied well by caring adults, they help children learn to accept rules and develop competencies important for achieving their potential when they are fighting the process of accepting responsibility. It is important for children to accomplish age-appropriate tasks and to know they can affect their own state of being and circumstances.

Logical consequences are part of life. We may be resistant to learning there are consequences, for we want to have the freedom to do anything we want any time we want. But time and the universe have a way of ensuring we will eventually learn. Everyday examples: When you pet the cat gently, she purrs. When you pull the tail of the cat, she will run away, hiss or scratch you. When you eat, your hunger goes away. When you touch a hot stove, you get burnt. When you go outside in the rain without an umbrella or raingear, you get wet. When you don't wear a jacket when it's cold, you get cold. When you wash your body and clothes, they smell good. When you don't wash your clothes or your body, you smell bad. When you do your homework well, you get a good grade. When you don't do your homework, you get a poorer grade. When you don't change the oil regularly, the engine doesn't function as well. When you go to work, you get a paycheck.

Relate the consequence to the behavior

A logical consequence is always related to the task to be learned. When a child is not doing a needed behavior, the adult who wants to apply a logical consequence will need to think about what it would be. For example, if a child is not doing his work in class, a logical consequence is staying after school *until* it is done. It would not be a logical consequence if the child has to stay one hour after school when the work is accomplished well in ten minutes or if the work is not finished at all.

If the children are making too much noise in the house, a logical consequence could be put in the form of a choice: "If you play quietly, you can stay indoors. If you want to make a lot of noise, you will need to go outside and play." Or, if you are feeling a bit tired of the noise and know they will continue to be noisy, you might say, "You're making a lot of noise, you need to go outside for a while."

Give meaning and then a small consequence, if necessary

To build greater understanding, compliance and success, give meaning first and then a small logical consequence if the behavior continues. For example, if a child is throwing a ball against the wall of the house and you don't wish her to do so, tell her why and discuss other places to throw it. For example: "When you throw the ball against this wall, the ball hurts these plants. When you throw the ball there, nothing is hurt." Or, "Grandma has a headache right now, so the noise of the ball against the wall bothers her."

If the child throws the ball against the wall after you have asked her not to, then a logical consequence is to take away the ball. Take away the ball for one to three minutes for a small child, and somewhat longer for an older child, and then give it back. If the ball begins slamming against the wall of the house again after you've given it back, then you might decide to take it away for 30 minutes or the rest of the morning.

State the consequence in a kind and matter-of-fact manner

Logical consequences are effective when they are kindly stated in a matter-of-fact manner. Communicating about a consequence with a negative emotional charge defeats the purpose of having the child look at his behavior as it triggers the dynamics of blame, resentment, anger and retaliation and can set up a power struggle.

When you state a rule and know you have control over the consequence, it is much easier to not get upset. State the rule sweetly but firmly, "You can play with the ball if you throw it over there. If it goes against the wall again, then I'll take it away until after lunch."

Follow-through on the consequence

One mother I worked with was frustrated with her child for not picking up his toys. She wanted the child to pick the toys up in the living room before dinner. The mother would remind the child many times and the child would demand that the mother help him. The mother, in desperation, had been giving in to the child's demand.

The new plan we worked out was for the mother to explain to the child that she would tell him ten minutes before dinner that it was time to pick up his toys. Any toys not picked up would be put away in a box until the end of the week. The mother agreed to tell the child only once and not remind or nag the child. The toys were put in a box at the top of the closet. The child learned in a couple of days to pick up his toys without demanding his mother's help. Carrying out the consequence quietly, calmly and efficiently also helps the child to listen to the parent as the parent is doing what he or she said.

Positively reinforce their appropriate actions, such as cooperating, listening and being helpful. Note how well they did a task or how nice it looks instead of complaining or moralizing about their old behavior. Always make a positive comment, even if it is a simple "Thank you," with a smile rather than moralizing: "See, if you would only have done what I told you to do the first time, we wouldn't have to be doing all of this.…" Moralizing creates the same kind of resistance that nagging does. Be peaceful and let your actions speak.

Discussing the consequence with the child — and the aim of the desired behavior

Sometimes you might wish to ask the child what the consequence should be. Often, children will give themselves a heavier consequence than you would have. When you share you think the consequence is too big, they are usually grateful and accept the smaller consequence easily.

Sometimes, it is important to talk about the aim of a behavior, especially with tweens and teens. For example, if a tween is piling her clean clothes on the floor along with the dirty clothes, you might want to sit down when you are feeling calm and respectfully ask your child what she thinks is the purpose of having clean clothes. Share your thinking about why you think clean clothes are important and your feelings about working to help her have clean clothes and how you feel when you see how your efforts are made worthless by having the clean clothes mixed with the dirty clothes. Perhaps share your feelings: "I don't feel like doing your laundry when I see all the clean clothes mixed with the dirty clothes." Generate possible solutions together. One logical consequence is for the child to do her own wash for a week. Together, decide on a plan that is fair to both of you. Show your child how to work the washing machine in a pleasant manner. Do not be unpleasant as you demonstrate as that would make it into a punishment rather than a logical consequence.

If the dirty clothes and clean clothes are mixed on the floor again, then perhaps the child does her wash for another week, or two. Observe. Does the child need a bit of help? Are there enough hangers? Would she benefit from a little help with organizing? Observe what help is needed and give it with love. Then allow the child to resume responsibility. Positively reinforce her new skills and allow her to complete the consequence.

Allow children to take fair consequences

Sometimes parents want to "protect" their child from fair consequences given by teachers, principals or other adult authorities. This does not protect children. Contrarily, it teaches them to try to weasel their way out of taking responsibility. It can reinforce children for whining or enhancing the story to the parents. Allow the child to take the consequence, unless it is blatantly unfair. Help your child understand not only his own rights but the rights of others. Help him or her respect others and think about the values within the lesson.

A positive and light attitude

Logical consequences can help children have a positive and light attitude toward life even when things go wrong as they are free of blame and guilt. I remember when a wonderful little girl dropped a plate of spaghetti on the floor of the family room. She looked crestfallen and looked up at me with a sorrowful expression. Her expression changed when I asked lightly, "What do we do when we drop food on the floor?"

"Pick it up?" she asked.

"Yes," I smiled and we picked it up together.

When we are light when something goes wrong, we are teaching an attitude toward life. What is more important, people or things? If things go wrong, it's much easier to get through it when we stay loving and kind.

~ 17 ~

Correcting — When Kids Engage in Wrong Behaviors

Sometimes tweens and teens make serious mistakes. When there is a behavior you are really concerned about, such as stealing, it is time to reflect and talk. Think about your values and what you want for your son or daughter before you sit and chat.

When you are calm, and can be serious but loving, sit down with your child. It may take a couple of days to think it through and calm down, but it is well worth the wait. Correction with love can build relationship and result in real change. It can empower your tween or teen to do what is right. The fire of anger usually destroys as it invites resentment. When anger occurs repeatedly, it can open the door to opposition. It is our fear for children and the loss of a bright future for them which fuels emotions that can explode into anger. Under the fear is your love. Wait until you can calmly communicate your love and your values.

Four Steps

> ➤ Step One — Positives: Tell your child you love him or her very much. Talk about some of their qualities.

> ➤ Step Two — Concerns: Tell him or her what behavior has you feeling concerned as you stay in the space of feeling love for the child. Describe the behavior.

> Step Three — Effects: Share the value and positive behavior you feel is important and the benefits of that value and positive behavior. Be specific about the effect the negative behavior is having in the present and/or might have on their future if it were to continue.

> Step Four — Listen and Plan: Listen to your child as well as your own intuition. The first three steps might have accomplished the intent. However, perhaps your child would like to share or would like to suggest something. Perhaps he would like a few days to think. Ask if he or she would like any help from you if the child does come up with a plan.

Stealing

When there has been stealing, a parent might do the above process in the following way. "As you know, I love you very much. You are a wonderful young woman — loving, kind and funny. But I want to talk with you now as I was really surprised and concerned when some money went missing. I want to share something with you from my heart. (By the way, if you know the child has stolen something, don't ask if he or she stole the item, simply state it as a fact.) To me, integrity is the mark of a person. You are getting older now, and I want to talk with you about why I think honesty is so important. When you are honest, you are _____."

I suggested the above approach to a parent. He told me afterwards that his daughter and he had the best conservation they had had in a long time. They talked for a couple of hours and his daughter never stole again.

During the conversation, ask your child if there is anything she needs. Perhaps discuss needs versus wants. If there is a strong want, create an opportunity for your child to obtain that or work toward it, if possible.

While you are engaged in dialogue, check to see if anything is bothering her. At the end of the conversation, tell your child you love her again.

If stealing has occurred, be a little more aware for a few months to be sure the stealing has stopped. If it occurs again, or if it has already happened more than once, consider doing some of the activities in the Honesty Unit of *Living Values Activities for Children Ages 8–14* or *Living Values Activities for Young Adults*, as appropriate for the age of your child. Enjoy the activities together. Don't engage with a punitive attitude of "You had better learn this, this is your punishment because you stole," but with an attitude of "Honesty is not really understood in our society right now. There's a lot of pressure on people to have certain things and acceptance of greed and corruption. I want to do these activities with you so you can deeply think about the role of greed and corruption in our society — and the effect honesty has on relationships."

Take at least an hour or two once a week to be with your child. Do an activity and spend some time together. Do something you both enjoy after the values activity. Be available emotionally, be interested and make the process pleasant. Mind-map together on a large piece of paper. Mind-map honesty and corruption and their effects on the self, relationships, business, society and the world. Ask your child for her answers and share yours. It may be fun to do it with the whole family. Perhaps you can find videos of the effects of honesty and corruption on YouTube. Make sure there is some Us Time daily — and some healthy family time.

Cheating

The steps and approach noted above for honesty are recommended whenever a serious correction is needed. At Step Three, Effects, share the benefits of being honest and not cheating and be clear about some of the consequences of cheating when one is an adult. For example, what would happen to a researcher who cheated by falsifying results? Allow the child to answer, but if not mentioned, share that the researcher's career would be ruined as the integrity of his research would be in doubt.

In Step Four, as you are listening, ask if there is pressure to cheat. Where is the pressure coming from? Listen. It may be coming from peers, from the child's own desire to do well or even be an effort to get into college or to please you. Discuss what is important to you. Discuss how one feels when one earns something honestly versus when it is unearned.

I-messages

"I-messages" allow the parent to share in a non-blaming manner. Rather than "You really scared me, how could you _____?" you could say, "I was really scared when _____." In the honesty section above, the parent gave several I-messages: "I was really surprised and concerned when some money went missing. I want to share something with you from my heart."

I-messages allow parents to share what is underneath the anger. For example, instead of exploding when the child is late, communicate your feelings. "I was frightened when you were so late. I was scared something awful might have happened." Allow the child to respond before generating an alternative, such as "If you think you are going to be late, I would appreciate a call or a text 30 minutes before the time you are supposed to be here."

If you have already exploded with anger over a situation, I-messages can be helpful in explaining what was happening with you. Instead of blaming the child for your anger: "If you would behave properly and come in on time, I wouldn't get so angry," you might say, "I was angry when you came home so late because I was scared you might be hurt." Or, you might say if trying to manage your anger at that moment, "I'm angry right now because I was scared something bad might have happened to you. I'll talk to you when I'm not so angry."

I-messages are useful in many situations. For example, perhaps you have been actively listening as your 15-year-old daughter shares that she wants to go out with a 21-year-old man. After actively listening, your I-message might be, "I'm not comfortable with _____." It would be good to share your concerns so your child understands why you are saying no.

Importance of a correction

I remember a wonderful intern I was supervising. An intelligent, warm, caring young man with an ability to relate easily, he came in one day to tell me about an incident related during his counseling group with five middle-school students. Two of the boys had broken the rear window of a car. They did this at random one night and did not even know to whom the car belonged. I asked him what his response was. "I listened," he replied.

"Yes?" I replied.

"I listened," he said again.

"And?"

"Nothing," he said. He added, "I can tell by your expression that listening wasn't enough."

"Don't you care about these students?" I asked.

"Of course I care," he replied.

"What would you have said if these boys were your own children?" I asked.

"I would have told them it was wrong," he said. "But, I'm doing counseling. Aren't you just supposed to listen?"

"No," I replied. "First you listen, but then it is important to get them thinking about their action and the consequences. It's important to run a correction as otherwise they will think you think it is okay to do such things. I bet by the time you return to that school next week some of the other boys will have done something wrong." Unfortunately, I was right. We discussed some of the other things he could have done which he did at the next session.

The following are a few things you can do when a child has caused hurt to a person or damage to property. A caring, authentic manner while carrying out the below suggestions is a million times better than a blaming, judgmental, accusatory manner. You are attempting to get the child to really reflect and think something through. People are able to think better, and change toward positive responsibility, in a calm, respectful atmosphere. The following items would fit into Step Three and Four.

Develop empathy or compassion for the person hurt. "How do you think the owner of the car felt when he came out and saw the rear window broken?" "How would you have felt if it was your car?"

Develop understanding of the consequences. "What would have happened if you had been caught doing that?" Confirm the consequence(s) and add any further consequences they may not have thought of. For example, one consequence is getting arrested and going to juvenile court. Another is the feelings of parents and extended family.

Discuss the consequences of those consequences and help them build their dream. Another possible consequence would be spending time in a youth-detention facility. "What do you want for your future? How could this affect your future?" "What attitude and actions are going to help you get there?"

Confirm the small-actions-matter lesson – and reinforce values. Small decisions and actions can dramatically affect our future. "What values would keep you safe and on track toward your dream?"

In the above example, these five teens were already troubled and acting out. Counseling was providing an opportunity to be valued and understood, and an opportunity to develop empathy and new perspectives to deter negative behavior and support positive action.

You may have noticed that in the first two examples in the beginning of the chapter about honesty and cheating, there was no shaming or punishment from the parent. The primary consequence for stealing the money and cheating was a values discussion and an opportunity to reflect on values and anti-values. Getting young people to reflect on their actions while in a respectful and caring relationship is far more effective than shaming or punishment. A values reflection with a trusted adult can be a positive lesson they will remember for the rest of their lives. As you help your child gain a greater understanding of a value and its consequences, you are helping them develop an internal guiding compass.

However, there was another consequence in both examples, a secondary consequence. In the first example of stealing, the young person shared she had also "borrowed" money to tease her friend. Hence, at the end of the discussion, parent and child mutually and naturally agreed that the money needed to be returned. In the second example, the school gave a consequence for cheating and the parents wisely allowed the young man to do the detention. In both cases these consequences alone would not have had nearly the effect as the dialogue with the parents.

Restitution or another kind of compensating action is appropriate when possible. Discuss this with your child toward the end of your dialogue as part of Step Four, perhaps asking, "What do you think should be done now?" Examples of restitution include returning stolen money, the child working to earn money to pay for damage to property or repairing the property of another. This might include replacing a cell phone dunked in water or painting over graffiti. If a younger child of a neighbor has been hit, then part of compensating for the action could be apologizing to the child and her parents. Ideas for a compensating action flow easily when there is the understanding of the value. It is naturally a little more difficult to carry out, but taking responsibility is essential.

The four steps can be used effectively for less serious behaviors. There is an example in Chapter 24, "'I Hate You' and Disrespect."

Section Four

Healthy Food
for the Body and Mind

~ 18 ~

Healthy Foods — Help Children Be Happy and Function Well

Children are very affected by their diet, physically, intellectually and emotionally. A healthy diet contributes substantially to a child's health, cognitive development and good temperament.

One of my nieces asked me what to do when her pediatrician said her baby was ready for protein at six months of age. "Yogurt, nutritional flakes and brown rice," was my reply. My niece mixed the nutritional flakes with yogurt. She would puree cooked brown rice and vegetables for the baby. She often used part of what she and her husband were having for dinner. After pureeing, the extra went into an ice-cube tray to freeze for use later in the week. She also pureed fresh fruit. It was easy, cost efficient, and the food was natural and healthy. It did not have the sugar or additives of bottled baby food. It was not months-old food that had lost much of its life force. It was fresh and often organic. She continued with a healthy diet as the child grew. His favorite drink at two years of age was fresh carrot and apple juice, and when I offered him a sliced cucumber with some brown rice at lunch one day, he was delighted with the taste. Interestingly enough, this child has had very, very few days of illness.

The more natural, the better

The general rule for a healthy diet is: The more natural, the better. Whole grains are more beneficial nutritionally than refined grains. Brown rice has more protein than white rice. Indeed, the first vitamins were made from the outer husks of brown rice. Enjoy whole grain breads, brown rice, quinoa, potatoes, legumes and fresh fruits and vegetables.

Eliminate everything with white sugar as the first ingredient! Give healthy cookies as an occasional treat rather than as a snack between meals. Cut up fruit for toddlers. Provide healthy snacks between meals, such as fruit, raisins, raw veggies, raw nuts and whole grain breads and crackers. Almond or peanut butter without sugar is wonderful, unless the child is allergic to peanuts. Add fresh fruit to plain yogurt. Make yogurt smoothies with bananas or a seasonal fruit. Bananas are high in potassium and yogurt and kefir provide beneficial bacteria.

In *The 150 Healthiest Foods on Earth*, Jonny Bowden rates oatmeal, quinoa and brown rice as the three healthiest grains. Oatmeal is a great breakfast for kids and adults. Add raisins, cinnamon and a little cane-evaporated sugar, maple syrup or the natural sugar of your country for sweetener, a little milk and a banana or another fruit, and your children will have a breakfast that provides fiber, protein and has a low glycemic load (meaning it does not affect your blood sugar very much). Oatmeal is one of the best foods on the planet, and it is not expensive. A real grain like this has much more life-force energy than boxed cereals.

Consider making fast food an emergency stop-gap rather than a regular diet. The effect of soda, refined sugars, high-fructose corn syrup and unhealthy fats can create havoc on health. Olive oil and organic coconut oil receive high marks from many nutritionists. Explore real foods. Fruits and vegetables in their natural state create wellness.

Let them help

Involve kids in the making of their food. They will have a good time, you can enjoy the relationship and they will develop competency and confidence in the kitchen as they learn about good food. Allow them to cut up vegetables and grate cheese for a pizza, cheese toast or quesadillas. They can toast bread, make pancakes and peel potatoes for mashed potatoes. Let them help make cookies. The amount of sugar suggested in the recipe can be reduced by 50 percent and result in a better tasting cookie!

Children who begin early with healthy, natural foods like to eat them, and they are much less fussy eaters than children raised on sugared-baby food, sugar-coated cereal, white-flour crackers, candy and cookies. One day when I was packing a snack for a trip to an animal petting farm, a couple of children who were used to white-flour-with-sugar crackers and cookies as their primary snacking food were astonished, and not very pleased, to find their only choices were raisins, dates, carrot sticks and apples. (No need for a lecture on healthy foods, just present their choices!) Once they realized no hidden cookies were going to come out of the cupboard, they accepted all the items — and quite happily munched on them at snack time later.

Lunch can be healthy foods that don't require cooking. Give them healthy choices if they take their lunch to school. Let them be creative in the way they put it together. I love simple picnics under the trees with children with a mixture of fresh fruit, healthy crackers and cheese or humus, perhaps olives, cherry tomatoes, carrots and cucumbers. We all enjoy — and it is easy.

Introducing a healthier diet

If you decide to introduce a healthier diet, you might want to begin with healthier alternatives to things they are accustom to eating. For example, provide whole grain crackers instead of the white-flour-with-sugar crackers, offer fresh fruit instead of canned fruit, provide 100 percent juice instead of a juice drink with 10 percent juice, start using almond butter or a natural peanut butter instead of one with sugar, provide raw nuts instead of roasted nuts and use real cheese instead of cheese food. Find a cereal with whole grains and natural sugar rather than the white sugar-coated variety. Perhaps add something healthy to one of their favorite foods.

In the summer, you might want to put grapes in the freezer, and make icicles out of peach, mango or another of their favorite juices instead of purchasing ones made of white sugar and flavored water. The frozen grapes taste like sherbet and the kids can have as many icicles as they like!

Sodas and colas — Once a month, if you must!

You may be surprised to learn that sodas are one of the worst things you can give to your child. For sixty years, medical researchers in Japan and South Korea have explored the relationship between various illnesses and the acidity or alkalinity of the body. Alkaline indicates a pH of 7 and above; acidic indicates a pH below 7. When the pH of a human's blood, urine or saliva is just above 7, then the body is considered alkaline. A pH of 7.30 to 7.45 is consider optimal for the human body. An alkaline body is associated with health. You might wish to do a web search on acidic versus alkaline diets and find a food chart which categorizes various foods according to their acidity or alkalinity. As you may suspect by now, brown rice, whole grain foods and fresh vegetables are higher on the pH scale than white rice, refined grains and processed food. According to some doctors, the body rarely gets ill if the pH of the blood or salvia is slightly alkaline. Pain and illness are frequent with bodies that are acidic. Colas have an acidity of 3.5 and hence lower the overall pH. Lack of exercise and sodas, with their low acidity and high levels of white sugar, are major contributors to the alarming rise of obesity and diabetes in children. Water and healthy drinks are important for children and adults.

A trick for success

This is all fairly easy to do if you shop when you are *not* hungry and only bring healthy food into the house. It's much harder to resist sodas, cakes, cookies, candy and ice cream when they are in the cupboard or freezer. Perhaps buy them for special occasions or an occasional treat. For daily fare, experiment with fresh healthy choices. Soon the whining will stop.

Sorry, but the microwave . . .

I learned a few years ago that microwaving food destroys much of its benefit. Dr. Linda Page, a leading nutritionist and naturopath, considers microwaving to be one of the worst things that ever happened to the modern diet. Microwaving food kills its enzymes. As she noted: "Enzymes are the catalyst for every body process. None of your vitamins, minerals or hormones can work without the right enzymes." Enzymes allow your food to digest and your cells to heal. Fresh fruit and vegetables, yogurt, kefir, and sprouted legumes such as lentils and mung beans, are full of enzymes.

Breakfast is important

Research has correlated a high percentage of morning discipline problems in schools with poor diet. Some children had an inadequate breakfast while others did not get breakfast.

Years ago when I was working as a school psychologist, I was asked to quickly come to the playground before school in the morning as a child with Down's Syndrome was out of control and hitting as many children as he could. When I arrived, his arms were flailing around as he was reaching out to hit. He was about nine, but small for his age, so I took his hand, led him over to a nearby bench, sat down and scooped him up on my lap. I wrapped my arms and legs around him so he could not injure me or anyone else. He knew me and communicated he was quite content with his new situation by relaxing and leaning back, giving a big sigh as he snuggled in. "What's the matter this morning?" I asked quietly, "Is something wrong?"

"Yeah," he said, with another big sigh, "I'm hungry."

"Well," I said, "let's go get something to eat." We got up and made our way to the cafeteria. His mother said she always gave him a good breakfast, but this young lad had a long bus ride. We agreed that if he was hungry again, he would tell his teacher or go to the kitchen rather than hit.

Help and get help

Sometimes a hungry child is a sign of troubles at home. School breakfast programs have been helpful to many children and families. Poverty is more prevalent than many would like to recognize in some developed countries and a horrible reality for millions in many developing countries. In all countries, sometimes parents are so overwhelmed with life they do not have it together to get up in the morning and make sure the child has a good breakfast. I remember a boy who would bring popcorn for lunch to school. When I questioned him, I learned his mother was grieving over the death of his father who had been murdered. Popcorn was what was available in the house and what he knew how to make.

Friends, family and the community can be a great help to parents in need. There are often community resources if poverty is temporary or persistent. We can also help those mired in sorrow, grief, hopelessness or helplessness to find resources, and have the courage to take help from social services, 12-step groups or faith groups. A friendly telephone call or visit once a week can give emotional support, encouraging the one in despair to move toward hope and wellness.

- 19 -

Video Games and Films — Humanizing
or Dehumanizing?

I remember going to a movie about the end of the world in my early 20s. In the movie, plants were no longer able to grow, so the food supply became scarcer and scarcer. At the end of the movie, two brothers who led opposing forces were facing off to kill each other. After the movie as we were walking down the sidewalk, I thought, "If someone approached me right now and I thought he was going to attack me, I would shoot him if I had a gun."

I was horrified at my thought, and surprised at the influence of the movie on my mind. I decided to be much more careful, and conscious, about the films I chose to see. Media, be it movies, cartoons or video games, are powerful. They can be humanizing or dehumanizing. They can create healthy, positive perspectives or move children, youth and even adults to demoralizing, pessimistic, aggressive, violent and even sadistic perspectives.

I am sure most of us can think of wonderful humanizing movies which have some violent content. Films such as *Karate Kid, Taming Your Dragon* and *Man of Steel* come to mind. It is essential to know there is bullying, violence, corruption and wrong-doing in societies and the world. Through movies teenagers can learn about some of the tragedies and injustices of history in order to comprehend that acts of senseless brutality and violence are wrong and should not be repeated.

Humanizing films with some violent content depict protagonists who have the courage to work for what is just. That is very different than watching a movie or playing a video game in which the protagonist is into violence for violence's sake. The victimization of children and adults for the pleasure of the abuser is a degrading message harmful to the spirit and the psyche. Exposure of young people to meanness, brutality and violence through films and video games has increased many times over in the last few decades. There has been a direct negative impact on children.

The horror of teens murdering classmates in recent years, and even children killing children is unprecedented. It has been documented that teens in two of the mass attacks in high schools in the USA were influenced by films. Granted, these teens had feelings of hurt and anger inside — but who doesn't? How we manage our emotions, relationships and challenges shapes not only our personality but the rest of our life.

What are your children watching?

If you don't know what your children view, you might wish to be observant for a week or two to see which cartoons, television shows and movies your children watch and which video games they play. If there are young children in the house, observe what they are exposed to when older ones, including the adults in the house, are gaming or watching television.

While watching movies, most people put themselves in the emotional space of the protagonists and wear some degree of the portrayed emotions. Hence, those emotions are being played through the mind. When you watch a show or movie with the characters displaying acts of kindness, camaraderie, courage and happiness, how do you feel afterwards? How does media of this kind influence you, your children and your thoughts and behavior?

When you and your children watch shows or movies full of sadness, fear, tension, meanness, anger, betrayal or revenge, how does this affect you, your children and your thoughts and behaviors in the next hour — or the next couple of days? Children and adults often replay scenes in their mind, so the influence of powerful scenes can last for days, or for some individuals, for years. Do you remember a scene from a frightening "thriller" in certain settings?

There is a huge increase in the number of young people who are depressed and being treated medically for depression. I feel this is a reflection of what is happening in our homes, schools and the society. While relationships, diet, exercise and the school and social culture have a major impact, I feel another contributing factor is exposure to shows and films which are demeaning or not appropriate for their age. What vibrations are running through their minds when they are spending hours on video games? Some children and youth are addicted to video games. They become angry if they need to stop the game and do not want to engage in normal childhood activities with their families. Children and youth need warm, loving relationships with their parents and friends, and age-appropriate activities. This includes exercise and sports — and learning about the beauty and wonder of nature. Hours of violent and degrading video games and films are not good for young people.

Think about limiting television and gaming time

A woman I know experimented with not allowing her children to watch television or play video games during the school week. The school suggested it as a one-week experiment. Much to her surprise, during the one week without television and video games her children got along better and were much more peaceful. She permanently implemented the no-television-or-video-games-during-the-school-week policy.

I was met with loud protests years ago when I told my partner's two children they could only watch 30 minutes of television a day. They were accustomed to watching as much as they wished. I never heard another word of protest after the initial reaction, as they thoroughly enjoyed doing so many other things. We played, did board games, made cookies, went to the beach, went on outings and simply spent time being and doing things families do. We had a wonderful time. Their confidence and happiness grew.

Reflect with your partner

Reflect on the impact of violent and dehumanizing films and video games and your beliefs and goals in life, for you and your children. Discuss this with your partner. Are you, the adults, able to give these up? Are you willing to renounce a certain type of violent or dehumanizing movies and not others? Decide what your parameters are, and then think about whether you want to limit your children's access to these at home. If you are unsure, observe the mood of your children after they watch the next three violent movies. If they are accustom to watching violent movies, you may need to try a month without violent movies to see if there is a difference. Observe your own thoughts and moods after watching a violent movie, and after watching an uplifting or fun-filled humanizing movie.

Discuss this with your partner again. If you agree to renounce violent and dehumanizing movies, and see no benefit in violent video games, talk to your children and share the decision with them and the rationale behind it. Perhaps you are doing this because of your belief in peace, or you wish to have a more peaceful household. You may be choosing to take this action as you know that whatever you watch, those emotions run through your mind and the minds of your children. You may feel it is better for your children's emotional and spiritual development. If you decide to implement this policy at home, don't cave in at the first bit of opposition. You may wish to propose it as a trial of three months and then re-evaluate with the whole family.

If you do the above, please also look at the free time you have created. What would you and the children like to fill it with? Is there the possibility of more family time together, play time, walks, outings, sports, music and creative activities? What can you enjoy together?

With older teens

If older teens choose to see violent movies with their peers outside the home, or quietly view them on their iPad, stay detached and content and listen to their experience. Keep the door of communication open. Be respectful and willing to talk about the movies and hear what they think. Value your teenagers as you watch them in the process of exploring what is helpful and what is harmful, what has merit and what does not. They are kids, they will explore. Just be the model of your values and be aware of their choices.

Ask them what values they saw during the film — and what anti-values. Perhaps chat about the message. What did they like about the message? Were there other messages? If they were to do a similar movie, what would be different? Intervene if the content is damaging or degrading, such as pornography, or sadistic or sexist violence. Such movies would call for a longer and more serious dialogue.

With babies and toddlers

I personally suggest no television for children before 18 months of age and limiting the time in front of the television to a maximum of one hour a day thereafter. Research has shown that more than four hours a day of television limits a child's development in several ways. They do not develop as well physically or in expressive language, creativity or social skills.

Please be aware of violence and try to eliminate exposing your children to violence, be it young children hearing violence on television, radio, within the community or listening to arguments and fighting of parents. Be aware of the child when older siblings or adults are watching movies. Is the child being exposed to images, noises and words too grown-up for her or his age? Be aware of the impact of the environment. A child under the age of three cannot place events in time and space, but does record the emotional impact of events.

Carefully choose videos and cartoons. Many cartoons are not suitable for children under three because of the violent content. There is a wonderful increase in programs with friendly cartoon characters and funny, nurturing characters. Explore what is available and allow small doses of the best. In which direction do you what your child to grow? What emotions do you want your child to experience? What emotions do you want to experience?

Please also be aware of the impact of music on young children. Choose peaceful and happy music which naturally creates the emotions you want your children to experience.

And the rap music? A story . . .

Once a mother who had attended one of my parenting groups came up to say, "Diane, my son is playing all this horrible rap music. The words are so violent and awful. I hate it. It's like it is invading the peace and serenity of my home. What do I do?"

I looked at her. She was a very pleasant woman with a deep nurturing spirit. I asked, "How is your relationship going with your son?"

"Very well," she replied. "I'm continuing to do all the things we talked about in the parent group."

"Terrific," I said, "then I'll tell you what to do." I modeled for her a conversation with her son, communicating her love for him and her feelings about what their home meant to her, and then her feelings about the rap music.

She then looked at me curiously and asked, "What would you have told me if I told you my relationship was not good with my son?"

"I would have told you to work on your relationship for three weeks, and then to come back to see me about communicating about the rap music. Cooperation follows love. If the relationship is good, you can always find a positive solution together."

When I saw her the following week, she gave me a big smile. "I tried it! I was so surprised. After I told him how I felt, he didn't even argue! He just looked at me and said, 'Okay, Mom, I won't play that kind of music anymore.'"

Good news. There is growing body of positive rap music about kindness, gentleness and values!

Section Five

Taking Care
of You

~ 20 ~

Taking Care of the Self — Nourish Your Body

Parenting can be fulfilling, with boundless moments of love, contentment and happiness when things are going well. There can also be times of worry, uncertainty, heartbreak and exhaustion. Taking care of the self helps immensely. When we are feeling well, it is much easier to handle life, children, partners, work ... and the unexpected. Our relationships are more positive and healthy. It is easier to laugh, to be patient and kind, to enjoy our children and partner and the ordinary tasks of life. It is not selfish, but essential to eat a good diet and nourish the self emotionally and spiritually.

Eat Well

Part of feeling well is eating well. A good diet is important for physical health and emotional stability. Good nutrients fuel the energy and health of the brain and body. Whole grains and fresh fruits and vegetables help our bodies stay healthy and have the energy we need to enjoy life.

Whole grains are much better nutritionally than refined grains. Brown rice, quinoa and oatmeal have more nutrition than white rice and couscous. Raw vegetables and fruit give instant energy, vitamins, enzymes and cancer-fighting anti-oxidants. Use a variety of fresh vegetables, fruits, grains, legumes and raw nuts in your diet. Fresh vegetables, lightly cooked, have more nutrients and fiber than when canned or fried. Frozen vegetables have more nutrients and less salt than when canned. Enjoy oatmeal or smoothies with bananas and yogurt in the morning and salads with fresh vegetables and a healthy dressing of your choice once a day if you can. Add a few sprouts and sunflower seeds or nuts to salads. Sprouts have high levels of life-force energy. You might want to consider organic when possible — for the health of the body and the planet.

Does your energy dive in the mid-morning or mid-afternoon? A large part of maintaining a healthy diet is having healthy foods readily available. Plan for those mid-morning and mid-afternoon energy dives. My cardiologist recommends fresh fruit every day in the mid-morning. A healthy, yummy protein drink or a large glass of carrot juice, or cucumbers, celery, whole grain crackers and humus, serves us much better later in the day, emotionally and physically, than a bag of chips and a cola. It also serves us better later in life. Shop when you are not hungry, and read labels for a few months! Some salad dressings on the market list the first ingredient as high-fructose corn syrup, the opposite of healthy.

When the body is slightly alkaline, it is easier to maintain good health, have less inflammation and greater freedom from pain. Many health food stores carry little rolls of pH-indicator paper, Litmus paper, for a few dollars. If you are curious about your pH, use it first thing in the morning to test your saliva, before you eat or drink. With a healthier diet, you will see positive change in time.

Sugar

Many women, myself included, reach for chocolate when things are upsetting emotionally. Chocolate contains neurotransmitters which create the feeling of being loved, but only for 20 minutes. However, when that fades is there the desire for more chocolate? In the book, *Sugar Blues*, sugar consumption is correlated with emotional instability and monthly blues. Sugar is a nutrient robber; it robs B vitamins. While some sugars are harmful, others are relatively healthy. The rule: The more highly refined, the less healthy. The vitamins and minerals naturally found in sugar cane or sugar beets are removed when refined.

Whenever possible, limit your white sugar intake and use natural or unrefined sugars. Explore healthy sugars. Consider cane-evaporated sugar. Aspartame, an artificial-sugar substitute, is considered to be more harmful than white sugar by many nutritional experts and has been found to contribute to depression. It is found in many diet foods and diet drinks. If you are concerned about the calories in sugar, you might wish to try a healthy sugar substitute such as Stevia, an herb from Brazil.

I have worked with many people experiencing depression. At the end of the first counseling session, I always ask about their consumption of sugar and sodas. I have found that if they get off the sugar, artificial sweeteners and sodas, and onto a healthy diet, they feel better within a few weeks.

Salt

Not all salt is equal. Some salt is highly refined, others have 50 or even 80 minerals. Again, the more unrefined, the better. A good salt with its natural minerals intact results in better tasting food and is better for your health.

Drink Water

Two quarts of water a day is said to be optimal for most people. But if your body is little or big, calculate the amount of water you should drink by dividing your weight (in pounds) by two. The result gives you the recommended number of ounces of water to drink daily. Tea and juice are not substitutes for water. The body functions better, and keeps itself more toxin free, when it receives adequate water. You may wish to consider using a water filter at home and filling a reusable glass or metal container when you go out. Avoid the toxins and trash from buying and drinking water from plastic bottles. Do your body and the planet a favor!

Adequate Sleep

Listen to your body and respect the amount of sleep it needs. Many adults are sleep deprived. Adequate rest helps us stay relaxed and happy. Little "power naps" are quite helpful and ease stress.

Regular Exercise

Regular exercise is recommended for good physical health and emotional wellbeing. Walking 30 minutes a day has been found to be one of the most helpful things a person can do to combat depression. It helps rebalance the neurotransmitters in the brain. You may feel you get plenty of exercise running after your children, but can you carve out at least one time a week to do an exercise you really enjoy? Some people prefer walks, others prefer a workout at a gym, dancing, basketball or hatha yoga. Perhaps you love hiking, biking, swimming or playing soccer or tennis. If your children are old enough, you might all enjoy some of your favorite activities together.

~ 21 ~

Taking Care of the Self — Nourish Your Spirit

Research on happiness began to increase in the early 1980s and took a leap in 2000 with the positive psychology movement. Martin Steligman, Director of the Positive Psychology Center and the leader of the positive psychology movement, notes "happy people are more productive at work, learn more in school, get promoted more, are more creative and are liked more." They also have better relationships and are healthier. This branch of psychology focuses on what helps people be mentally healthy rather than on pathology.

In her research on happiness, Sonja Lyubomirsky and her colleagues studied identical twins along with other research and concluded happiness is 50 percent genetic, 10 percent circumstantial and 40 percent intentional, that is, under our control. While many people think if they won the lottery, got a new car, a new house or a promotion they would be much happier, studies show this is not the case. People adapt to their new circumstances with time and return to the same level of happiness. Getting out of a toxic relationship, a difficult job situation, or another situation which feels confining may increase happiness for a while, but to maintain that level people need to control how they think and act.

Sonja Lyubomirsky studied twelve strategies that measurably increase happiness levels. In *The How of Happiness: A Scientific Approach to Getting the Life*

You Want, she details these strategies. To name all twelve (not in order): *1. nurture relationships, 2. do activities that truly engage you, 3. savor life's joys, 4. count your blessings, 5. practice kindness, 6. cultivate optimism, 7. take care of your body, 8. develop coping strategies,* 9. practice spirituality, 10. avoid over-thinking and social comparison, 11. forgive, and 12. commit to your goals.

I have italicized the first eight strategies in the above list to indicate that we have already touched on these topics in this book, especially in regard to children. To me, the first seven strategies are important components of mindful parenting. These ingredients along with the many parenting skills presented become "coping strategies," that is, part of your way of being and interacting as you nurture and guide your children. Healthy, loving, respectful, appreciative relationships increase the happiness and wellbeing of adults and children.

In this chapter, you will be asked to think about the ninth strategy: practice spirituality. In the next chapter, the tenth and eleventh strategies, avoid over-thinking and social comparison, and forgiveness, are taken up along with a myriad of other ways to decrease negative emotional energy by transforming negative mental habits. The twelfth strategy, commit to your goals, is something I trust is already your intention, as you are reflecting and experimenting with new ideas and skills and making them practical in your life and with your family.

Do you remember the line at the beginning of the book about Aristotle's reasoning when he did not include happiness in his original taxonomy of emotions? He felt happiness was not an emotion but simply a result of virtue. Choosing to act with love, respect and peace, practicing kindness and compassion and being one who is honest and does the right thing — these are some of the ways to live our values. When we live our values, happiness automatically increases. When we act in accordance with what is at the core of the human spirit, the soul, the self, automatically feels happy.

Take time to fill the self with peace and gratitude every day

Each person has his or her religious or spiritual path and methods to fill the self with peace and love. Some of us pray, some of us meditate and some enjoy affirmations while others take walks remembering God. Some people go to churches, others to temples or mosques while some gather quietly in homes or centers to share. Everyone enjoys taking in the beauty of a sunset and many of us treasure a few quiet minutes with a cup of tea or coffee in the morning or evening, just being.

I think it is worthwhile to take time to fill the self with love and peace every day. Some people have a daily religious or spiritual practice. If you don't pray, meditate or consciously engage in filling yourself with positive energy every day, please consider it. Perhaps start by saying good morning to God and spend a few minutes taking in love from the Supreme.

Perhaps end the day by talking with your children for two or three minutes, thinking of things you liked or were grateful about during the day. Perhaps say a prayer with your children or fill up with God's light of love in your own private way as you say good night to each other and to God. Long periods of time are not needed. A few minutes to center and fill with peace and love help anchor us in our own serenity, love and strength. You may wish to experiment with writing down a few things you are grateful for before you go to sleep. Gratitude increases awareness of how fortunate we are, what is important in life, and our happiness.

A friend of mine experimented with increasing her experience of peace. One evening when she arrived home, she was so peaceful that when she walked in and her 16-year-old son was running around creating a bit of chaos with a younger sibling, she didn't react in her usual manner which was to yell at him. Instead she looked at him and said, "I'm happy to see you." As she hugged him she felt like the peace she was feeling was shared. He didn't brush her off like he usually did, but stood there quietly. When they separated, he said, "Thanks, Mom." She said he was peaceful the rest of the evening. One's way of being is communicated to children.

Consciously increase positive thoughts

We all live in our minds. We feel and picture things in the mind. We may feel peace or anger, love or fear, but not both at the same time. Sometimes we dwell on the past, or worry about the future. How often are we truly present, enjoying the self, our children, our partner or the beauty of nature?

There are different kinds of thoughts. One way of classifying thoughts is in accordance with the energy they create in our mind. Some thoughts are negative, others are waste, necessary or positive. Once I was teaching a stress-reduction course. During the second session, a woman who was a hospital administrator commented, "I realized this week that every morning when I get up my first thought is 'What shall I worry about today?' That's how I start my day!" Thereafter, she chose to change the first thought into a positive one.

Many people have negative or waste thoughts circling in their minds, not because they need to think of those things at the time, but because the mind likes to be full. It needs to be filled with something. One way to gain more positive emotional, spiritual and physical energy is to feed the mind positive thoughts. How many times do we need to think about what happened at work or what we need to get at the store?

There are many moments and minutes in the day when we don't need to think about what we are doing. An example: When I was working at one particular school, it was a long walk down a corridor and across the playground to get to the special education class. I knew what I was going to do when I got there, so I had three minutes free to be totally present and enjoy the thought as I walked, "I am a jewel of contentment." Negative thoughts drain out our energy while feeding the mind positive thoughts about our core qualities or values increases emotional, spiritual and physical energy. When we fill the mind with the vibrations of peace, love or contentment, the mind feels full, allowing us a few minutes of inner silence.

You may wish to think about one or two of your positive qualities, virtues or values — ones you feel are part of who you really are or ones you would like to further develop. Create a positive thought around that quality or value. A few examples of positive affirmations: I am a loving being. I am peace and light. I am a compassionate soul. I am a loving soul. Respect informs my every action. Peace enters my mind whenever I am still. I am a jewel of light.

Experiment with choosing a positive thought as a screensaver for your mind, that is, revert to your affirmation whenever you don't "need" to think about something. The mind slows down when you fill it with the energy of peace, love or contentment.

Be mindful and enjoy being in the present

The above is one way to increase the experience of our natural qualities, and to train the self to be more mindful. Being mindful implies focusing in the present moment rather than thinking about the past or the future. The more present and aware we are, the more our thoughts slow down. Being in the present allows us to enjoy the moment, be present with those we love and build emotional and spiritual energy.

If you are tense, or your thoughts are scattered and fast, jumping from one to another, you may wish to begin by focusing on your breath as you slowly breathe in and out…. Notice the sensations in your chest and abdomen as they rise and fall with each breath. Experiment with bringing in a positive thought, such as "I breathe in the light of peace … the light of peace fills me…. It fills my mind and surrounds my body…." Slowing down thoughts sufficiently to allow ourselves to be in the present allows us to experience "being," the sensations of what we are doing, and to be present to that which we are seeing or feeling.

When one is present in a mindful way, we notice what is occurring, without judgment. To cultivate being mindful, softly observe what is happening … enjoy the light on the leaves of a tree as you take a walk, be aware of the scent of freshly-cut grass, be conscious of radiating peace as you stir a pot of soup, be aware of your feelings and emotions, those of joy, of vulnerability or of sorrow … without resisting. Allow emotions that are painful to be lovingly accepted so they can pass through. When we are aware we can consciously surround our own sorrow with love from our wise core self.

You may wish to experiment with being in the present moment as you do simple tasks and as you play with your children. When your child is talking with you, let love, contentment or peace flow through your mind as you observe the play of emotions on their face. Enjoy the sparkle of sunlight on your child's face or hair when you play outdoors. Enjoy looking into their eyes as you notice their feelings and enjoy feeling love for them. Be fully present.

See the positive qualities

Notice the positive qualities of your partner, children, family and friends, and enjoy feeling good wishes for them. Notice your own positive qualities. Have you heard the saying: Where attention goes, energy flows? When we focus on the negative, emotions of hurt, fear, frustration, resentment and/or anger build. Are you focusing on one negative and ignoring 30 positives? That attitude is instantly transmitted when the object of our thoughts walks into the room. Conversely, our positive attitude is also instantly transmitted.

A friend of mine had a son who dressed as a punk rocker when he was 15 years old. A psychologist advised her to ignore the black clothes, spiked hairstyle and black belt with studs, and focus on his inner positive qualities and their relationship. He was well-behaved at home, he was just dressing differently. One evening her son was going to a school dance. He had asked his mother to drive him to the home of his date to pick her up. My friend was engaged in a stern, repetitive silent dialogue with herself as her son went up to the door of the girl's home: "Now, don't react when she comes out dressed all strange. Just be warm and friendly. Now don't react when . . ." Much to her surprise, the girl looked quite sweet. My friend almost collapsed in surprise and relief. Her son went on to do very well. In a year he abandoned the need to dress differently.

With detachment from the situation and a focus on loving your child, it is easier to have good wishes and to maintain a successful relationship. In an atmosphere of love and trust, children more easily develop self-respect. The positive energy they receive makes it easier to do what is good.

Notice if you are making negative comments. Negativity can destroy relationships. It quickly decreases happiness and increases unhappiness, for both you and the receiver. Negative comments chip away at self-esteem and add to feelings of unworthiness. Positive comments build wellbeing. Some adults still painfully remember negative comments said to them as children.

Stay in your core values

Think about which values you would like to use in different life situations. When we are experiencing our values it is easier to relax and be worry-free as the core self is in line with our words and actions. Be positive and operate from your values in relationships with others. What we give comes back to us. As you succeed in accomplishing even small actions with your natural positive qualities, trust in yourself and natural optimism will grow.

To play with switching on your inner core values, you may wish to experiment with the following …

What qualities or values would you like to keep with you all the time? Love, peace and respect? Lightness, caring and humor? Courage, hope and compassion? Contentment, integrity and authenticity? Write down two or three. Play with holding one of them in your mind and in your heart. Visualize yourself speaking with that feeling inside. Now hold the second quality. Experiment with holding one . . . two . . . or three. Be mindful as you slow down to the present moment and play with experiencing your qualities as you take a walk, play catch or do a task.

~ 22 ~

Taking Care of the Self — Transform Negative Mental Habits

Negative mental and emotional habits can be automatic, and accepted by the self as a normal reaction to the stressors of the world. However, it is these old mental habits that contribute to discontentment, sadness, anxiety, anger and greater stress. They prevent us from enjoying life when they are present in our mind, and their negative energy lowers or negatively affects our emotional, spiritual and physical energy.

Some people doubt their own goodness, others have a tendency to be preoccupied with fear, guilt, blame, resentment, worry or jealousy. Some people have a negative view of themselves, others or the world. The consequent effect on one's own happiness can result in poor decisions for the self and decreased effectiveness. Relationships often suffer.

If you have old negative mental habits you would like to change, you may wish to consider the following suggestions. Start by selecting one or two you think will be fairly easy to do. Perhaps put a reminder in your phone and a note to yourself on the mirror. By the time you are successful for three weeks, the new habit will be easier to maintain and you may wish to try another. Good luck!

From critical to nurturing self-talk

Listen to your inner voice the next time you speak to yourself inside your mind. What is your tone of voice like? Is it critical and harsh or is it encouraging and loving?

If your inner tone of voice is harsh or critical, observe your self-talk for a couple of days. Write down some of your statements to yourself. Are some of them critical, depreciating, guilt-inducing or blaming? Do you call yourself names? The voice of the internal "critical parent" has good intentions. It is trying to help you be good. However, the result of constant negative comments weighs on the self and can result in feeling discouraged, hopeless, anxious or angry.

What would the voice tone of an inner "nurturing parent" be like? Each one of us has a wise core self. When we nurture and encourage the self, positive emotional energy and positive actions are the result. Refuse to use negative labels with the self. Choose your words to the self with care. Note your positive efforts and see if you can create a space of loving acceptance and silence inside from which your wise voice can emerge. A nurturing voice and encouraging words create hope and courage. These ingredients help bring about positive change.

Go back to the list you created during the first two days of observing your self-talk, if you found you were making critical or harsh comments. Write a positive or encouraging comment you could substitute for each negative statement. When the critical tone re-emerges, say "Stop," to the self. Go into a moment of patience or serenity. What positive comment can you say to the self instead? Look at the list of alternative positive statements you made and create others. For example: I am okay. I am moving toward loving and accepting myself. I am a person who loves my children. A good parent is kind — that means being kind to myself, too. I grow in the direction I want with the power of love. When I am patient with myself, I am learning to be patient with others. I am learning to give love to everyone — that includes being loving with myself.

Be gentle with yourself ... suspend the judgment. When we develop compassion for ourselves, we are simultaneously developing more compassion for others.

Don't compare — Accept and value the self

A common trap people fall into is comparing the self with others. What is the point of comparing? To feel better about the self? Avoid feelings of inferiority and superiority, for there will always be people who are more intelligent, sweet and successful than we are, and less intelligent, sweet and successful. There will always be people who are more beautiful or handsome or less so. Neither self-doubt nor arrogance serve us, nor their companions of constantly apologizing for the self or boasting. Know your qualities and talents so you can use them well, and be grateful for your blessings. The balance of self-respect and humility allows us to be light and take things lightly.

Try on the idea that each one of us is unique and has an important part to play. In a machine, each part is essential. If a part is missing, the machine either will not work or it will break down after some time. There are many pieces in large puzzles. If one piece is missing, the puzzle is less beautiful and the pieces around it may be incomplete. Each of us has a purpose. Make your own puzzle piece as beautiful as it can be. Each smile, each loving word and each act of giving adds beauty and makes a positive difference to those around you.

Forgive

Forgive others. When we are hurt or angry with others, the first person we hurt is the self. If you feel you had a part in creating the situation, begin by forgiving the self. We are all doing the best we can, and we all make mistakes. What did you learn? What will you never do again? What would you have liked to do instead? What virtue or value would help you do that if a similar situation occurs? Pray or mediate to rekindle the virtue or value you want more deeply.

If the person you are upset with is a close friend or relative, explore your own feelings, including considering if a positive solution is possible. If so, you may wish to communicate about your feelings of hurt or fear under the anger and what you would like them to do next time. Listen to the other person's feelings and what they would like.

You may need to set limits and boundaries with some people so a harmful situation cannot reoccur, including the choice of not seeing the person again. Some people are so toxic that it would only create more trauma to communicate with them directly. If so, perhaps write a letter to them, not to send, but to give yourself a voice. Know it is your right, and the right of your children, to be safe.

Don't gossip

Never gossip. Gossiping is a form of bullying. How do you feel when someone makes a negative comment about you or spreads a false story? Gossip is hurtful and can be damaging to others. It often creates the fear that others will gossip about you. If you have a real concern about someone, process your own emotions and then communicate positively and constructively about your concern. If they can hear you, wonderful. If they cannot hear you, enlist the help of a friend or set a boundary.

If you are the victim of gossip, surround yourself with the loving support of friends and family and then take the high road. The high road is the only road to happiness. Revenge rebounds unpleasantly and can have disastrous consequences for all involved. One of my favorite quotes by the late John Wooden, renowned UCLA basketball coach, is "Never worry about your reputation, only worry about your character." Let it go. The truth will be revealed in time.

If someone gossips about someone else . . .

When someone gossips to you about someone else, you might try saying something positive about that person to interrupt the deteriorating conversation. For example: "One of the things I admire about her …" "But, look at where he's coming from. He's getting a lot better." "I think she is a nice person, she …." Or, "I think he has a lot of courage, he …."

A benevolent response provides an opportunity to the gossiper to develop more empathy or a broader understanding of the situation. It also lets him know you are not into gossip. You could also encourage the gossiper to be a friend to the one being gossiped about. You might say something like, "This must be difficult for her. Do you think there's something we can do to help?"

Don't blame — Accept responsibility

Some people learned as children, from the adults in their life, to blame others for things that go wrong. If their parents were blamers, they probably were occasional targets and developed a defensive attitude fueled by low self-esteem. This attitude does not serve us well as adults. Adults with a habit of blaming others for almost everything, including their unhappiness, the problems at work, their anger, the upheaval in the home, and even their own shortcomings, are far from fulfilled. The false belief that others are responsible for our life and happiness makes one feel powerless. The consequent bitterness and frequent complaining drive people away.

If you are stuck in thinking others are responsible for your happiness, you might want to experiment with challenging that belief. Instead, perhaps try on the following: I am responsible for my happiness. I am responsible for my thoughts and feelings. No one can make me feel a certain way. I can choose to observe a situation, see the other person as separate from me, and stay in my self-respect and power. When I stay in my self-respect, I am empowered to act instead of react. I can respond calmly and positively to situations that occur. I am responsible for me and I choose happiness.

When your child, partner or co-worker does something wrong, do you blame? "It's your fault!" "Why did you do that? What's the matter with you?" Blame is often used when people are angry, or when people are trying to escape being blamed as they do not wish to be seen as less than or incompetent. Blaming is destructive to relationships. Those who are continually blamed usually hold onto consequent resentment and anger. They may feel victimized and powerless. With frequent blaming, homes and work environments become unpleasant places of manipulative games, anchored in pressure to prove one's worth. Resentment and anger rob people of positive energy and negatively affect health. When people are not blamed, they are likely to see their own responsibility more clearly as they are not so busy defending the self.

You may wish to experiment with learning to be okay with making mistakes. Stay in your self-respect and accept responsibility for a mistake you made. A quick apology is easy to offer when one has the balance of self-respect and humility. You are not what you do, you are an invaluable being. It's okay to make mistakes; it is part of being human. It is much better to make 1000 mistakes than to not try.

Be patient with yourself in learning to not blame as you take responsibility for your thoughts, feelings and actions. It takes time and practice to master this, but each success results in a greater sense of personal freedom. You will discover happiness is a choice.

No more than five minutes of guilt!

Despite our best intentions, we occasionally blow it, doing something we wish we had not done. Guilt serves us for a few minutes as a mechanism to get our attention, but to dwell in guilt and shame depletes our energy and courage. Let go of the past and forgive yourself. Reflect on how you would like to feel and act the next time in a similar situation. An *accepting dialogue* with yourself when you are embarrassed might look like: "Okay, I'm really embarrassed about what I did … I guess I too am human. I wish I hadn't done that, but I need to look at this with perspective. This is one little negative compared to many positives. What quality would I like to have in the same situation next time? If I can see the virtue, it is mine." Play the scene over in your mind, substituting the more positive quality, feeling and action, and thereby developing your power to do that in the future.

Deal with your fear, hurt and anger

Everyone I know succumbs to fear, hurt, sadness or anger at least occasionally. It can help to name the emotion and detach a little, as this allows the intensity of the emotion to lessen. Talking to a positive trustworthy friend about the situation can help put things in perspective, as can a walk in nature, journaling or having a private conversation with God.

Choose a loving positive confidant

Choose your confidant with wisdom. You may need to help a good friend or partner learn how to listen when you are hurting. I remember two people in my life, whom I loved and trusted, who were very willing to help but simply did not know that what helped me most when I was troubled was to be listened to. With both of them, I momentarily stopped my tale of woe to say, "I just need you to listen and let me know you love me. I'll be fine." Then I returned to my tale of woe, and bless their hearts, they did their part as requested, listening, and then telling me they loved me.

Confide in someone who can listen and love you, and if you wish guidance, guide you in a sensible positive direction. If the advice is harmful to yourself or harmful or vengeful to another, it is not good advice.

Walk when distraught

A walk in nature can also help put things in perspective. Nature offers us her peace and tranquility, the opportunity to look beyond the immediate with her beauty and unlimited horizons. You may need to stomp in the sand or make up a song of your fears and sing to the wind, but often expressing allows us to understand more deeply and see with more clarity.

Journaling and the inner child

Journaling is helpful to many people. Some people journal every day for a few minutes, others only when they are troubled. Some write about their day and feelings. Others write down their dreams. Others look at life lessons.

There are many books on the "inner child". I think of the inner child as the sensitive part of the self which is hurt or scared easily. When "things happen" the reaction of the inner child pops into the mind, and in turn most people have an inner critical parent that tries to suppress the reaction. When we try to squish down our emotions, suppressing them with our critical parent, the inner child only feels worse. In time the emotions will rise to the surface with more force. Lovingly accepting our feelings and emotions, both positive and negative, is extremely important, for it allows us to know the self and discover what is beneath the surface so we can process it in a healthy way. When we can comfort and protect the inner child, that part of the self can grow into a somewhat more mature child who can share her or his sensitivity and wisdom.

I like to journal with the inner child when I am in a quandary of emotions, writing the emotions of the inner child in longhand on the left side of a piece of paper, and listening and responding on the right side from the wise, loving core self. Listen to the inner child, the part that is sad, scared or having a tantrum, for a long while first … and then dialogue. Many people have experienced this method to be helpful and are able to understand and resolve something in five or ten minutes that they have been mulling over for days.

Try seeing the beauty of your inner child and appreciating what that part of the self is saying. Does your inner child always know how others "should" act? Of course! You might say, "Okay, so she should have acted like that. Suppose we act like she should have acted. Since that's the right thing to do, shall we do that?" Your support in doing the new right action helps the child move from feeling like a victim to feeling empowered. Promise your inner child you will protect her by leaving if the situation is uncomfortable. Make a deal with your inner child. Hold her by the hand when she is scared, surround her with love, and you will both feel better — more courageous and stable.

Taking in God's love and light

Taking in God's love and light to heal old hurt can also be very helpful. Know that God loves you immensely. Allow the self to be open to receiving God's love, and let the light of love surround the entire body and the place where you hold the pain in your body. Some people hold pain in their chest, others in their throat, stomach or gut. Be still for a few minutes, breathe slowly and deeply, fill with peace and then love, and let the love around the entire body begin to slowly seep into the dark space, softening the edges and slowly dissolving a little of the darkness. Be comfortable with the pain of the old hurt. Accept it, and surround it with love. Take in God's love and light daily in this way, even if only for five or ten minutes, until you can feel love and light in the area where you hold hurt.

Seek help when needed

If you are dealing with long-term fear, hurt, depression, anger, grief or emotions elicited by abuse or severe trauma, you may wish to see your primary physician to find out if the difficulty is health-related. If not, please consider seeking help from a support group or a mental health practitioner. Learning to deal with your own pain in a loving healthy manner is essential for good long-term mental health and wellbeing. Counseling can be very helpful.

Hospitals and faith centers often have support groups to help people deal with the death of a loved one. For alcoholics and those addicted to drugs, there are many kinds of 12-step programs. This includes Alcoholics Anonymous, Narcotics Anonymous and special programs for partners and families. There are also 12-step groups for incest survivors, overeaters, codependents and gamblers, etc.

Nurturing the self and transforming negatives you wish to change will increase your happiness and the happiness of your family. We are all changing constantly. You can change in any direction you choose.

~ 23 ~

With Your Partner and Family — Keep Love Flowing

It is easy to be happy and give love to others when we feel full of love and are surrounded by loving people. Love flows when we are full. In the last two chapters, we've looked at ways to increase positive emotional and spiritual energy and stop some of the leakage of energy by transforming negative mental habits. In this chapter, let's explore ways to maintain a loving relationship with a partner, prevent damaging relationships by limiting and managing negativity, and keep love flowing in the family.

With your partner . . .
Keep your relationship alive — Enjoy time with each other

Enjoy a morning, afternoon or evening at least once a week with your partner — without the children. When children are small, it is sometimes hard to have a normal conversation with another adult. Take time with your partner to keep the flame of respect and love alive. Perhaps take a favorite long walk together, visit a new place or go out to dance or for dinner. Perhaps bike, take a dance class together or go rock climbing. Enjoy each other — have fun together. Perhaps grandma or a favorite aunt would enjoy some time with the children.

Be positive with each other

Research by Dr. John Gottman shows happy couples have five times as many positive interactions as negative interactions. When there are more negative interactions than positive, divorce is usually the result. Be present and positive with each other. Pause and enjoy saying hello when your partner comes home. Smile, be interested in each other and thank each other for small things you appreciate. Laugh, be affectionate and compliment your partner. Take time to enjoy being grateful together at the end of each day.

Toss the constant corrections

Don't talk down to each other. I remember being surprised when there was a change in a friend's marriage. A couple of years after the birth of the third child, the husband began to use a righteous tone of voice with his wife. A normally pleasant man, he began to correct her about every little thing, even interrupting conversations with others to do so. A few months later was the first time she mentioned thinking about divorce. Marriage counseling was remarkably successful for this couple. Not surprisingly, the superior voice tone and the continual mini-corrections disappeared on his side. And of course, there was more balance on hers. Love, affection, respect and attention are important for each and every member of the family, not just the children.

A family friend once sweetly told a friend who had the habit of correcting his wife whenever she mixed up the word order of a sentence, "Don't listen to what she says. Listen to what she means!" He got it — and stopped the corrections instantly and permanently. I think it allowed the ratio of five positives to one negative to be re-established!

Create a loving safe space to share

I hope you are enjoying actively listening to your children. In the same way, actively listen to your partner. Try detaching from the need to offer solutions if you have that tendency. Sometimes we offer solutions because we just want the complaining to stop. Stop, relax and be content. If you're physically tired, put on some background music and lay down while you listen. Be the understanding ear — and the thinking partner, when invited. Use the time to relax, be present and understand. Accepting the other person and what is happening with him or her, empowers them to accept themselves and work on a solution at a different level.

Some people are afraid when their partner has a different opinion about something. If you have this tendency, entertain the idea that it's okay to have different viewpoints. You are both unique individuals. Be interested rather than defensive: "So you think _____ is important." If you wish, share some of your thoughts: "Sometimes I feel the same way about _____, but I also think _____." Different viewpoints can have the same value at their foundation. Be interested in knowing your partner as you both grow and pass through time together.

Manage anger

Anger is harmful to the self, emotionally, spiritually and physiologically. It is also harmful to others. A child may feel he is a bad person when a parent gets angry frequently. A partner may feel stressed, anxious, hurt, sad, unloved and/or angry about being on the receiving end of anger. That feeling can last for days, weeks and even months. If anger is frequent, waiting for the next explosion can be a constant source of anxiety and stress and dramatically decrease the amount of happiness in the home. It is important for our wellbeing and the wellbeing of our family to learn to manage our anger.

Be aware of and responsible for your own feelings and emotions. If you are frequently angry or feel a need to constantly control your partner, then you may wish to take an anger-management class and go into counseling. Frequent anger and the need to constantly control another signals deep hurt, fear, feelings of inadequacy and shame. These emotions usually accompany people into adulthood, the result of childhood experiences. Deep hurt and anger can be dangerous for the self, one's partner and the children, especially if there is a tendency toward depression or a tendency to rage and be violent. Some people have this under control when they are sober, but unleash these emotions and behaviors when drinking or using drugs. If you have these tendencies, please consider renouncing drugs and alcohol for your own safety and the safety of your partner and children. Work on the underlying emotions. A 12-step program and counseling are recommended.

If you are the partner of a person who rages, please know there is no excuse for abuse. You and the children have a right to respect and dignity, to love and safety, to a home free from verbal and physical violence. Watching abuse of a parent is almost as harmful to the child as being abused. Please know you are an invaluable being. It is not that you are not good enough or that your partner would not abuse you if you were good enough. Every person deserves to be treated with dignity and respect — every person deserves to live without violence. Find a safe place for yourself and your children.

Fight fair — with kindness!

I remember complaining to a gentleman I had seen for many months who was also a therapist. He was driving. I complained to him about him for at least 20 minutes. When we arrived at the destination, he turned off the car, turned to me and calmly said, "Now suppose you tell me what's really the matter." It was easy to look inside: "I don't feel loved."

Learning to communicate feelings in a healthy way takes courage and willingness to practice. It's possible and rewarding to do so when both people recognize the need and are committed to kindness in their relationship. Work on transforming your negative mental habits and behavior so you can leave behind blame and criticism. Blaming, calling names, labeling, saying mean things and being derogatory to your partner is unfair fighting — and a recipe for destroying the relationship. Only hurt people, hurt people. Deal with your own hurt so you don't hurt others.

When you are upset, sort out your own emotions and then communicate with your partner when you can do so calmly and with kindness. It may take a few hours or a few days to calm down and figure out what you want to communicate. You might get a little upset as you share, despite your best intentions, but don't stay with the secondary emotion of anger. Make a pact to listen to each other nondefensively as the more upset person begins to share. Be committed to communicating about your own underlying primary emotions of hurt or fear. Share what is going on with you when you do feel hurt or upset by something your partner did do, or forgot to do. A useful formula is: "I feel _____when you _____ because to me it means _____." When your partner is sharing, listen well. Perhaps ask, "Is there something I can do that would help?" Or, "Would it help if I did something differently?"

One of the joys of co-creating a safe space to listen to each other and to share with kindness is developing so much trust that you are comfortable feeling vulnerable with each other. Be such friends that you can do this with each other. Go into marital counseling if you need help learning to communicate with respect.

Communicate what you need . . .

Tell your partner what you need. Some people believe that if their partner loves them, they will know what they need. That is not true. Communicate: "I feel loved when you _____. When you don't _____, I'm afraid _____." Other examples: "Right now, I'm upset. I need you to just listen. You don't need to say anything, just hold me and stroke my back occasionally." Share what you want. For example, "I want you to make sure you are home for little Ana's birthday — that's important for Ana and important for me." Or, "I know you're really stressed with work right now, but I need some Us Time. I think 30 minutes of your undivided attention, every evening, with the phones off, will do it." Pay attention to the little things you know your partner appreciates. Fill yourself with love and be loving.

By the way . . . don't argue in front of the children

Perhaps it can go without saying, but just in case! Please don't argue in front of the children, and especially don't argue about the children in front of the children. As all people have a tendency to want what they want when they want it, including children, it is good to communicate as partners and decide on things together regarding the children rather than allowing them to play the splitting game. If one parent has said "No," then no it is … at least until you can get together privately and discuss it. You may want to read some of the chapters in this book together, talking, reflecting and sharing as you decide what you want for your family.

With the family . . .
Daily family time

Throughout this book, suggestions are sprinkled about spending time with the children, your partner and yourself. I hope reading this is a time for reflecting on what you want less of, and more of, in your family and in your life. If life seems too busy, reflect on your priorities. Children grow up so fast. Their young years are precious. They need time with you, your love and protection, your affection and guidance, your laughter and play. Reflect on how you can enjoy time with them every day. Separate from the time together as you go shopping and do chores, always find some Us Time every day for listening, playing or rough-housing, and a bedtime ritual.

Turn off the cell phones, iPads and video games for at least two, three or four hours in the evening as you enjoy yourself and each other and have some family time together without electronics. Perhaps put a bowl or basket out to collect the cell phones and iPads, if they are a big temptation! Perhaps if someone wants to use their cell phone (for five minutes only) during those three hours of no-electronics family time, they have to make popcorn for the entire family! Enjoy making up your own rules. For example, the electronics could come out if the game involves several family members. Those two, three or four hours will fly by with homework, making dinner together and eating, chatting and Us Time. Maybe one night is cooperative chore night (amazing what can happen in 30 minutes when everyone helps) with a movie afterwards, perhaps another night is game night! Create your own rituals.

Whenever possible, have dinner or your main meal together. Turn off the television as you eat together, relax and share about your day. Perhaps you can plan to spend one full day a week with your children and partner. Play and eat together, enjoy nature or do something special.

Love low? Create a flow!

We all get out-of-sorts sometimes when we are tired or don't feel valued or loved. Sometimes we don't feel love for the self or perhaps we are just feeling a bit low or unappreciated by our partner, children or others in our life. Sometimes our partner or the children are grumpy.

In the love unit of *Living Values Activities for Children Ages 3–7*, teachers are asked to say to the class if the children are having a grumpy day: "Do you know what I know when people are grumpy? . . . That there's not enough love inside. Shall we choose love over being grumpy?" This is a lovely thing to do with children. It allows you to stop struggling with getting a task done when children are grumpy or resistant, settle into the moment and look at the process causing a low or off mood.

You may wish to actively listen about the mood you see or describe what is happening. Perhaps the child or your partner will share in response. You may wish to ask, "Do you want to share why you're grumpy/stressed?" Acknowledge the response and take care of any physical needs. Perhaps the child is hungry or your partner is stressed by something that happened at work. Then proceed to filling up with love.

You may wish to create a flow of love in one of the following ways. Or, you may have other favorite ways to fill up with love — be creative!

☆ You can softly say, just to the person in front of you: "Fill up with love time!" And give him or her a special hug and/or kisses.

☆ Call out: "Fill up with love time!" You can create a tradition in your family where one person calls out and everyone in hearing distance comes to give love. In your family it might be hugs or kisses. You may enjoy group hugs.

☆ Ask: "How many kisses will it take the grumpies to go away?" Give them the number they ask for.

☆ Call "Peace Tent Time!" When you are sitting together, say, "Let's go to the inside love factory. I picture a soft rose-colored circle of light all around us … as we breathe in love, the clouds of grumpiness begin to fade…."

Bedtime Rituals

Ending the day well is important for children and adults. It is said our thoughts and feelings in the 30 minutes before going to sleep more deeply affect the subconscious than the rest of the day. It is not a time for scary stories, bad news on television or arguments. Bedtime rituals will change as the children age. May they always include each person sharing a few things about which they are grateful, some peace time, be it a prayer or reflection, and telling them you love them.

Bedtime rituals can begin at a young age. You may wish to softly sing as you tuck in your infant, share how you love them and hold a moment of peace in your mind. With toddlers, the ritual may start with the practicalities of a bath, brushing teeth and getting into pajamas. It may continue with a bedtime story, before you share what you are grateful for and say goodnight to God. My mother used to sit all four of us children on the couch in the living room for a story after we were in our pajamas and ready for bed. We would sit close together as she read a chapter from a favorite book.

When the children enter school, you may wish to prepare for the next morning as part of the bedtime ritual, such as setting out clothes for school. This can avoid frantically hunting for things in the morning and children getting upset when what they want to wear is not available.

A family of a friend of mine gathers every night around the bed of their youngest child. For the extremely busy father, this time is sacred. The parents and children sit on and around the bed of the youngest to share the highs and lows of their day, fix any problems with openness and give thanks. Doing this when it's time for the youngest to go to bed is sensible, for then the whole family can be together and share together.

You may wish to experiment with and change the components of your bedtime ritual over time. If the children are squabbling a little, you may wish them to share something kind one of their siblings did or what they love about each one. It's a good time to take up different values or qualities you feel are important for the family. You could go around the circle, each person sharing one sentence about peace, love, respect, or honesty, etc., such as "I think peace is important because _____." You might want to have them reflect on sweetness, understanding, compassion, cooperation or responsibility.

Family meetings

Family meetings are a wonderful option to mutually solve any problems, plan the week's activities, know everyone's schedule and have a good time together. This is especially practical when the children are older or there are many children. Jane Nelson, in her book *Positive Discipline*, beautifully describes the process. To sum it up quite simply: Meet once a week for an uninterruptable session and begin with every person complimenting each person there or sharing something for which they are grateful. Go through the agenda items which have been accumulating on the refrigerator door during the week, coming up with positive solutions which are taken up when everyone agrees. If a good solution is not apparent, put in on the agenda for the following week. Get to know each one's schedule and needs, schedule special chores and plan fun family things to do. End with a game for the whole family and/or a dessert. You might wish to read Jane Nelson's suggestions and great stories about this process if you are considering doing this.

Family outings

Many of my childhood memories are those of family outings. Those of swimming in the waves at the beach during the summer and my brothers and I taking turns burying each other in sand. Driving day and night as we set out to national parks for camping trips, my mother and father driving all night, watching the sun come up as we drove, putting up the huge tent with each of us kids holding up the poles inside, building fires and making pancakes on the camp stove early in the morning, hiking up steep trails, loving the wildflowers, icy water and meadows, hiking down from Half Dome in the dark, floating down rivers on air mattresses, singing at night around the campfire and making s' mores. We went on vacation for three weeks each summer — and would take several weekends a year to visit my grandparents, occasionally going to visit museums and amusement parks in the city where they lived.

Some parents can afford to take their children to fancy hotels and others can't afford to take time off to get away for a week. Do what you can. To a child what is important is quality time together with parents and siblings — and exposure to different experiences. Together, enjoy hiking and visiting science museums, nature centers, observatories or whatever your area has to offer. It doesn't matter if you get to the lake, the museum or a nature center by foot, by bicycle, in a bus, car or limousine — but get there. Enjoy exploring together.

Allow your children to have different opportunities

One of the roles of the family is to provide opportunities for children to engage in a variety of activities so they may develop different skills, confidence and explore who they are. Help them enjoy learning and get the best education possible. Support creative thinking and encourage art and music. Teach them love for our Earth and her oceans and how to be a friend of the Earth.

Let them have as much freedom as is healthy and sensible for their age. Control your fear about worms in order to allow them to learn about them with a sense of curiosity and joy. Control your fear about them falling from a tree. Close your eyes if you need to when they climb a tree or hang from a limb. Allow them to be children and explore. Seek out opportunities for them with scouts or guides, your faith group, dance or music lessons or whatever is good for them in your community. Perhaps you are into tide pools, studying insects, birds or dolphins, making native musical instruments, painting, drawing, creating and filming skits, skiing, skating, surfing, hiking, rafting or archery — share your interests and your passions. Don't let them work or study all the time. Play, relax and be, watch the sun set, enjoy them and allow them to have time for friends.

What is success?

You want your children to be successful. But what is success? Is success being able to have the privilege of doing the work you want, being surrounded by kind people, living your purpose and being happy? Is it knowing how to be peaceful and content, and how to enjoy others and be of benefit to the world? Be happy yourself, know you are making a positive difference as you raise your children well and share values which benefit them and the world. Stay in your values … and happiness will follow you like your shadow.

Section Six

Practicalities
in Everyday Life

~ 24 ~

"I Hate You" and Disrespect

The five-year old stares up at you, his face contorted and says passionately, "I hate you." How are you going to deal with this? You've read the sections on *Nurturing with Love and Wisdom* and *Disciplining with Peace and Respect* — so you have even more options. Let's apply it.

Option One: Thinking time

You're at home, so it's easy and effective to use this option — if you've already had the talk about family and have been using a thinking-time timeout. "Thinking time," you say, pointing to the direction of his thinking place. This is a good option if the child's statement has you feeling hurt, shocked or angry as it gives you time to calm down and center. Know he doesn't hate you. He's just angry. After five minutes, go to the child's thinking place, sit or lean down so you are at eye level and ask, "What do you think would be a good idea to do instead?" Listen to the child's response. If he comes up with something appropriate, say, "Yes, that's a good idea." Some children may cry and say they are sorry. Give them a hug and tell them you love them too — and proceed with the next steps.

Describe what you saw happening, such as "What I saw was you wanted to do something and you weren't getting your way, so you got really angry. Sometimes you really, really want your way." Provide the space for the child to share and actively listen. Then explain why you would not give in to his wish. "I know you want to have ice cream, but you've already had a sweet today and I want you to be healthy and strong. Too many sweets is not good for you."

Before you separate, say gently but seriously and firmly, "It's wrong to use words to try to hurt people's feelings. We don't use words to hurt people in our family." You may wish to add: "When you're angry about something, what can you say to share your feelings with me instead of using words to hurt?" Actively listen and validate as appropriate. Perhaps ask: "What words do *you* like to hear in our family?"

Option Two: Actively listen in the form of describing the behavior and then give an I-message

Parent, speaking calmly: "I see you're really angry. You want ice cream and Mommy said "No." You got angry when you didn't get your way." Wait for the child to respond and actively listen to his next response, even if it is giving a nod of understanding. This is a good option if you aren't reacting to the child's words. If you get upset when he says mean words then it is best to use timeout. If the child goes into a tantrum, use timeout. Don't give the child the ice cream.

Provide a calm space for the child to share and actively listen. Explain why you would not give in to his wish. "I know you want to have ice cream, but you've already had a sweet today and I want you to be healthy and strong. Too many sweets are not good for you." Don't argue with the child if he tries to convince you to give him the ice cream; simply repeat your reason kindly and firmly.

Before you separate, say gently but seriously and firmly, "I don't like it when you use words to hurt. It's wrong to use words to try to hurt people's feelings. We don't use words to hurt people in our family." As above, you may wish to add: "When you are angry about something, what can you say to share your feelings with me instead of using words to hurt?" "What words do *you* like to hear in our family?" Actively listen and validate as appropriate.

The only absolute in this book is that it is wrong to hurt people. If you feel it is important for people not to say hateful things to each other and want this to be one of your family rules, then it is important to explain this family rule to your child. Another example would be if one of your children calls another person a name.

With teens

If a 14-year-old girl is distraught over something and cries "I hate you, you're ruining my life," to a parent, the same options as above apply, but it will take longer to actively listen and communicate. It is very important to peacefully and lovingly communicate with teens when they are distraught. Don't slam shut the door of communication by shouting, "How *dare* you speak to me like that, young lady! You are *so* grounded! Go to your room — *without* the cell phone!"

Keeping the door of communication open is keeping the door of safety open. Instead, you may wish to start with, "Let's have peace time (or thinking time) for ten minutes and then talk." Afterwards, ask her what is happening. Actively listen. Make sure you understand the entire situation. Reflect. As you listen to your child and reflect on the situation, do other options come to your mind? Can the situation be adjusted so it fits in with your values? Is there another alternative? Don't give in to what is not okay with you and your values, but be open to exploring alternatives.

If you think there may be an alternative, perhaps say: "You know I'm not comfortable with _____. Is there another way to achieve your aim that would work for both of us? What is it that your heart wants?"

If it seems an option is not possible, explain your stance with an I-message. "I'm uncomfortable with you going to/doing _____ because _____." Explain why you think it is not a good idea for the child to engage in the behavior or activity. Perhaps explain the possible negative consequences for the present and/or future, so the child can understand your concern. Perhaps share a story from your experience. End with "I love you and I want you to be safe." Add what fits for the situation, such as "You are only ___, so this isn't something you can do now. My answer will be different when _____."

At the end of the conversation you may wish to say, "I don't like it when you use the word hate and tell me I'm ruining your life. I know you were upset, but I would rather you tell me you're upset because you're scared your friends won't like you any more if you don't go with them. I don't like us to use hurtful words like hate in our family. It is important to communicate with love and respect."

Disrespect

The general rule for values, qualities and virtues seems to be to give what we wish to receive. If you want respect, give respect. If you want love, give love. However … sometimes children do test us!

I remember a nine-year old who dropped something as we were on our way to the car. "Pick that up," she said in a commanding tone of voice. I was unpleasantly surprised. But given my profession, several alternatives ran through by mind.

One alternative: An angrily delivered, "How dare you talk to me in that tone of voice," was obviously not going to strengthen our relationship. That would have probably been my option before learning about parenting skills!

A second alternative: Pick up the object she had dropped? No, it would not be good to be bossed around by a child. That would only reinforce her disrespectful behavior.

A third alternative popped into my mind. An I-message would be okay: "I don't like the way you just spoke to me. It feels disrespectful."

I quickly settled on a fourth alternative and delivered it in a kind, respectful tone: "If you want me to consider doing something for you, you'll need to ask me in a way I like." I walked past her to the car.

She picked up the dropped object and got in the car. That was the first and last time she ever spoke to me disrespectfully. The delivery is very important. If the same thing had been said with anger, it would have acted as a punishment rather than a gentle but firm lesson. It would have created resentment and been a step toward an unharmonious relationship.

Don't cooperate if a child asks you to do something in a disrespectful way. Instead, stay in your self-respect and give a message in a kind, respectful tone of voice or in a light manner, such as the following. Pick one you are comfortable with — adapt it as you wish!

☆ Oops, I think I just went deaf! Could you try another tone of voice?

☆ I don't feel like helping when you speak to me like that, buddy.

☆ Hmmm, I couldn't hear your sweetness just then. Would you like to try that again?

★ I can't hear you when you speak in that tone of voice.

★ Oops, I think you left out the love when you asked just then. Can I hear that same request with love?

★ Let me hear that with love.

A brief thinking time is an option as well, if you are at home. Afterwards, ask the child for a suggestion about another way to ask, and have a little discussion on the importance of treating each other with love and respect.

Using the four steps

You may wish to apply the four steps for correction, noted at the beginning of Chapter 17, if the child has been verbally disrespectful for a few days or weeks. The parental side of the conversation with a tween or teen might go something like:

Step One — Positives: "Denise, let's sit down for a few minutes. I want to talk with you about something. You know, I love you so very much. You're my wonderful daughter with so many abilities and talents. I love your sweetness and kind, loving nature."

Step Two — Concerns: "Your kind, sweet nature has been missing the last few days/weeks. You've made several comments in a rather disrespectful tone — to me and your Mom. I feel disappointed and a little sad."

Step Three — Effects: "I feel love and respect are the two most important values in our family. When we use love and respect, relationships are positive and grow in healthy ways. Disrespect causes hurt and anger. When you are disrespectful to me, I don't feel like doing things for you."(If a second talk is needed, you may wish to talk about the importance of respect for her future, such as "If you use respect with your friends and teachers, things will go well. If you use disrespect, disrespect will come back to you.")

Step Four — Listen and Plan: Actively listen to the child. After you have listened, arrange a signal, that is, make a plan to say or do something in case the child uses a disrespectful tone again, such as saying "Big oops," or "Oops. I think you forgot the love."

The clear message is that disrespect is not okay in your home. If you need to give the signal, the child has the opportunity to say, "Sorry, Dad," and make a respectful response. If she does, wonderful.

What else is happening?

If the child is disrespectful after your talk and doesn't instantly apologize and correct herself, then another talk is called for. You may want to ask if something is bothering her and check to see if things are okay at school and with her friends. Does she need help with anything? Think about her diet with your partner and make sure it is healthy. Reflect with your partner on the amount of Us Time and family time your daughter is receiving. What else is happening that might be making her feel hurt or angry? If more Us Time is needed, great. But, the family values of love and respect still need upholding by all.

Or, is it that she is so accustom to her parents being loving and considerate that she feels she can get away with it? Is she testing the limits as a teenager? Is there the balance of nurturing and discipline? Yes, children have rights. So do parents. She has the right to a respectful tone of voice as a human being — and so do you. It is important to guide children and set limits. You may wish to dust off thinking-time timeouts if another disrespectful comment is made. Implement it in a non-punitive matter-of-fact matter.

Sometimes peers can have a negative influence. Perhaps some of her friends are disrespectful to their parents and she is copying them. Stay in your self-respect and communicate your love and the importance of acting with the values of love and respect — as you set limits and house rules.

The value of staying in a place of respect . . .

I remember a story from Paulo Barros, a wonderful high school teacher in Brazil and a leader of the LVE team there. A new LVE teacher, he did values activities with students as well as teaching other subjects. One day, a student who habitually sat at the back of the class and hardly ever did his work, called him a name. Paulo said the entire class went into shocked silence, waiting for his explosion. He turned away from the class, toward the board, and said to himself, "I am the Living Values teacher, I must be peaceful. I must be peaceful." He got control of his anger, put peace in his mind and turned toward the waiting class and student. "Is that a name to call your friend?" he asked quietly. The teen walked out of class and Paulo continued teaching. The next day the student came in and took a seat at the front of the class instead of the back. He was respectful, did the assignments and became one of Paulo's best students.

What would have happened if Mr. Barros had reacted with anger? Would the teen have felt cared about? Would he have decided to learn and cooperate? It takes control to give respect at times. The many benefits include self-respect, not engaging in power struggles … and caring, respectful relationships.

~ 25 ~

Homework

Homework time can be frustrating for parents and children. It is actually an important time — for your relationship, their sense of accomplishment and capability, and their future attitude toward work and difficult tasks which need doing. Ideally, we want our children to do their homework independently and well and without complaint. But, what if they are resistant to doing their homework or avoid it at all costs?

Some might say, it's their homework, let them bear the consequences of doing it or not. Ultimately, that will have to be the case. That attitude works well with some children, especially teens who are motivated. However, it can be an abysmal failure with others, who do the minimum, struggle when help is needed or give up and fail completely. Before you are tempted to have your children be totally responsible for their homework, you may wish to share some ways of being and doing.

Reflect for a moment . . .

❖ How would you like them to handle work as an adult?

❖ What attitude from others helps you persist when something is hard?

❖ When you feel positive and capable, is it easier to get a task done?

❖ What helps you do things when the task is difficult?

Individuals do different things to help them get things done when their energy is low. For some, it's a cup of coffee. For others, a cup of tea and a snack. Some play meditative music and light a candle, others play rock and dance. Some read an inspirational passage, others deliberately decide to tackle the task after working out. And there are certainly less healthy options.

As with adults, children are more easily able to tackle a task they perceive as difficult when they have positive energy. They benefit immensely from a parent who is willing to be positive and patient at homework time.

If your child does his homework well, and is happy and independent while doing so, that's wonderful. The aim has been achieved. Don't change what doesn't need fixing. However, if your child resists doing homework, think about what usually occurs.... Has your child just come from school? Has she had time to play? Is she hungry? Has he been eating candy? Do you get upset when they don't start their homework on time? Do you feel, sound or act angry when the child is not "getting it"? Is there gloom on his face even before he starts?

Homework guidelines . . .
1) Establish a consistent, fairly quiet homework time — after time for physical activity and a healthy snack

Doing homework right after school is a drag. Children need time to play or engage in exercise or sports, do a creative activity they love, or have some down time. Having fun is an important part of life, as is time away from electronic games and videos.

A healthy snack helps brain functioning and blood sugar levels, especially if it has been a long time since lunch. When are they hungry, just after school? Or does it work better for them to have a snack just before homework time?

Establish a consistent homework time, if at all possible. When does she focus best? Perhaps before dinner works for you, or after dinner. Are there a couple of times that would work for you? If so, give the child a choice of the time, if his focusing power is the same. Which would he prefer?

2) Stay peaceful and positive

Children work better when the person with whom they are working is calm, supportive and positive. (Did you ever have your parent yell at you when you were doing your homework? How did that feel? A bit harder to do your homework afterwards?) Be determined to stay light — peaceful and positive. Most children can feel their parent's vibrations sooner than they do, so if you start to get frustrated or upset, excuse yourself for a few minutes. "I'll be back in a bit, I'm going to get …" A consistently peaceful and positive attitude will help the child not dread the time. If you have been a nagger or criticizer during homework time, it may take a few weeks before the child trusts you to stay peaceful and patient, and relaxes into being able to focus more on the task.

3) Make sure she knows how to do the task

Does the child know what she is supposed to do, and how to do the task? If your child gets out her homework and begins independently, great, you need do nothing more. If there has been difficulty in a certain subject, you may wish to make sure the first problem or two are correct. If they aren't, patiently guide her in doing it correctly. Perhaps ask how her teacher explained or look it up on-line. Guide: "Start by adding the number on the right side…." Be patient and encourage as needed as she learns. You are not there to do the task for her, but there to give just enough support for her to do the task.

4) If he resists starting the task, or starting to work, set up the opportunity for frequent positive feedback

I remember being in a classroom once to observe a particular child who was known to tear out the hair of other children. During the observation, I noticed another child. He had sat with his math worksheet in front of him during the entire 20-minute observation and had not done a thing. I wondered if he could do it, so afterwards I went over and asked him to do the first problem. He did it quickly and correctly. I smiled, said "Great," made a little x at the end of the row and asked him to call me when he had finished the problems in that row. His hand was in the air by the time I sat down. I went over, gave him another smile, checked to see if the problems were done correctly, made another little x, this time down a couple of rows. With two more repetitions, the entire paper was done in five minutes, correctly.

The above method can be quite useful when helping your child if he tends to resist starting the task or sits and does little.

A: As above, ask him to do one or two problems to make sure he knows how to do the task correctly. If not, positively teach. Then ask him to do another couple of problems to make sure he can do the task correctly.

B: Make your best guess about how long you think he can work independently. Three seconds, ten seconds, one minute? Young children may initially need frequent positive attention. They appreciate positive comments, such as "Good work," "You really thought about that one," "Good thinking," "Well done," and "You're getting all those problems right!" If they do need positive attention frequently, then it will usually go much more quickly to make a little x at the end of the first row, then down two rows, then down another two rows, etc. You shouldn't have to do this more than a week or two for most children, once they discover homework time can be positive and quick! After a couple of weeks, you might be able to simply say, "Call me when you're done with the top half of the page," or "Call me when you're done with the page." Go over to see his work when called and make a positive remark. You may need to check for correctness — positively. "Five and two are how many? Let me see you count on your fingers." "Great!"

Please note, if children are rested, and have had some exercise and a healthy snack, it is unlikely to take long to do their homework with the above approach. But, for that time, be it 10 or 20 minutes for younger children, be close by with something you need or like to do, such as preparing dinner, sorting through mail, reading, etc. Gradually, as the child becomes more independent, you can move a little further away, if you choose. You are there to provide just enough support until the child can accomplish the task independently and with a feeling of success.

5) Dealing with procrastination

Some of us tend to be procrastinators. It is sometimes hard to start a difficult task because of the anxiety we will not do well. Then, when the fear of being a complete failure by not doing it at all increases, we are in a mad rush to do it. It is useful in life to learn the benefit in tackling the difficult things first — or at least second!

Some children don't procrastinate or are consistently outstanding students. If this is not the case, it is wise to monitor your child's homework. Ask: "What do you have to do tonight?" and perhaps, "Are there any projects due this week or next week?" If a task seems overwhelming to a child, help her break it into manageable segments.

Share a way to overcome procrastination. For example, say, "What would you like to do first? The easiest thing or the hardest thing?" Let her decide. If she chooses the easiest thing, say, "Great, doing the easiest thing first lets you know you do things well. Then let's tackle the hardest thing, because once you do the hardest thing, everything else is going to be simple!" Avoiding the hardest thing creates a tension inside. Once the hardest thing is done, the tension will lessen and it will be easier to emotionally handle the rest.

Growing the experience of feeling competent and successful — and being competent and successful

The experience of feeling competent and successful usually begins with a parent's positive attitude and encouragement. The above methods help build the feeling of success. These methods can be used in any area. Your way of being is important as it conveys your belief in the child and his ability. You are helping create the opportunity for the child to experience his competence.

Some children absorb like sponges, learning without effort. Others struggle with each task. If the latter is true, break down the task so the child can be successful. Smile with their success at each step, perhaps say "See, you focused and did it." As the child feels successful, there is more enthusiasm, an internal release of tension and greater attention. Learning will then begin to occur more automatically. Build interest and enjoy small successes with them. You are communicating your love and belief in them.

Be interested in your children's school work and help them understand things when needed, by engaging with them or finding someone else to provide tutoring. If they are struggling with learning a language, perhaps enjoy learning it together. Laugh and have fun with it. There are now free foreign language tutorials on the internet which are terrific. Fifteen minutes a day of practice really helps.

Value each child and help each one feel successful as a person, whatever ability he or she has. Each person has a unique set of abilities and talents. There are many kinds of intelligence. Not all children do well in traditional schools. I have frequently suggested engaging your child in a variety of learning experiences, at home and in the community. Why? Learning to do builds abilities, talents, competencies, the feeling of competency, and prepares us with skills for life. Learning a variety of things allows young people to discover what they are good at and love doing. As we learn a variety of things in a variety of ways, the brain develops new neural pathways which allow further learning to take place. It opens up possibilities and opportunities to experience and think at different levels. As children are successful in learning, they are more likely to develop an attitude that it is possible to learn anything. This is a wonderful attitude for life and their life work as an adult.

Find many things at which your child can succeed, whether they are naturally good at academics or not. What else can your child succeed at? Let them explore, inside and outside of school. It may be art, music, reading and studying about elephants or stars, graphics, math, soccer, learning different languages, gymnastics, building traditional musical instruments, learning about comets, beadwork, cooking, building canoes or _____? Creating opportunities to develop their abilities and talents lets them not only feel competent and successful but have an art, craft or skill to contribute to their community and the world.

By the way . . . is the television on or do video games draw their attention?

An elementary school principal and teachers in California once asked parents to turn off the television and all electronic games for the school children for one week. The parent I know who did it said she and her husband decided to continue the experiment as they enjoyed their children much more. Plus, they had more family time, the homework was done more easily and there was less grumpiness, whining, complaining and fighting.

It is sensible to turn off the television, video games, cell phones and electronics during homework time — and family time. Research shows young people, and adults, focus and learn better when they do work without multi-tasking. However, some children do study better with music!

~ 26 ~

When Siblings Squabble and Fight

"I want to do it!" cried one child. "I want to do it!" cried the other. They were both behind me, two lovely little girls, a six-year old and an eight-year old, arguing about who got to stir the cookie dough first. I had just asked if they would like to help stir. "When you decide who gets to stir first, let me know," I said quietly, and continued stirring the dough. A quiet conversation took place behind me, then, "She can go first," said the eight-year old. I whispered to the speaker, very softly, "That was sweet of you."

Support them sorting out their own squabbles

A general but useful guideline is to allow children to sort out their own squabbles. It helps the parent avoid favoring one child over another and it helps the parent have more time to do needed tasks — and to enjoy playing, being, guiding and positively supporting.

Sometimes children fight more when the parent is nearby and rarely squabble (argue) when you are away. If that is the case, reflect for a few minutes. Is it possible they get more attention from you when they are fighting? If so, turn it around. Play with them occasionally, enjoy being with them periodically when they're getting along, and don't rush in when they are fighting. If they begin to squabble or fight, you may wish to try one or two of the below statements and see which works well for you and your children.

⭐ "I'm sure you can figure it out."

⭐ "I hear fighting in there. I want you to figure out a way to get along." Sometimes add: "When you figure out how to get along, come and tell me what you decided." Actively listen to their solution when they come in to tell you about it and positively comment on their mutual agreement.

⭐ Say lightly, "Figure it out or timeout! Your choice, you have one minute." If there is still arguing after one minute: "Thinking time! To your thinking places. I'll be there in five minutes.

⭐ Let them settle the conflict, but point in a positive direction: "I'm sure you can figure out something that is fair." You may want to occasionally add: "When you've figured out something fair, let me know." Again, actively listen to their resolution and positively comment on them figuring out a solution.

⭐ "I'm hearing squabbling. Have you used peace and respect? Or love? Let me know which one works best." When they come in: "Which value solved the problem?" "Great — good thinking!" Or, if it is not resolved: "How would love help? What would you do if you used your love?" "How would it have sounded if you used respect?" Positively comment on any constructive ideas. If they are not constructive, help them think: "That's an interesting idea. What do you think would happen then?" "How would you feel about that?

Is one child being hurt?

If the children are similar in age and ability or are using their natural kindness, then the above approach is usually fine. However, if a younger or weaker child is being hurt, then it is best to move immediately onto a combination of Peace Time and learning conflict resolution.

I once knew a little girl with four older brothers who was frequently teased. The parents did not teach them to protect her or treat her kindly. Her rage and aggressiveness interfered in all areas of her life.

In general . . .

> Model peaceful and respectful communication.
> Do not favor one child over another. Make sure all the children are safe, and help them learn kindness.
> Listen when they come to you, and teach them how to do conflict resolution.

Don't favor one child over another

Sometimes one child is favored over another, perhaps because the child has been ill, is the first-born, or because you always wanted a girl, because you always wanted a boy or because the child is the youngest. Favoring one child over another is not helping either of them. The favored one may feel loved and special, but this can grow into feelings of superiority, arrogance, the feeling of being entitled, the tendency to act and think that he or she is always right, and an attitude of disregard for the feelings of others. The favoured child may boss others around and feel it is his or her right to tell others how they should be, and treat others as less than. Additionally, the child will be resented by his or her siblings, harming their relationship and increasing the frequency of squabbling and hurtful fighting at home.

If your children fight frequently, observe what is happening. Are you favoring one of the children? Is one child trying to get another into trouble? Is the favored one fighting as he wants to experience being favored, or is the unfavored one angry and trying to hurt the favored one? Is the favoured one getting back at her? Do you spring easily to the defense of one but tend to ignore it when the other is hurt?

If any of the above is true, take a step back and stop yelling and handing out corrections and punishments. Pause as you reflect about your own feelings — and your love for each of your children. Imagine how you would feel if one of your siblings was valued more than you. Think about the importance of each one being loved and valued. See your children as unique individuals and think about their positive qualities.

Please take the time to do Peace Time and teach them conflict resolution. Consider doing some of the LVE activities in the peace unit with your children. These are a great build up to teaching conflict resolutions.

Peace time and conflict resolution

I trust you have read the sections on *Nurturing with Love and Wisdom* and *Disciplining with Peace and Respect* and perhaps made a Peace Tent or Peace Place in your home. A Peace Tent or Peace Place and the talk you have with your children when setting up thinking time are wonderful ways to begin a conversation about peace, what families are for, and what makes us feel peaceful and happy. These activities, your active listening skills, and doing the LVE activities in the peace unit will make doing conflict resolution easy.

The role of the parent in facilitating the conflict resolution process with children is to be a peaceful, respectful, nonjudgmental being who helps them communicate and generate positive solutions. You are getting out of the unenviable position of playing judge. Sometimes it is a challenge to be peaceful and have a respectful attitude for both children. Sometimes we may feel that one of the children is being "bad" or mean. But it is a peaceful, respectful, nonjudgmental attitude which will help the children trust the conflict resolution process and learn how to do conflict resolution well and independently.

As the facilitator, you ask several questions to both children. One child is to listen as his or her sibling answers the question, and then repeat what is said. This process is repeated for each child and each question. This may take five to ten minutes the first few times you do this with the children. If they are teenagers, it may take longer. Within two to four weeks they should be able to do it by themselves if you are using it three or four times a week.

Conflict resolution questions . . .

- ◆ Please share what happened.
- ◆ How do you feel when that happens?
- ◆ What would you like him/her not to do?
- ◆ What would you like him/her to do?
- ◆ Can you do that?

Why would I want to do this?

One: This will dramatically decrease fighting in the home.

Two: You and the entire family will have more peace and harmony.

Three: You will not have to be the "judge" or referee at the end of each conflict, scolding and handing out punishments as one child resents you and the other feels favored and lords it over his brother or sister.

Four: It is important for children to learn to express how they feel and what they want another to do and not do when boundaries are being violated. This is terrific practice for life — and will help your children develop life skills.

These life skills include tuning into their feelings, expressing their feelings and emotions, listening when others express themselves, confirming they are listening by repeating or actively listening, and being able to generate solutions. As they experience the consequences of the solutions, they will understand the feelings and consequences different behaviors generate. You will be helping them do all of this with peace, respect and love. So, this simple exercise is not just about helping them get along in the present, it is helping them develop positive social and emotional skills for the future.

Five: Their ability to think and generate solutions will help protect them as they move through adolescence and into adult life.

A win-win approach

The focus in this method of conflict resolution is simple communication: hearing each other in an atmosphere of peace and respect. The act of speaking one's truth while being listened to is important. The listener is providing respect by listening and repeating what is said. When respect is given, anger cools. This is a win-win method in which there is no recrimination or blame about the past. The emphasis is on both children committing to positive behavior and leaving the negative behavior behind.

Beginning conflict resolution with your children

If your children get really upset when they argue or fight, it is a good idea to practice while they are not fighting. When you are not feeling rushed and have 30 minutes, do a LVE Quietly Being Exercise for children seven and under, a LVE Relaxation/Focusing Exercise with children eight and older, or another relaxation exercise in your Peace Tent or Peace Place. Then tell them in words you are comfortable with, something like:

"I've been thinking. I love you both so much. I hope when you are older you will be really good friends. Sometimes you are good friends now, but I don't like it when you call each other names and hit each other. You don't have to fight, you can come up with a solution. I'm going to teach you how to do conflict resolution. That means that if you fight, I'll ask you some questions so you can use words to say how you feel and solve the problem. People who care about peace learn how to do conflict resolution. People who care about peace have the courage to come up with solutions. I think both of you can do it."

Practice with a pretend situation, or use a situation which occurred earlier. Sit down with them, one on each side. Begin with the child who was the most upset. When they are learning this process, you will need to ask each of them the conflict resolutions questions and model listening for them.

Tell them: "I'm going to ask each of you the same questions. I want you to listen very carefully to each other. Each of you will have a turn to answer each question. I'll be asking both of you to repeat back what each other said."

If you don't know what happened between the children, begin by saying, "Please share what happened." Model respectful listening: "So you're saying that first _____."

If the children tell conflicting stories, don't react but stay peaceful and impartial. Continue to model listening and stay with the process. Ask the other child to repeat what was said. Usually the truth gradually comes out when the "mediator" (Yes, that's you!) stays peaceful, respectful and does not take sides.

Give encouraging comments as appropriate, such as "Good listening and repeating what was said." Continue to ask them to repeat what each other said.

If a child interrupts, say: "You'll get a turn to share how you saw things in a minute. Listen carefully to what your brother is saying because I want you to give him the respect of letting him know you are listening."

If you and the children know what happened, then you can begin by saying: "Please share how you feel when _____." Initially, model respectful listening by repeating the essence of what was said and asking the other child to repeat what was said. When you do this you are showing you understand and value their feelings. While you might say, "So you feel _____ when _____," after a couple of practice sessions you can prompt them to say to the other child, with direct eye contact, "I feel _____ when you _____." Continue with this process. It might sound something like:

Sam, I want you share with your sister <u>how you feel</u> when she _____.
　　　Good sharing how you feel. So you felt sad when _____."
Maggie, what did he say?
　　　Good listening.
Maggie, how did you feel when Sam _____?
　　　Good sharing how you feel. So you felt angry when _____.
Sam, what did she say?
　　　Good listening.
Now, Sam, tell Maggie <u>what you don't like</u>.
Maggie, what did he say?
　　　Good listening.
Maggie, your turn to say what you don't like.

Sam, what did she say?

> Good listening.

Sam, what would you like Maggie <u>to do instead</u>?

> Look at her and tell her, Sam. … Good.

Maggie, what did he say?

> Good listening.

Maggie, what would you like Sam to do?

> Look at him and tell him, Maggie. … Good.

What did she say, Sam?

> That's right, she wants you to _____.

Can you both do that?

Encourage the children to come up with positive behaviors as solutions. What they come up with sometimes is surprising — and wonderful. If it is a fair suggestion for both children, stop there. If you feel it is quite unfair to one of the children, ask them to generate another solution. Positively comment on both of their efforts when you are finished.

Do this the next time they have a conflict. After they have decided what they are going to do, ask them if they can do that for a certain amount of time. Set a short enough time so they will be successful. Pay some positive attention to each during the practice time. At the end of the time, describe to them both what you are pleased about.

To summarize, take turns asking each child the following questions. Each child listens to his or her sibling and repeats back what is said after each question.

- What happened?

- How do you feel?
- What would you like _____ not to do?
- What would you like _____ to do?
- Can you both do that?

The parent can set a short amount of time for them to do the new positive alternative. Please specifically praise, that is, describe their success at the end of the time period.

After you have done a few conflict resolutions sessions with the children, put up a list of the last four conflict resolution questions in the Peace Tent or the Peace Place. You and/or the children can write out the questions. If they are little, perhaps draw a picture for each question.

Bring values into the conflict resolution process

After the children can do the basic conflict resolution steps, introduce values into the process. Comment when they act respectfully during the communication process. If there is not a lot of respect going on, ask them to bring respect into the process. Talk about what respect is. You can find age-appropriate definitions on the Reflection Points posters for the 3–7 and 8–14 age groups on the livingvalues.net website. Perhaps print out the poster and discuss the reflection points or do some of the activities in the Respect Unit. Model what respect would look like. Play with the contrasts: What is a respectful look and a disrespectful look? What is a respectful tone and a disrespectful tone of voice? Laugh and have fun as you model the contrasts. Another time, talk about respectful words.

When they are quite accustomed to conflict resolution, and are managing more respect, introduce love after a conflict resolution session. Say,

"Let's look at love. How could you have used love to prevent this problem?" As the weeks go by, continue to support them by listening to their ideas and helping them think of peaceful, loving or respectful things they could do before the squabbling begins!

After a few weeks, ask them to think about adding another question or statement to the list of conflict-resolutions questions. Which one would they like to add? Or, is there another question or statement they would like to add?

⭐ What value would have stopped this from happening?

⭐ I would like you to use the value of _____ with me.

⭐ I think I could have helped prevent this if I used the value of . . .

Soon the need for conflict resolution should decrease dramatically. But, don't hesitate to send them to the Peace Tent or Peace Place to do conflict resolution if they do have a conflict. It helps them clarify their feelings, to themselves and each other, and communicate in a healthy way.

Building kindness . . . Growing peace, love and gratitude every night before bed
If your children have been fighting more frequently than you would like, you might wish to do a Quietly Being Exercise, Relaxation/Focusing Exercise or another relaxation exercise which helps them center and fill with peace, love or respect every night before they go to bed.

Follow this with a Peace Circle, Kindness Circle or Gratitude Circle (Choose the name you like best.) in your Peace Place — or another place where you are all comfortable. Talk about your day. Actively listen, validate and problem solve as appropriate if there has been hurt feelings or challenges during the day at school or at home. Then do one of the activities below for a few minutes before you end with thanking God — and hugs goodnight.

- ✸ Ask everyone in the circle to finish the sentence: I think peace is important because _____ .

- ✸ Ask each person to finish the sentence: I feel peaceful when _____ .

- ✸ Share how you see each child growing in peace. Describe his or her positive behavior and quality or way of being.

- ✸ On little pieces of special paper, draw a symbol of a virtue or value each child has demonstrated. Tell them about their virtue and give each child their paper.

- ✸ Ask each child to share how they feel when someone is kind to them, and name a way someone can be kind. Ask them to do one kind thing the next day. Tell them they will be able to share what they did at the next circle meeting.

- ✸ Ask the children to share about their kind action. Actively listen as an acknowledgement. Ask them to do another kind action the next day, if you would like to continue this.

- ✸ Ask the children to finish the sentences: I think respect is important because _____ . Do a second round, finishing the sentence: When people are disrespectful, they need to know _____ .

- ✸ Allow the children to take turns making little cards for each member of the family. They can draw something or write a word or sentence. Ask them to give them to each person with respect.

- ✸ Ask everyone in the circle to share two or three things for which they are grateful.

- ✸ Ask each child to share how they feel when being loving — and ask each one to do one or two loving things the next day. They can choose to use loving words or actions.

☆ Ask them to share about the loving things they did. Actively listen. If you wish, ask them to do one loving thing the next day.

☆ Ask the children to finish the sentence, I think love is important because _____.

☆ Note a quality you see in each child's heart, or write a sentence about why you love them. Give each child their piece of paper with love.

☆ Ask everyone to finish the sentences: When people are loving, I feel _____. When people are mean, they need to know _____.

☆ Share how you see each child living a value. Describe what you are observing — perhaps it is the look in their eyes, the way they smile or speak, something they said or an action.

☆ Have a contest for two nights in a row and see how many virtues or values you can name in 90 seconds. Each person who names a virtue can only say it when they feel it first!

☆ Ask everyone in the circle to name three virtues or values that they think are important. Actively listen to their comments as a form of acknowledgement.

☆ One person can tell a story he or she loves — and why. What is the main virtue or value in the story? Would everyone like to practice that virtue or value the next day? At the next circle time, another person gets to share one of his or her favorite stories.

☆ Ask everyone in the circle to share something they love about each one.

~ 27 ~

When There's Change — Helping Children Feel Secure

Children often feel insecure when there is change. In one corner of my office, I kept a pile of plush toys and puppets on top of a low filing cabinet. I always knew older kids were having difficulty when they immediately headed for the animal puppets, playing and interacting like younger children when they came in for their weekly counseling session. They were usually unsettled about something and wanted to be little again, free from the pressures of being older — enjoying the loving interaction playing with puppets can bring. I would always accommodate, picking up a puppet to play with theirs. Later we would chat about what was happening.

There are many things to be unsettled about in our world, for both children and adults. Divorces are difficult for all. Moving, deployment, a death of a relative or friend, arguments and fights, the loss of or change in a job, etc., make real differences in the lives of children and the family. For older children and adults, there are also concerns about the state of the community or the world.

Help children make sense of the world by attaching meaning to events

It is important to explain to young people what is happening. Tell them what is occurring, and help them attach meaning to the event, using language and concepts appropriate for their age. For example, for a three-year old: "We will be moving to another house in another town because Mommy got a new job. It will be a house almost like this — and all our things get to come with us. Ana sees us every day for a couple of hours, but she is not going to be able to come with us to the new town, because she needs to stay with her family. So, we will need to say a special goodbye to Ana and tell her how much we love her." Answer any questions about moving and then perhaps plan together how to say a special goodbye to Ana.

Understanding why things happen helps children feel included and safer. It is also an opportunity for you to interpret the world for them and to share your values. For example, if there is a murder in the neighborhood, discuss it with your preteens if they have heard about it, or are likely to hear about it at school or through the media. One view I share is that sometimes people do horrible things because they don't have enough love and peace inside. The darkness of hate and meanness is inside their heart and they don't know how to get rid of it. All people are naturally good, but they can become mean when people are unkind and awful things happen in their life. You might add, "We are lucky because we know how to keep love and peace alive." You might ask, "How do you keep love alive?" "How do you see your Dad and me keeping peace and love alive?" "Who else in your life do you see spreading peace and love?"

There is no need to tell young children about tragic events unless they have somehow heard about them. If so, you might wish to actively listen to their comments and feelings and engage in a discussion: "Why do you think people do things like that?" Share your views with age-appropriate language and concepts.

If adults do not help children attach meaning to an event, often children will create their own meaning. Young children, because they are egocentric, are likely to decide they are responsible for an event if it is not explained to them. Hence, if the thing that happened is "bad," they will decide they are to blame. A small child, for example, may think it is his fault if the parents fight or divorce. For small children, keep it simple. It is important to explain to children as young as 18 months why one parent or grandparent is not there. For all children, keep it healthy and kind, that is, do not label your now-separating spouse as a liar or cheat. Reassure your children that both of their parents love them immensely and will always love them. Make a pact with a separating partner, if possible, to always talk kindly about each other in front of the children.

Re-establish routines when there is change

With change, some children become withdrawn and depressed, others whine or become aggressive. When the parents are experiencing turmoil or the situation is chaotic, the usual routines can stop. Re-establish Us Time and the routines as soon as possible. Young children find comfort in set sequences of events or rituals. It gives them a feeling of security as they know what is going to happen next. The morning routine may be a parent coming in to wake them up with a song, making the beds, having a certain drink at breakfast and saying a blessing together. Or perhaps the routine might be a snack after school, or a chance to play with Dad before or after dinner. A ritual may include a set bedtime, with a bath before a bedtime story. Tell the story on the bed or a couch where all the children can cuddle around. Perhaps share what you are grateful for and say a goodnight prayer or do a Quietly Being or Relaxation/Focusing Exercise together. For tweens and teens, it may be a little chat at a certain time of the afternoon or evening, including sharing what you are grateful for, a walk together, and a kiss goodnight at bedtime. If you want to continue the story time ritual when the children are tweens or teens, allow them to take turns picking out a book. They can read one chapter a night to everyone. Routines help immensely. They help children feel reassured and secure, build relationship and give happiness.

~ 28 ~

Rebuilding Relationships

Years ago, I worked with a wonderful intern. She came in one day with an unusual story. She had woken up, a few hours after she had gone to sleep for the night, to find the lights on and her husband and children out of their beds. There was a young girl she did not know in the house, sitting at her dining room table. Her husband and children were outside, along with some policemen. A car was on top of their fence and there was another preteen she did not know. One of the preteens had taken her parent's car late at night and driven it — crashing it onto the stone fence.

When the child's parent arrived, she was furious, and promised to beat her child when they got home. This wonderful intern asked a policeman to tell the parent that if she beat her child at this time, if the child was in trouble in later years she would not likely come to her. My friend received a call from the parent the next day, thanking her for sharing her advice with the policeman and sharing that instead of beating the child, she listened to her story. They talked and shared for a couple of hours. It was the first time in over a year they had had a real conversation and a time of sharing and closeness. The young girl shared during the conversation that she and several friends had all been planning to take their parents' cars in a few weeks and drive to a town 100 miles away. Imagine how many lives might have been lost.

This incident provided an opportunity for the parent to seriously examine the role she wanted to play in her child's life. Punishment sometimes appears effective for a few days, but the long-term result is more hurt, resentment, anger and alienation. A loving relationship with a parent who knows how to listen with love and respect is an important protection for tweens and teens — for they are much more likely to come to the parent for help when needed.

It's never too late to begin anew. If you wish to rebuild the relationship with your child, consider the suggestions below.

- ☆ Spend some Us Time every day. Ten to 20 minutes daily will make a difference. Give your child your full attention during that time as you talk, play or enjoy doing something together. Don't answer the phone or text during the time. Don't look at incoming messages. Your full attention lets him know he is important. Hold love for the child in your mind as you stay in the present and enjoy him.

- ☆ Keep your promises. If you say you are going to play a game, play a game. If you say you are going to take the child somewhere, do it. Keeping promises is immensely important in developing trust.

- ☆ Make at least three positive statements daily to the child. These might be in relation to something the child did. A simple "I appreciate you doing that," is great. Reread the section on acknowledgement. "I love you," is always important. You may occasionally want to share a favorite memory of her as a child.

★ Study the chapter on active listening again — and listen daily. As you are listening to your child, attend to the feelings of love and good wishes in your heart for this unique soul who chose you as a parent.

★ Choose well your rare words of advice — and make sure they are rare! Engage in a dialogue about what matters only when you are both in a good mood — when ears and hearts are receptive.

If there has been a lot of anger in the family, please read Chapter 33.

Section Seven

Prevention
and Intervention

~ 29 ~

Bonding and Comforting Have Many Gifts —
One is Self-Regulation

A peaceful loving attitude is a special gift for children from the time they are in the womb. Some parents are aware of the child's ability to perceive while in the womb, and they begin bonding and teaching before the child is born by talking to the child within, reading aloud or playing music. Research has shown that infants recognize the voices of people who had been talking to them while in the womb. Infants also have a relaxation response to the music they heard while in the womb.

Infants and toddlers are especially responsive to the attitude and emotions of their primary caregivers. They respond in a healthy way, emotionally and physiologically, to loving care, and poorly to irritation and peacelessness. They become distressed when the parent is grieving, depressed or angry, and are more stable and happy when the parent is unhurried and happy. It is nurturing to be held by a caregiver who is peaceful and loving. The vibrations of peace, and the love in the face of a caregiver, nurture and teach a way of being.

In recent years there has been considerable research on the ability of infants and toddlers to self-regulate. The ability to self-regulate, also called the ability to self-modulate or self-soothe, means the ability of the child to calm him or herself. When an infant or toddler becomes upset and the parent consistently stays calm and soothes the child, the child begins to learn how to soothe the self. If the child becomes upset and the parent gets upset with the child, the child becomes more upset. This process of escalating emotions is harmful to the child. You can imagine a child who becomes upset and a parent who screams in response. This not only decreases the chance of learning a self-regulating response, neurological development is negatively impacted, and the infant or toddler develops insecure rather than secure attachment.

I remember a story about a three-year-old boy who became upset and began sobbing when his aunt was babysitting. When she tried to comfort him, the little boy continued to cry. But soon, he picked up a small plush animal and handed it to his aunt. He continued to sob as he said, "Here, pet me on my back." He started to settle down as soon as the soft toy was rubbed lightly down his back. The little boy's mother confirmed later that when her son was upset, she would often stroke him on his back with her hands, or a little plush animal. The child wanted his aunt to do the same.

Often we see children comfort themselves with their favorite blanket, plush toy or teddy bear. That item is associated with love and comfort. They use it to feel nurtured and okay again. When we are loving, nurturing and peaceful with children, we are helping them develop emotionally and neurologically — we are helping them form ways of responding to life.

The experience of many teachers implementing LVE is that a values-based atmosphere and regularly doing Quietly Being or Relaxation/Focusing Exercises helps children enjoy quiet time, concentrate better and self-regulate. One teacher from Italy told me a story of a four-year-old boy who would ask for quiet time. A teacher of young adults at a college in Australia said students would ask for relaxation time at the beginning of the class, telling her it helped them de-stress and focus more. We collected surveys from 623 students in two Karen refugee camps in Thailand who had taken one 90-minute LVE class a week for one or two years. Ninety-four percent self-reported being able to concentrate better.

You may wish to experiment with doing Quietly Being or Relaxation/ Focusing Exercises with your children in your peace place, daily or several times a week. This is especially helpful to children who have difficulty self-regulating, that is, children who become upset quickly and have difficulty calming down. These relaxation exercises help children learn to fill themselves with peace, love and respect. You can download the Quietly Being Exercises for children three through seven years of age from the livingvalues.net website. For older children there is a greater variety of exercises and they are encouraged to create their own. Imagine what would happen if all children could fill themselves with the feelings of peace, love and respect whenever they wished.

I remember the first child I taught to fill herself with love. "Kim" was eight, and I was desperately searching for a way to help her manage her hurt and anger. On her first day in the school at which I was working, she took a pair of scissors and tried to attack the teacher, and did attack other students, kicking them with her thick boots. The principal and I ended up holding an arm and a leg each, as we sat in a row on three chairs. I told her, "We'll let go when you are calm." She yelled at us, spat at us and called us names. I was struck by the way she would lean toward me to spit, and at home that night I thought, "Hmm, she really wants contact." So, we gave her contact. Positive contact. I would get real close to her when she was doing something appropriate, such as simply holding a pencil. I would look into her eyes with affection as I said something positive, and asked her teacher to do the same.

It was slow, but with this and counseling, there was change. After a couple of months, I knew we were making progress when during play therapy Kim offered me something imaginary to eat from the tiny clay bowl she had just made. Shortly afterwards, I taught her to fill herself up with love and asked her to do that every night before she went to sleep and every morning before she got out of bed. She did. She loved it.

About a month later, her teacher came into my office at the close of recess and asked me to see Kim. I was pleasantly surprised to learn she had gotten off of a swing when asked to do so by another child, actually obeying a rule and being pleasant instead of being verbally or physically violent. I asked her why. She looked at me, grasped her elbows with her hands and rocked her arms backed and forth while saying, "I wanted to stay in my love." She had. There was a long way to go, but she was on her way.

As caregivers we teach values and a way of being constantly as we act and respond peacefully, respectfully or lovingly — or act and react with blame, fright, anxiety, irritation or anger. The importance of peaceful and loving ways of communicating and nurturing continue as children pass through their teenage years for these allow relationships to grow in a healthy way. While the overt methods of communication and nurturing change over time, a healthy relationship with parents keeps teens safe. A nurtured teen with values, who can use her or his cognitive skills to think about alternatives and consequences, is better equipped to navigate the world safely, with respect, confidence, purpose — and happiness.

When a child becomes upset, it does not mean you are a bad parent. It simply means the child is upset and has a need. For you as the parent, it is an opportunity to be in a state of peace and love and hear what needs hearing. Listen with love. This will help your child learn to self-regulate and become more secure.

~ 30 ~

Drug Prevention — Begin by Age Six

One of the fears of parents is their child becoming involved with drugs. It is wise to take preventative steps. The greatest preventions are a good relationship with your child, including the ability to listen and share with love and understanding, drug education, and family time together.

Listen, and talk together

The ability to listen and share with love and understanding usually goes hand in hand with children sharing their feelings and emotions. This includes not just love, joy and enthusiasm, but also sharing emotions of anxiety, worry, doubt, insecurity, fear, hurt, sadness, grief and anger. It is invaluable for children to be able to open up with their parents and be heard, to not have their emotions discounted, but understood and accepted. This allows children to lovingly accept their own emotions and be able to process them in a healthy way. People who are unable to deal with their emotions are much more vulnerable to becoming addicted to substances and engaging in maladaptive behaviors.

Family time

Family time is important for many reasons. Loving and being loved is one of the key joys of life. Family time allows children to learn social and emotional skills. When family time is full of love, it gives meaning and happiness to life. That said, even when family time is not happy, children are still learning — about the mores of our society and how to communicate when there are challenges. Even if a family is dysfunctional, many still impart a sense of belonging. Family time is essential for children of all ages. Tweens and teens who do not feel a strong sense of belonging may get into drugs and/or gangs in their effort to attain attention, acceptance and a sense of belonging and identity.

As parents, spend time with your children, be available daily to talk and "hang out" together. Turn off the television, video games, computers and cell phones for at least a couple of hours each day. If you choose to watch a movie together, make it a humanizing one which you can enjoy and discuss together. Create traditions on holidays, birthdays and special occasions. Traditions can be simple and inexpensive. What is important is the flow of kindness, recognition, acceptance, love and laughter with one another.

Educate about drugs

By the time your children are six years of age, make sure they know it is not safe to accept pills from people other than their parents and caregivers. This means not taking pills from their friends, their friends' older brothers or sisters, other kids at school, adults they know or strangers. In drug-infested neighborhoods, please begin to educate about drugs at an even younger age. Educate yourself about the different kinds and forms of drugs available in your area, be it prescription pills, joints or inhalants, so you can inform your child of what to be wary. A couple of stories appropriate for young children are below.

By the time your child is eight or nine, discuss drugs again and inform him of some of the effects. You might want to say something like, "You are smart and doing well, and I want you to stay healthy and smart. Drugs can damage your brain. Different kinds of drugs harm people in different ways. For example, when kids breathe in glue or _____, some of their brain cells are killed. Kids who are addicted to glue harm their brain so much they become dumb. I want you to be safe. I want you to enjoy life and be able to achieve anything you want to achieve." Discuss the drugs which are available in the neighborhood, answer any questions and discuss the advantages of staying smart and drug-free.

If your child knows people who take drugs, ask her why she thinks people take drugs. Listen carefully, and add any other reasons that are age-appropriate to share. Ask about the effect she thinks drugs have on people her age and older and inform as needed. For example, many teens smoke marijuana. Their motivation to study, do well at school, and achieve in life suffers immensely. One of the dangers of smoking marijuana is joints laced with other drugs. Some teens have a psychotic break during drug trips with laced joints. This can catapult them into serious mental illness.

It is important for the child to know how to be able to resist peer pressure to take drugs. Perhaps role play things people might say to him and possible answers until he finds one he is comfortable with and can say easily. For example, "Thanks, but no thanks. I like my brain just the way it is." "No artificial highs for me, thanks." "Hey, none of that for me! I want to keep my smarts." Take turns role playing the two roles, acting out different ways of being approached. Role play until he or she can deliver the preferred line with self-respect and confidence.

Continue to bring up the subject two or three times a year as your children grow, perhaps in response to a movie with a drug scene, or in relation to news about a drug overdose, or a neighbor or schoolmate affected by drugs.

If the child questions the effects of drugs, for example, saying marijuana or alcohol is not harmful, get on the internet together and research. There are websites which give information about deaths due to alcohol poisoning and how the developing brains of young people are much more adversely affected by marijuana than those of adults.

Two stories about the effect of drugs for young children

I once created a series of stories for young children who were vulnerable to taking drugs because of their difficult life circumstances. Taken from *Living Values Activities for Street Children Ages 3–6*, two of these stories are adapted below. They are appropriate for children six and above, should you wish to have stories about drugs and selling drugs to use as a springboard for discussing the issue. Do not tell the stories to children of five years of age if they are not vulnerable. Wait until they are a bit older.

A story about drugs: *I don't want to be trapped in a glass ball!*

Once upon a time there was a boy named Fred. Fred and his mother and little sister lived together in a house in the city. They loved each other very much. Fred's Mama always told him each child was loved, valuable and important, especially him and his little sister, Katie.

One day when Fred was outside playing with Timmy, he saw his mother get upset when she talked to the next-door neighbor. Later that night, he asked, "Mama, why did you get upset when you talked to Ana?"

His Mama frowned a little, like she didn't want to tell him, but then she looked at him seriously, took a big breath and said, "Ana was worried. She said her younger cousin, Alan, started to work for some drug dealers. She's worried about him and she's worried about you kids, too. She told Alan she loves him, so he has to find a way to quit. She also told him to not come around here until he does. She doesn't want you or Timmy or any of you kids to get into drugs. She's afraid Alan might give you some.

"What are drugs?" asked Fred.

"Well," Mama said, "drugs are things people put in their bodies to get high. There are many kinds of drugs. There's marijuana and pills, sometimes they have glue to sniff or _____." (Note: Kindly fill in the blank with whatever drug is most common and available for children in your area.) Some people take drugs to try and forget their problems or to try and feel happy.

Mama said, "I want you to promise me to never take drugs."

"But Mama, you said people take them to get high and feel happy," said Fred. "Charlie up the street said he got a pill and it made him feel good."

"Yes," said Mama slowly. "Sometimes a person feels good for a little while. How can I explain it to you?"

Mama sat down next to Fred and said, "Okay, I want you to pretend you have a glass ball around you."

"A glass ball?" asked Fred.

"Yes," said Mama, "all around you so even your hands and feet are inside. When you take drugs, it's like having a glass ball around you. The person starts looking at the glass ball and watches how the light shines on it. It looks pretty. And because it feels like there is something between the person and the world, sometimes the person feels safer. But, it's much safer *not* to be in the glass ball. What would happen if you were in the glass ball when a car came by? You wouldn't notice it's close enough to hit you because you're only looking at the light on the glass ball."

Illustration by Joanne Corcoran

"After a while, the brain is really hurt. It gets slow and it's hard to learn. The person slowly gets dumb and then dumber. And then," continued Mama, "when you want to get out of the ball you can't, because your body and mind only want the drug. So, you take more drugs and you get trapped in the glass ball."

Fred said, "I don't want to be trapped in a glass ball!"

"Then don't take drugs! It's no fun inside a glass ball after a while," smiled Mama. "When you are outside the glass ball you are free to grow and go where you like."

"Thanks, Mama," said Fred, giving her a hug. She gave him a big hug back and her special smile.

Discuss

- ♦ What did Mama say drugs are?
- ♦ Why is taking drugs like having a glass ball around you?
- ♦ What can't you do if you are trapped inside a glass ball?
- ♦ What happens to your arms when you are on drugs?
- ♦ What happens to your mind when you are on drugs?

- Why do you think some people take drugs? (Discuss as appropriate.)
- Do you know anyone who takes drugs? (Discuss as appropriate.)
- Do you have any questions about drugs?

Activity

Ask the child to pretend to be in a glass ball. Put a little spot on one arm and ask the child to pretend that is where the light shines on the ball. The child is to look at the spot on his or her arm while pretending to be in the glass ball.

You, or the other children, can take out peace puppets, or a favorite plush animal or toy, and play with those and each other. Ask the child pretending to be in the glass ball to pretend he or she can't understand them very well. So the one child just sits and looks at the spot while the others play. Do this for just two minutes and then ask the children to share their experiences. Listen as they share and answer any questions they may have.

End with the Respect Star exercise. It is downloadable from the livingvalues.net website.

A second story about drugs: *Drug Sellers Pretend to Be Nice at First*

Fred enjoyed stretching as he woke up the next morning. It was a pretty day outside and the early morning sky was blue. He could hear the birds singing. He thought about what Mama shared yesterday about how being on drugs was like being trapped in a glass ball. Now he got to enjoy the blue sky, and the sounds of the birds, and his family and friends and toys and everything. He didn't want to be trapped! He pulled on his clothes and ran to the kitchen where he could hear the sound of dishes clinking together.

"Okay, Mama, I promise," Fred shouted as he ran in.

"Promise what?" asked Mama, looking up in surprise.

Fred gave Mama a hug and said, "Remember what you told me about last night? About Ana's cousin and how taking drugs is like being trapped in a glass ball? I promise never to take drugs."

"Wow — great!" Mama said with a happy smile. "So you want to stay smart, hmm?"

"Yes," Fred said.

Mama sat down at the kitchen table. "I should tell you one more thing," Mama said. "You have to be very careful about people who sell drugs. Drug sellers pretend to be nice at first, but it's only until you are hooked on drugs."

"What do you mean, hooked on drugs?" asked Fred.

"After you take some drugs a few times it's hard to stop taking them because your body craves them. That's called being hooked on drugs," explained Mama.

"Drug sellers are very selfish. Often they offer drugs free the first few times. Then once you are hooked they charge you money. It is wrong for people to make money on kids."

"I think that's probably what's happening to Ana's cousin. That's why she is so upset," said Mama. "He's only a teenager. Somebody probably got him hooked on drugs. Now they're telling him they will give him the drug free, *if* he brings other people. If you love your friends, you would never ask them to take drugs."

"I love my friends," said Fred.

"I know you do," said Mama. "You're a good friend. Drug sellers can be selfish and very mean too. Sometimes drug dealers want kids to be hooked on drugs so they can use them like slaves."

"Slaves?" said Fred.

"Yes," said Mama, "if they can get you hooked on drugs they know you will do anything for them in order to get the drugs. They can do what they want with the children because they are trapped in the glass ball. It looks like they may be doing that with Ana's cousin."

"I'm not going to be anyone's slave!" protested Fred.

"No, you're not," said Mama. "You're free because you don't take drugs. People who take drugs begin to lose their smarts. They get less and less smart and can get dumb, especially on some kinds of drugs. When you learn, you get smarter and smarter. You'll be able to do what you want in life."

"I like to play ball, and I like to run and I like to read," said Fred.

Fred's mother gave him a big smile and said, "Yes, you are smart, you are kind, you like to play and you are learning to read. You will never be trapped inside the glass ball of drugs."

Fred looked up, with a worried look on his face, "Mama, will you tell this to Ana, so she can tell it to her cousin?"

"Great idea, Fred," smiled Mama.

Discuss

- ◆ Did Fred promise not to take drugs?
- ◆ Why do drug sellers pretend to be nice?
- ◆ Are they nice? (No.)
- ◆ What does "hooked on drugs" mean?
- ◆ If you love your friends, what will you not do?
- ◆ Why do the drug sellers want to sell drugs to kids?
- ◆ How do drug sellers make kids like their slaves?
- ◆ Are you slaves?
- ◆ Are you smart? (Yes.)
- ◆ What can you say to someone if they offer you a drug and pressure you to try it?

Activities

Discuss the different kinds of drugs available in the neighborhood. Then discuss how they think other people could offer drugs. Role play what people might say when offering them drugs and possible answers, until they find a response with which they are comfortable. For example, "Thanks, but no thanks. I like my brain just the way it is." "No artificial highs for me, thanks."

"Hey, none of that for me! I want to keep all my smarts." Role play until they can deliver their preferred line with self-respect and confidence."

The following week …

Ask the children if they would like to hear the stories about Fred and drugs again. When you've finished reading, ask them if they have any more thoughts they wish to share or any questions.

Say, "Some people don't have enough love inside so they are selfish and mean. We are fortunate because we have love inside and know we can give happiness." Ask: "What's one way you like me to give happiness?" (Perhaps a hug, a special smile, etc.) Ask: "What are ways you give happiness?" Positively acknowledge their answers. Perhaps ask them to draw a picture of someone giving happiness on one side of a piece of paper and someone giving sorrow on the other side.

Are you a binge drinker? What are you modeling?

Check your own behavior. Are you a binge drinker? Do you drink daily? If you are more than an occasional drinker, and you allow your teenager to drink, you are asking for your behavior to be copied no matter what you say. Many adults with a good education and a successful career use alcohol to manage their stress; others struggle to hide their addiction and continue to succeed at their profession. However, as they are already adults, they have their education and their brains are developed. This is not the case for preteens and teenagers.

Drugs and alcohol are doubly harmful to tweens and teens, not just because of the damaging effect on their still-developing brain, but because of the other behaviors to which they can lead. Being high or inebriated usually imparts a sense of false confidence and results in extrovert behavior. False bravado can be fun when it results in jokes and silly laughter; it can be meaningful when a person feels free to share something they would not usually be comfortable sharing. However, false bravado can also lead to harmful or dangerous acts which would not even be considered if not under the influence, the influence of the substance and the influence of peers who have a history of engaging in risky behavior.

Camaraderie under the influence of substances is viewed as very special by many teens, and even by some adults. If they think the camaraderie, or the enhanced feeling of confidence, can only be experienced while under the influence, they are seriously limiting their potential. They will then be less likely to want to spend the time to achieve academically, in sports or in any other worthwhile pursuit. Their attention will be on the next drug or alcohol-enhanced experience. Drinking and drugs do not lead to achievement or lasting happiness in the real world. They take many people down the path of addiction, drug overdoses, underachievement and maladaptive relationships.

When children are using . . .

Protect your child from drugs and alcohol. Zero tolerance is the best policy while they are underage. Allowing a little allows the attraction to grow. With time they are more likely to have the values, maturity and wisdom to make sensible choices and indulge wisely, that is, as an occasional choice rather than a compulsive need or an attempt to prove themselves. Know where your child is and with whom. Be aware of your stock of alcohol and prescription drugs, if they are in the house.

The legal age for drinking, and official entry into adulthood, varies from country to country. A teen having a beer with friends at 18 is a far different story than a 10-year old or 13- and 15-year olds taking drugs or drinking until they vomit or pass out. If the latter is the case, it is time to reassess.

How is this child doing in school? What does he need in order to do well? What are the peer influences? Where are the tweens or teens getting the substances? Is there adequate parental monitoring and supervision? Is there adequate family time and Us Time?

You may wish to meet your child's friends if you have not already. If the child has good long-term friends in the neighborhood, who are also now getting into drugs or alcohol, you may wish to call the parents of these friends and invite them over for a discussion with the tweens or teens. Tell them of your love and concerns, perhaps in a similar fashion as outlined in steps one through three of the correction sequence in Chapter 17. Create the opportunity for them to share and set up some new guidelines.

If some of your child's friends are completely into drugs or alcohol and you do not wish that for your child, you will also need a new set of guidelines. Tell your child of your love and concerns. Your concerns might include brain development, alcohol poisoning, overdoses, lower academic performance and a changed vision of the future should there be lack of entry into university because of poor grades. Concerns might also include the possibility of a greater chance of being sexually active and hence greater vulnerability to sexually-transmitted diseases and teen pregnancy. Listen to your teen and ask about their vision of the future and their hopes, and then share your hopes and vision for their wellbeing.

You may wish to explain in a loving and sensible manner that one of your main jobs as a parent is to make sure your children are safe and get a good education. One of the main jobs of a tween or teen is to make effort to do well at school. As you make a plan together, don't hesitate to include logical consequences. After a lapse of judgment on the part of the child, one consequence may be limited social outings with approved friends only. Random home-drug testing is an option to consider if you suspect there may be a lack of compliance. Look at other social activities. Is there a team sport the child can get into or a club which fits with his or her interests? Encourage good grades, be positive about helping with homework if necessary, and set up tutoring if needed. It is logical to permit certain privileges, such as driving a car, only if the teen has good grades and is drug and alcohol free.

Do not punish the child through your looks or attitude. Continue to enjoy and delight in him or her while letting the consequences take place in a matter-of-fact manner. Listen, be open to discussion and nurture. Increased family time and Us Time are, as always, one of the key ingredients for success. Stay loving and positively engaged with your child as you encourage the development of healthy interests.

~ 31 ~

Help Children Deal with Bullying and Social Media

Many parents are concerned about bullying, violence and the many ways in which children can be rejected, ignored or treated meanly by their peers. As human beings we thrive in a culture of peace, love and respect. In such a culture there is a sense of belonging and harmony.

At the beginning of this book, you were asked to think of two values that would change the world. Would living those values create a culture of peace, love and respect? Are you willing to live those? Many people have been taught by their families and society to judge others by their race and religion. More subtle, but equally devastating, it seems almost all of us have been taught to judge others by their status, appearance and possessions. We have been taught to respect some and value others less, even to be prejudice.

Are we willing to treat all others with respect and dignity? Are we willing to live our values in such a way that we are part of creating a culture of peace, love and respect? Are we willing to teach our children to do that? In such a culture, not one child would be taunted. In such a culture, *every* child would be safe.

The situation is worse than I think most of us ever expected it could be, from teens shooting and killing their peers at school campuses and a movie theatre in the USA, to teens killing their prefects/monitors in Kenya, to children killing children in England, Japan and El Salvador. The perpetrators can be young. This last year there was a story of two boys, a 9-year old and a 10-year old in the state of Washington, who planned to kill an 8-year-old girl.

While senseless acts of brutal violence are horrific, the percentage of children and families directly affected is relatively low. In contrast, bullying and a culture of disrespect affect most children, even if they are only frightened by someone else being bullied, fearing it could happen to them. However, the consequences of bullying can negatively affect people for many years, indeed, for the rest of their lives. However, bullying can be equally tragic — it can result in death. In 2014, a 12-year-old girl in Florida committed suicide after peers urged her to kill herself through social media. A Massachusetts high school 15-year-old freshman endured months of taunts and threats before she hung herself. Six of her classmates face charges.

Research shows children do better academically in a culture of care. I think we all know they also do better emotionally and socially. So, how can we help our children not be bullies, not be bullied, and form positive relationships with their peers to cooperate in stopping bullying while creating a culture of peace, kindness and respect?

What is bullying?

Often people think of bullying as physical bullying, with boys picking on other boys or girls. But it is also name-calling, taunting, deliberately spreading rumors and ostracizing others, by girls and boys. Bullying in any form, including belittling, harassing and threatening, causes not only emotional distress to victims but can result in some victims engaging in self-harm. While bullying is most prevalent in fifth through eighth grades, it can occur as early as preschool and can continue as a mean, hateful, desperate or cowardly action in high school and throughout adulthood. In Australia there is a nationwide campaign to stop bullying in the workplace. It costs businesses billions in lost productivity every year.

The "Stop Bullying Now" campaign of the U.S. Department of Health and Human Services defines bullying as:

"unwanted, aggressive behavior among school aged children that involves a real or perceived power imbalance. The behavior is repeated, or has the potential to be repeated, over time. Both kids who are bullied and who bully others may have serious, lasting problems. In order to be considered bullying, the behavior must be aggressive and include an imbalance of power: Kids who bully use their power— such as physical strength, access to embarrassing information, or popularity—to control or harm others. Power imbalances can change over time and in different situations, even if they involve the same people. … Bullying includes actions such as making threats, spreading rumors, attacking someone physically or verbally, and excluding someone from a group on purpose."

Social media, chat rooms, texting and emails provide opportunities for non-face to face and anonymous attacks, resulting in even more vicious statements than would usually be said in person. The ease of taking photographs with cell phones can result in embarrassing pictures being posted in moments. Years ago, a mean statement said to a victim was bad enough. For a rumor, mean statement or embarrassing picture to spread to a hundred classmates is far, far more devastating socially and emotionally. To millions? I can't imagine.

To not create a bully

Some people believe only children who are victims of violence and bullying by parents and siblings at home will become bullies. These "victim bullies" do suffer from low self-esteem, hurt, anger and poor interpersonal skills, but bullies can also be attractive young people with intact interpersonal skills who use bullying as a method to try to belong to a certain group, to be popular and/or to stay popular.

To not create a bully? Nurture with love and wisdom and discipline with peace and respect. Carefully select the books, movies and video games to which children are exposed. Choose tales of peace, love and kindness where those with the courage to be good are rewarded. Teach your children that treating every person with respect and kindness is important — and model that at home and in your interactions with the larger community.

If you think it would be good for your children to practice giving and receiving positives, do the "Building kindness … Growing peace, love and gratitude every night before bed" activities at the end of Chapter 26. Perhaps do some of the Living Values Activities in the respect and love units to increase social awareness and intrapersonal and interpersonal skills.

Be aware of your children's relationships with siblings and friends. If there is quarreling and fighting, teach them conflict resolution skills. If your child is an only child, when he or she is fighting with a friend or cousin at home, engage them in learning conflict resolution. Does your child have good social skills? Make sure he has the opportunity to play and interact with others. He or she may benefit by boy or girl guides, sports, activities organized by your faith community and adventures in nature with friends.

Be aware of your children's statements about friends and what is happening at school. Listen when they talk about their feelings toward school and classmates. Actively listen to their comments. Be aware when they are undergoing changes and feeling low about something. Help them understand and manage their emotions.

When someone is negative toward them, actively listen and perhaps share if something similar happened to you. Help them understand that only hurt people hurt people. Gently acknowledge the hurt and/or fear under their anger rather than allowing them to stay stuck in anger. Sometimes a statement such as "It sounds like your feelings got hurt," can create an opportunity for them to share. It can be helpful to reaffirm their natural qualities if another person was mean to them.

I remember doing the latter with a five-year old. She nodded after my active-listening statement of, "Your feelings got hurt when 'Sally' said that." I continued, "Sometimes people say mean things when they are feeling grumpy. But I know who you are. You are not what she said. You are a sweet, wonderful, smart little girl who I love very much." She leaned up against me and said softly, "I'm so glad I came."

Continue to enjoy family time together and positively reinforce kind social skills. When you hear about a bullying incident, either at school or on the news, discuss those that are age-appropriate and build empathy. Ask how they think the victim would feel. Teach them positive social skills to support peers who are being bullied as noted further on in this chapter. Be involved with your children's teachers and school.

Help your child be sensitive and positive when engaged in social media
Before your child begins to use a cell phone or computer, have a talk about texting and emailing manners. Ask what values he thinks would be important. Ask her to think of phrases or sentences which would create

positive feelings and feelings of friendship and belonging. Ask how he might feel, or another person, if he were to receive a rejecting, unkind or mean text or email. Try out positive messages and neutral messages. Experiment with saying neutral messages in different voices to see if they can be interpreted negatively. Tell them that text messages and emails can be saved for many years, so it is very important to only send something they are going to be proud of years later. Perhaps ask them to send their first emails and texts to you and other relatives. Ask them to make a rule for emails and texts. For example: Kind or helpful. Or: I would like to get this! Perhaps they can make it part of a graphic and post it as wallpaper on their device.

Discuss the effect of gossip on the person being gossiped about, and ask them to never gossip about others. Discuss the importance of never hitting the "send" button on a text or email when angry. Explain that when people are angry it is easy to want to hurt — and it is wrong to use words that hurt. The test: Does their message leave people with a positive feeling? A few weeks later, revisit the subject.

For tweens and teens who are already texting, engaged in live chats and involved with social media sites such as Facebook and Instagram, have a similar conversation as above. However, also visit the bullying.about.com website and talk about the mean messages which have contributed to suicides. Talk quite seriously about what they share on social media sites — messages and photographs.

Let your child know there is no such thing as privacy on social media. Suggest that anything they post should be something they are okay with everyone seeing — including you and aunts, uncles and grandparents. You might wish to mention sexting, the disturbing trend in which suggestive pictures meant to be private have been circulated after a couple have broken up. Is what they are sharing or posting something they want everyone in the school to see or that they will be proud of in ten years? Is the message or posting embarrassing to anyone? Is it hurtful to anyone? Ask them what two values will help them decide what is okay to say and what kind of pictures to post. Please do this with all of your children, boys and girls.

Avoid being bullied

The school of your child may have an anti-bullying program. If so, they are likely to have discussed how being bullied might feel. Some anti-bullying programs have conflict resolution steps and small group interventions if there are specific incidents of bullying. If your children are in a school implementing LVE, our experience has been that bullying disappears when a culture of peace, caring and respect is established. Children do have disagreements, but they use a language of values to solve their problems. As one principal of a K–8 school said, "There simply is no bullying."

There is a considerable amount of information about bullying on the internet. If your child mentions bullying or is concerned about bullying as they become nine or ten years old and enter higher grades, ask them if they would like to learn more about bullying. If so, visit together the bully.about.com website and become aware of the different kinds of bullies and bullying. The About.com site mentions six types of bullies: bully victims, popular/aggressive bullies, relational bullies, serial bullies, group bullies and indifferent bullies. Their general recommendations include strategies such as students at school avoiding being bullied by staying with a friend and staying in areas where teachers are present.

Kids are kids. It is possible they may be influenced by peer pressure. Perhaps there is an attractive or popular peer who wants someone to do something slightly negative — and your child wants to be accepted by that person. Consider implementing the sections above, "To not create a bully" and "Help your child be sensitive and positive when engaged in social media." The "Building kindness" activities can help heighten their awareness of the effects of giving and receiving positives. This is a useful contrast when discussing what feels bad. One little mistake can be magnified on social media, so discussing values and increasing their sensitivity to the effect of positive and negative is an important part of preventing being a bully — and receiving bullying. The best defense is self-respect and the value of respect for all.

In much of the literature, the words bully and victim are used. For the rest of this chapter, I will use the word "target" instead of victim as target is a more transitory term with less emotional impact. I would suggest being careful about calling someone a "bully". It is more transitory to describe the behavior: "When you bully," or "when she bullies." Change is possible. It is kinder to not label people and keep the door of change open!

When alone — Help your child be assertive when trouble appears

Do you remember the story about benevolent assertion in the chapter on "Positive Alternatives, Modeling and Choices?" I used to teach this to boys who frequently fought. With only two ready alternatives in their social tool kit, name calling and fighting, they were frequently in trouble. We would discuss what happens when people reply aggressively to being called a name, and what happens when people respond passively. They knew what happened when they responded aggressively as that is what they were accustomed to doing: it led to a fight. They were not comfortable being passive as they felt they would look cowardly. Children responding passively to a person bullying, such as apologizing, crying, looking sad or pleading as mean things are said, can actually lead to further bullying as the person bullying feels more powerful. A sensible alternative is an assertive response. The person bullying does not get the feeling of power over a person when the target stays in self-respect.

You can help your child develop assertive responses at a very young age when someone is unkind. Begin teaching your child at two years of age to "use words" if other children call names, pinch, hit or bite. Two- and three-year olds can say, "No hitting. Stop." Or, read your child *The Star Story* in the Peace Unit of *Living Values Activities for Children Ages 3–7*, and teach him to say, "Stop. Be a Peace Star." Read the same story to his hitting or biting friends and engage them and your child in playing with peace puppets and visiting the Peace Tent.

Four-year olds can learn to say, "I don't like you to call me names, I want you to stop." I teach this same assertive statement to nine-year olds who are behaving either passively or aggressively as both invite trouble.

Listen if your child comes home with a story about being called a name or hit. Actively listen to his feelings and validate in a supportive manner. Then teach an appropriate social skill. For example, if he was hit, you might want to teach: "I don't like it when you hit me, I want you to stop." Model it a couple of times, then ask the child to say it. Ask the child to tap you and say it again. Say, "Look how I am saying this with self-respect. Now I want you to stay in your self-respect and say it." Then say, "Okay, now I'm going to tap you and I want you to say it." Tap him very lightly on the arm and say it again. Practice with him another three or four times till he can deliver the line with self-respect, even when you tap a little harder.

In the same way, do this with name calling. Listen carefully to her story, being supportive with active listening and validating as appropriate. Then teach: "I don't like it when you call me names, I want you to stop." Model it a couple of times, then ask the child to call you a name. Your child will be surprised, as hopefully she has been brought up to never call you a name. Ask the child to call you the name a couple of times, and say your assertive sentence each time. Then say, "Look how I am saying this with self-respect. Now I want you to stay in your self-respect and say, "I don't like it when you call me names, I want you to stop." Then say, "Okay, now I'm going to call you a name and I want you to say that." Call her "meanie" very kindly and encourage her assertive response. Then call her the name a little more loudly. Positively encourage her to say the assertive response clearly and with confidence. Finally, call her the name she was called by the other child earlier in the day, and practice a few more times till she can deliver the line with self-respect.

Benevolent-assertive responses

If your child is eight years old or above and is encountering situations he or she thinks are unfair, the child may be ready to learn benevolent-assertive responses. A benevolent-assertive response is useful in changing the dynamics when there is an atmosphere of discrimination, meanness or bullying. It can make a prejudiced person think, stop meanness and bullying — and even open an alternative door to kindness, understanding or even friendship. This can be used when someone is being discriminatory, or when someone is bullying your child or another child.

Please teach the child the assertive response skills noted above: "I don't like it when you hit me. I want you to stop," and "I don't like it when you call me names. I want you to stop." Children should be comfortable with those skills before you introduce the social skill of benevolent assertion.

With a benevolent-assertive response, the child is deliberately not agreeing with the offending person by letting the person know in a non-offensive and nondefensive manner of a different view. The comment may include an acknowledgement of the goodness of the offending person or change the direction of the interaction to values, qualities or relationship.

Examples . . .

When someone makes a discriminatory remark — to your child or to another child.

⭐ Life wouldn't be so interesting if we were all clones.

⭐ God is a great artist. I think both of our colors are beautiful.

⭐ I was hoping to be purple this birth, but it didn't work out!

⭐ I think all the religions of the world are cool.

When someone attempts to start a fight with your child.

⭐ Why are we fighting? We have the same skin color.

⭐ Fighting stinks. Can't we think of anything better to do?

⭐ I think there's enough fighting in the world. Fighting or friends … what a choice!

⭐ Peace is a better choice than fighting.

When your child wants to stop the bullying of another child and it feels safe to do so.

⭐ Kindness is cool. Respect is cool. Come on, I know you have at least one of those inside.

⭐ <u>All</u> people deserve respect — that includes everyone here.

☆ I like to see your kind side, _____ (name). That's the you we care about.

☆ The world has enough wars. Do we really need another one here?

Say some of the above examples aloud with your child and see if he thinks any of them might work for his situation. Ask your child about a situation of concern and play with making up appropriate responses. When you find one he likes, role play the statement which is relevant to the situation until he can deliver the response with self-respect and confidence. This social skill can help children now and as they grow toward adulthood.

Use Humor

Now that your child has the practice of delivering a response while staying in self-respect and confidence, talk about using humor or agreeing with the bully. A humorous response which usually disarms when delivered confidently with a smile is: "If I had feelings, they'd be hurt!" When people don't get defensive and stay in self-respect, the bullying usually stops as there is no pay-off for the one bullying. Together with your child, think of things people have said in the past and come up with an agreeing or humorous response if you think it might work. Agreeing with a smile can also defuse the situation. "You're silly!" Response, with a smile and a touch of pride: "Sometimes."

A wonderful story I was just introduced to by The Joy of Reading Project is *Simon's hook* by Karen Gedig Burnett. Suitable for young children and beautifully illustrated, it introduces the concept of not buying into being bullied in the same way some fish learn to not bite a hook. Be a free fish and learn to not react, by agreeing, distracting or using humor. The Joy of Reading team kindly gave permission to post this story on the livingvalues.net website so it can be downloaded free of charge.

Avoid those who bully — Practicalities when there is a history of meanness

As adults, most of us have met some people who initially seem to be cold, offensive or defensive, yet they turn out to be wonderful people when we get to know them. However, I think many of us have also met one or two people who act mean intentionally or bully others consistently. Perhaps they are jealous, arrogant or have had a lot of trauma in their life. I believe in giving respect to everyone. However, I don't think there is any need to offer yourself as a target.

I would suggest talking to your child about avoiding those who bully. To say hello or give the person a nod or a smile when she is close by would be using the value of respect, especially if the child senses that this peer does not wish to stay in the role of bullying. However, it is only sensible for your child to avoid those who bully as much as possible until they behave with kindness.

Peer intervention — Working together to deter bullying

When peers intervene on behalf of the target, bullying frequently stops. Canadian research indicates the bullying stops 57 percent of the time within ten seconds if a peer intervenes. Bystanders passively watching bullying take place can add to the feeling of power the person who is bullying wants, so standing and watching can unwittingly reinforce bullying. Peer intervention is important as adults are rarely around when bullying occurs. Other children are frequently around when bullying occurs: 85 percent of the time.

Which of the following is the best intervention?

    A. Peers walk away from the bullying scene.

    B. One of the peer bystanders calls out to the target, "Come on, Sema. Don't listen to her." Or, "Come on, Tom, it's no fun listening to this." Then peers walk away from the bullying scene *with* the target.

    C. One of the peer watchers calls out to the target, "Come on, Sema, it looks like Pam is grumpy today. Maybe she'll be nicer tomorrow!" "Come on, Tom, it's no fun listening to this. It looks like Mack isn't his usual self today." Then peers walk away from the bullying scene *with* the target.

In Intervention A, the person bullying is deprived of an audience, but the target feels unsupported and may fear the bystanders think less of him or her. It is important for the target to walk away, but to walk away alone might be difficult. The target might feel shunned by everyone.

In intervention B, the target feels supported by the bystanders so does not suffer as much. It is successful in stopping the bullying.

In intervention C, the target feels supported by the bystanders and the intervention has been successful in stopping the bullying. Additionally, the person bullying has not been completely alienated. He's been offered a reason for his behavior. This opens a door for possible change. This is the best intervention as it does not intensify the feelings of being a victim or a villain — increasing the likelihood that neither child will feel as stuck in those roles. Possibilities are created, of a more positive interaction tomorrow, of a friend talking to the person bullying or ….?

Teach your children and their friends to intervene by calling out to the target

Children can easily learn this intervention. This can be done with students at school, with kids in after-school activities or by you with your children and a group of their friends. Perhaps another proactive parent would like to join you. If you, a teacher or a friend would like to do this, go through the following steps in an age-appropriate way, using language the children will understand. This activity can be done with children seven years old and above. Older teens could read this chapter and do the activities with their friends.

Step One: Begin by sharing your reason for bringing up the subject. Perhaps say something like, "I've been reading about ways to help stop bullying. I want to talk with you about it as there's something easy and safe you can do. I like all of you so much and would never want any of you to be bullied."

Ask any of the below questions that fit for the group of children in front of you. Acknowledge or actively listen to their responses. Give them time to share.

- Do you know what bullying means?
- Have you ever seen anyone bullied at school or in our neighborhood?
- How do you feel when you see someone bullied?
- How do you think the person getting bullied feels?
- Have any of you been a target of bullying? How did you feel?
- Have any of you acted like a bully? How did that feel?

Step Two: Share with them: "When someone is bullying another person, if someone speaks up for the target, the bullying stops more than half of the time.

If people just stand there and do nothing, the person bullying feels more powerful. So it is important to not just stand and watch when someone is bullying another kid.

Step Three: Say, "I am going to ask you to imagine different things that can happen when there is bullying.

> Scene 1: Someone is bullying someone else and everyone stands and watches.

> Scene 2: All the bystanders walk away from the bullying scene, leaving the person bullying and the target. The person bullying continues being mean and finally the target walks away alone.

> Scene 3: One of the kids calls out the name of the target and says, 'Come on, don't listen to this.' He and the target and all the other kids walk away from the bully."

> Ask:
> - In which scene is the bullying worse?
> - How do you think the target feels in scene 2?
> - In which scene is the target protected?
> - Do you think everyone should be protected from being bullied?
> - If you had a friend with you, do you think you would be comfortable helping the target?

Say, "In Scene 3, the helpful bystander called out to the target before leaving with him: 'Come on, don't listen to this.' Other statements could be: "Come on, Sam, let's go. It's no fun listening to this," or Hey, Mira, let's go. This is totally uncool."

Ask:

♦ What kinds of things could you call out to the target to let him or her know you are helping them be safe?

Make a list of their statements. As the children call out a statement, ask everyone in the group to echo them. Ask them to read aloud all the statements with self-respect when they have finished generating ideas.

Step Four: Tell them you would like them to role play Scene 3.

Ask:

♦ Who wants to be the person bullying?

♦ Who wants to be the target?

♦ Who wants to be the helpful bystander? What shall we call the helpful bystander? Peace Star, Courageous Bystander or something else?

Say, "The rest of you will play the bystanders watching the bully and the target."

Ask:

♦ Person bullying, what are you going to say? ...... Got it? Allow the children to generate a bullying statement and/or action they have witnessed before.

Say, "Okay, person bullying, stand here. Target, please stand a few feet away and look surprised when he says something that is bullying. Helpful bystander, Courageous Star (or whatever name they have decided upon), stand with the group. You can pick your lines from the list we made."

Have a good time with the kids as they role play the scene. If there are many children, divide them into groups of four or five so they all get to practice the helpful-bystander role. Positively reinforce efforts and encourage them to say their statements with self-respect and confidence.

Get together and practice again, perhaps a few days or a week later, adding the benevolent-assertive response below.

Teaching the group of friends to intervene with benevolent-assertive responses

Once they are doing the above skill well, you may wish to teach them about benevolent-assertive responses. If so, say, "There's another possibility. You've been practicing calling out the name of the target and saying something supportive to stop the bullying and help the target be safe, before you walk away with the target. But there's something else you can do called a benevolent-assertive response. In this, before our helpful bystander goes, he adds something a little nice about the person bullying! Examples are:

- ☆ Dana is grumpy today. Maybe she'll be nicer tomorrow.
- ☆ It looks like Mack isn't his usual self today.
- ☆ Hector is having a bad day. He'll be better tomorrow.

Say, "*Sometimes* if we are a little kind a few times, the person bullying will stop bullying. *Not all the time, but sometimes*! Some people get stuck in being mean for a few years, so during that time they just get meaner. But some people who bully can feel stuck in needing to be mean. So when someone is a little kind, it can open a door for the person bullying to change. Don't be too kind — just a little! But, the most important thing is always to stop the bullying and help the target get away feeling supported."

"Okay, the benevolent-assertive responses were ..." (Repeat the three starred statements on the previous page.)

Ask:

♦ Can you think of other things you could say to a person bullying?

Write down the benevolent-assertive responses the children come up with for the situations they are encountering, and have them echo each statement. Perhaps decide together which responses might work for one person who is bullying and which might work better with another person bullying. Have a good time role playing Scene 3 and the benevolent-assertive response scene until they can deliver the helpful-bystander statements with self-respect and confidence.

Distraction as an art of nonviolence — for children 11 years of age and older

A few years ago in the *Los Angeles Times,* I read an article about a police department that used distraction as a method to help them deal with domestic-violence disputes. Tragically, sometimes policemen and policewomen are killed when they are called to a home to intervene. Using planned distraction, this police department was able to reduce mortality. The example given was a policeman arriving as a couple were screaming and yelling. If the couple continued the argument after the police officer arrived, he would start talking about how tired he was, go into their kitchen and start rummaging through the cupboards to find a cup and some coffee. The couple would often stop their argument to follow him and ask what he was doing. One of them would usually help the officer make a cup of coffee. It changed the dynamics and decreased the level of violence.

I like the two bullying interventions noted previously, as the target is being protected and a door of possible change is being opened for the person bullying. In both Scene 3 and in the benevolent-assertive response, the helpful bystander is acquainted with the person bullying and the target. However, sometimes we come upon a situation where we don't know the person bullying or the target. Distraction can be quite useful in such a situation.

I remembered distraction as a method one day when I was out walking about ten years ago. In our quiet little town, all of the sudden a large white pick-up truck, jacked up on over-sized tires, appeared at an intersection, its brakes screeching as its driver jerked to a halt at the stop sign in the wrong lane. He was yelling at two Black men just a few feet away in a small older sedan. They had properly stopped, in the correct lane. Allergic to prejudice and not wanting harm to occur, I thought distraction might work as a safe intervention. I walked into the intersection toward the space between the two cars, looking up at the man in the white truck. I was planning to ask him if he knew where a particular street was. However, he looked at me and took off. Relieved, I put my hand on the arm of the driver of the sedan and asked if he was okay. His friendly look and reply assured me he was.

LVE has educational resource books for street children. "Distraction as an art of nonviolence" is introduced to 11- to 14-year olds as a method to stop violence. If you and your children and their group of friends are interested in distraction as a method to reduce bullying, you might wish to read the story below. "Crazy Like a Fox" is Story 22 in a series of stories about a street-children family who love and care for each other. Mohammed, Fred and Marion are main characters in the street-children family. Mohammed is the oldest of the three. Marion is a girl. At this point in their life they go to a school for street children. Tony and Keeman are two of their friends.

A Story: *Crazy Like a Fox*

Mohammed, Fred and Marion decided to visit Tony and Keemen after their workshop at the street-children school. As they walked down the alley, they heard Tony's voice shouting, "You want to steal something? You thieves. I'll give you something!"

"Let's go," said Fred. Fred, Marion and Mohammed started running toward the sound of the yelling and fighting. Tony and Keemen were on the ground fighting three other boys as they rounded the corner. Fred, Marion and Mohammed stopped running as soon as they saw the boys.

"Hello, Tony. Hello Keemen," said Marion brightly.

"Hey guys, I got some tangerines. Want one?" asked Fred.

"You guys all look pretty good at what you're doing, maybe you can help us with our next play. We're doing it in the park on Saturday. How about it?" asked Mohammed.

"Yeah, it's a great play," said Marion. "Have you seen it, Tony? How about you, Keemen?

"I think they would fit in really well in the second act, don't you Mo?" asked Fred. "You know, right after that terrific song."

Tony and Keemen had paused. The three boys they were fighting looked up, surprise and puzzlement on their faces.

"Well," said Mohammed, "do you think you could do this in one of our plays? It's a great scene."

"Are you putting me on?" asked one of the three strangers.

"Are you crazy?" asked one of the other boys.

Fred pulled out the tangerines, "Anyone want a tangerine?"

Tony started laughing. He reached his hand up for a tangerine.

Mohammed looked down at one of the three boys who were strangers. He offered him a tangerine and sat down beside him. He started to peel another for himself. "Being a street kid is hard enough without us fighting each other."

"These are the guys that stole our guitar!" said Keemen, anger rising in his voice.

"Okay," said Mohammed. "Let's be human beings for a minute and listen. These are our brothers. They probably had a real good reason for doing what they did. Do you know their story?" He looked at the boy who had accepted the tangerine. "My name is Mohammed. I bet you had a real good reason for taking the guitar. Would you like to share your story?"

The boy looked at Mohammed and shook his head. Another said, "Let's get out of here." The three jumped up and ran, but one paused before he rounded the corner and gave Mohammed a little nod, still holding the tangerine he had accepted in his hand.

"What's the matter with you?" Keemen asked Mohammed. "With you two we could have beat them up. It would have been four against three instead of two."

Mohammed looked at him in silence. He slowly ate his tangerine.

Fred said, "Great tangerine, Mo."

"Yeah, Mo, thanks," said Marion.

"I don't get you guys," said Tony. "You come and help and then don't help us beat them up."

"But we stopped the fight, didn't we?" smiled Marion. "Distraction as an art of nonviolence."

Tony started to eat his tangerine and Keemen sat and just looked at them. His eyes looked like he was trying to understand something new.

"Do you want to be like them?" asked Mohammed quietly.

"I don't know what you're taking about," said Keemen.

Mohammed was silent.

"I don't want to be like them," said Tony.

"What happens when you fight?" asked Fred. "They beat you up, you beat them up. They knife you, you knife them. They shoot you, you shoot them. It only gets worse. Gangs are like that. They just gradually kill each other off."

"What comes around goes around," said Mohammed.

"But how do you stay alive if you don't fight?" asked Keemen.

"You use your head," said Fred. "You gotta' be smart to survive on the streets. But to do better than survive is possible. You can create beauty. You can help others to see their beauty."

"Are you crazy?" asked Keemen.

"Crazy like a fox," smiled Marion.

The End

(Translator Note: A fox is considered clever in English. Please put in the name of an animal or mythical character which is considered clever in the culture of the children.)

When physical force is being used violently, adrenaline is flowing, fists are flying, hormones are pumping and peace isn't anywhere in the picture. Trying to restrain someone can result in the helper being hurt, sometimes quite seriously. Joining a fight to stop it is dangerous and **never** recommended. For serious violence, the first action should be to withdraw to safety and call the emergency number for police intervention. It is important your children understand this.

In the story, "Crazy Like a Fox", distraction was as option as three kids were fighting two others. The three strangers were not likely to take on two or three more. There were no guns nor knives. The situation was not out-of-hand. In the situation in my town, it was clear I was nonthreatening, so it was unlikely that the man bullying would feel threatened and hence become more violent.

Distraction can be used as to attempt to stop low-level fighting and bullying by people who are strangers *if* the person feels inclined to do so. Many people do not have this inclination, but some do. Distraction can also be used to stop bullying with people you know. This is easy to do. Sometimes it is hard to think of a benevolent-assertive response unless you have been practicing! Your protection is acting in a clearly nonthreatening manner. You are de-escalating tension, not increasing it.

Examples . . .
When someone at a distance is bullying someone you know — Call out to the target in a loud voice:

⭐ Dana, could you come over here? I need your help right away!

⭐ Hey, Dana! Mr. Murphy (name of a teacher) wants to see you right now!

- ☆ Dana, have you seen Mrs. Tey? I can't find her anywhere!
- ☆ Hey, did you see the really cool _____ Sam has?
- ☆ Hey, guys, is that a snake over there?

When someone close by is bullying someone you know — Call to the target:
- ☆ I can't find my phone! Have either of you seen it? If I lose it my father's going to be soooooo upset. I'll probably be working for a year to get another one. Have either of you lost your phone? Have you seen mine? Harry, would you help me look for it?
- ☆ Hey, have you guys seen that really cool new movie, _____? The part I like best was _____.
- ☆ Did you see the raccoon over by room 3? Awesome! Today it was just one, but the other day I saw one with two cubs....
- ☆ Do either of you remember what Mrs. Rami said about the _____?

To strangers:
- ☆ Do you know where _____ is?
- ☆ Excuse me, I'm lost. I'm trying to find _____.

Read the prior section to the group of young people with whom you are working. Ask them to generate statements, questions or dialogues which could work as a distraction and be safe. Allow them to role play. It will help give them a repertoire of responses, just in case they need it. Meanwhile, they are likely to feel more confident knowing this additional skill. The art of distraction is also useful in protecting yourself from violence.

Remember to include and be kind

I remember getting upset years ago when a principal told me about a group of sixth-grade girls who had written a very mean letter to another girl in their class. I went out to where the class was playing baseball and asked the teacher to send the girls to my office. They, of course, wanted to know what they had done. When I told them the letter had been read, they readily admitted to writing the letter. I talked about the importance of respect for every person. I remember saying, "I'm not asking you to be her best friend. You have the right to choose your best friend. But, I am asking you to give her respect as a human being. She can be an acquaintance you treat decently." We continued to talk.

I was the one who was surprised when the girls asked if they could come to see me the next week. We met two more times before we decided together to invite the girl to whom they had written the letter. We continued to meet for another four or five sessions after that. It was hard to tell by then which girl had been ostracized — she had been included.

As you work with your children and some of their friends, ask them if there are classmates who seem to be rejected by others or alone most of the time. While your children and their friends do not need to be best friends with children who are isolated or ostracized, would they be willing to be kind? To give respect through a hello and a smile? To comment favorably on something they did during class?

Often when I was working as a school psychologist, if there was a student who had no friends in a classroom or poor social skills, I would ask the teacher to choose two popular students who had a naturally kind nature and were friends. I would talk to those two students and ask if they were willing to include the isolated child, perhaps for one recess or one lunch period of the day. It works well when two or more students who are well-liked do this together. It does not diminish their popularity and the other students are given the message that it is okay to be friends with the isolated child. If your child is part of a group of friends who are all willing to hold their values of peace, kindness and respect, perhaps they would be willing to give caring and respect to those isolated through hello's, smiles and perhaps including them in conservations. It can make a real difference.

Protect your children when they are on-line

Children are playing games on-line at earlier and earlier ages. As they begin to play on-line at perhaps six or seven years of age, limit their time and choose carefully what they are allowed to play. There are some games which are healthy and sensible. Some build spatial skills and non-verbal reasoning. They can practice math and reading skills and learn about different cultures. Some games are fun and have good values. As they grow, on-line resources can be a wonderful tool for learning about a variety of topics. There are so many websites with up-to-date information about the environment, uplifting projects, the latest research on stars, etc. Other games and sites are not good for children and young adults.

If your children are engaged in on-line games or research, it is essential to know how to adjust the preferences and settings on the application they are using to limit access to what is harmful or inappropriate for their age. Your children need to know there are unsafe teens and adults in the world who are not kind to children. As they do not know who is a safe adult and who is an unsafe adult through the computer, it is important to have a family rule: Never share their name, age, address or city on the computer.

It is wise to set up the computer in a common area of the house. A friend of mine with several young children and a tween recently remodeled her kitchen. The kitchen has a roomy computer nook. This space is linked to the dining area and living room. It is perfect for her children to wander in and out, doing what needs doing on the computer or playing for a little while. It is natural and easy for her and her husband to monitor their activity and what is being watched on You Tube. Another friend set up a little table between the area joining the kitchen and living room. Sometimes the laptop is there for the children to play with, often not. Stay peaceful and friendly, loving and kind — and be watchful.

When your child wants to be on Facebook or another social media site, be their Facebook "Friend" so you receive all of his or her posts. An open respectful relationship in which your child is comfortable confiding in you is her or his greatest protection. Being a Friend on Facebook or whichever social media site they are involved is a natural extension of a good relationship. It is important for their safety — as is your eye on their demeanor.

The entry age for Facebook is 13. Some parents have caved into their child pressuring them to join Facebook at nine years of age as some of their friends are allowed to do so. It is not pleasant being pressured by your child; just as it is not pleasant for them to be pressured by their friends. Tell them you love them and explain why you are saying "No." Perhaps, "I love you immensely and want you to have real friends rather than hundreds of acquaintances. I want you to learn about science and space and all the other things you are interested in rather than knowing who is going to go where. These are your years for learning so many things. I know you are smart and I want you to have a wonderful life. Part of having a wonderful life is getting a good education — that means learning certain kinds of things now. I want you to have friends and you do. But no Facebook right now. Have real friends in real time. If your friends want to know why you can't be on Facebook, you can say, 'My parents said no,' or "My parents think I have better things to do with my mind than to think about what everyone else is doing. They said right now it is best to have a few real friends in real time rather than hundreds of acquaintances.'" Listen to them, yes. But stay firm on your no.

The number of suicides of children 11 to 14 years of age is increasing. Some of this has been linked to cruel comments on Facebook, Ask.fm and in response to You Tube postings of their own videos. Know what is happening in your child's life. Sites which allow users to be anonymous, such as Ask.fm, have attracted teens who specialize in meanness and bullying. It would be impossible to not be hurt by "Kill yourself," comments. It would be devastating to any normal adult.

When to cut social media

If your child is on the receiving end of hateful comments on social media, actively listen and validate the child's experiences and good qualities. Discuss with your child what real friends are. Real friends value, love and support their friends. Real friends are kind. Help the child understand the situation. Help them stay in self-respect and know that people who are acting in a mean or cruel way are not real friends. They are people who are damaged.

Ask: "If you were five years old and got to choose between three children the same age who were going to give you ice cream and share their favorite toys with you or three children the same age who were going to throw mud and rocks at you and call you bad names, which group would you pick?" Which ones are the real friends?" "Why would you even want to associate with people who act mean or bully others?"

Discuss with your child the benefit of not engaging in social media sites for three or four months. Ask: "What is the benefit of associating with people who get joy out of hurting others?" Tell your child: "You are a loving, sensitive, lovely person. You are _____, _____ and _____. (Name her qualities.) You deserve real friends. Don't listen to or communicate with people who want to destroy."

If someone is being hateful with your child on-line, it is best to deal with this as a team. Decide together, your child, yourself and your partner, if it is a good idea to delete an account and cell number and create new ones to which only real friends have access. Explore ways to help and get help. It may be important to notify school officials or other authorities. You may wish to consult the school counselor or school psychologist about what is happening at school. If your child is receiving kill-yourself messages, it is time to contact the police.

If your child really wants to continue with social media, then allow her the option of creating a new account if she promises to confirm as friends, real friends. Keep a loving, supportive relationship and help them manage things, but also keep the communication doors open so she can confide in you if further hurtful comments are made.

If hurtful comments somehow continue to get through, then discuss two options: Cutting all social media for three or four months, or allowing you, the parent, to view the postings first. Give them the choice. Explain no one can handle a diet of meanness — children or adults. In the same way you would not allow him or her to eat poisoned food, you will not allow him or her to read poisoned words. Do what is necessary to stop the hurtful influx.

Meanwhile, increase supportive positive family activities. Make sure Us Time is part of every day. Create opportunities for them to be with their real friends and practice the anti-bullying skills mentioned previously. If the child appears depressed, enroll the child in counseling. Exercising every day helps prevent depression and recover from depression. Perhaps your child can join a team sport or a dance group or you can talk together for 30 minutes while you chat. Take good care with diet and daily nurturing. Watch inspiring movies together, read uplifting books — let the child know how important he or she is to you and how special their qualities are in your family and for the world. Tell your child you know this is hard, but it will change, and you promise it will get better with time.

~ 32 ~

Help Children Be Safe from Sexual Abuse —
Begin by Age Three

The tragedy of sexual abuse is a nightmare for children. Adult survivors of sexual abuse and incest struggle daily as a result of childhood trauma. As a parent, I am sure you are already passionate about protecting your child.

Global statistics on child abuse are difficult to come by as many countries do not collect data. However, surveys in developed countries indicate approximately 20 percent of women and five to ten percent of men report being sexually abused as children, while 25 to 50 percent of all children report being physically abused. Scientific surveys indicate sexual abuse can be as low as seven percent in some countries and as high as 37 percent in other countries. What you and I know is that any sexual abuse is too much.

Most parents try to protect their children from abuse by telling them to never go with strangers. They tell children not to get into a car with a stranger and not to go with a stranger when offered toys or treats. This is important to tell your children. However, more than 90 percent of juvenile sexual abuse occurs with perpetrators who are known to the children. They are not strangers.

We have myths about who might sexually abuse a child and what a perpetrator might look or act like. Throw out the myths. Child abuse occurs at every socioeconomic level, across ethnic and cultural lines, within all religious groups and across all levels of education. Perpetrators can hold full-time jobs and seem responsible in every way.

Who do perpetrators sexually abuse?

"An estimated one in 20 teenage boys and adult men sexually abuse children, and an estimated one teenage girl or adult woman in every 3,300 females molests children. … Most families mistakenly believe that as far as molesters go, there has never been one in their family, and what's more, there never will be." (Source: Child Molestation Research and Prevention Institute http://childmolestationprevention.org)

Perpetrators sexually abuse members of their own family: Biological child, 19 percent of the time; a stepchild, adopted or foster child, 30 percent of the time; brothers and sisters, 12 percent of the time; nieces and nephews, 18 percent of the time; grandchild, 5 percent of the time. Perpetrators sexually abuse children in the neighborhood: Child left in my care, 5 percent; child of a friend or neighbor, 40 percent. Children who are strangers: 10 percent. Some may molest one child, others may molest 20 or many more.

Hopefully, you and your children are in a situation where sexual abuse is not even a possibility. Unfortunately, it is a grim and horrible reality for many. In one developing country there is a myth that AIDS can be cured by having sex with a virgin. In this country, abuse of younger and younger children is rampant. Protect your children by keeping them with safe adults, maintaining a good relationship, being aware of changes in their behavior, and educating them to recognize unsafe people and take assertive action when feeling unsafe.

Vulnerability ...

The following information, beginning with the word Fact and followed by sentences enclosed in quotation marks, is taken from The Children's Assessment Center website. You may wish to read all their sexual abuse facts at http://cachouston.org/child-sexual-abuse-facts.

Fact: "Perpetrators report that they look for passive, quiet, troubled, lonely children from single parent or broken homes (Budin & Johnson, 1989)."

Help your children develop the social and emotional skills to be full of peace, love and joy — and confident and assertive. Listen to them, play with them, encourage them and help them be responsible — these are essential safety factors!

Fact: "Age is a significant factor in sexual abuse. While there is risk for children of all ages, children are most vulnerable to abuse between the ages of 7 and 13 (Finkelhor, 1994)."

Fact: "Family structure is the most important risk factor in child sexual abuse. Children who live with two married biological parents are at low risk for abuse. The risk increases when children live with step-parents or a single parent. Children living without either parent (foster children) are 10 times more likely to be sexually abused than children that live with both biological parents. Children who live with a single parent that has a live-in partner are at the highest risk: they are 20 times more likely to be victims of child sexual abuse than children living with both biological parents (Sedlack, et. al., 2010)."

The last statistic is devastating, but worth knowing. Perpetrators are known to cultivate a relationship in order to have access to a child. Be aware.

Your child is your first priority. Don't rush into a live-in relationship with a new partner if you have children under the age of 18, but especially under the age of 14. Men interested in molesting children will often act nice in order to engage the child. Think very seriously before allowing a boyfriend to have access to your children or to babysit your children. If you think seriously about it, you will not do it. The results of sexual abuse are damaging for decades, emotionally and physiologically.

While the above research information about family structure as the most important risk factor in child sexual abuse is important, please note it stated children who live with two married biological parents are at low risk for abuse. It did not state there is *no* risk. When perpetrators were interviewed, one survey reported 19 percent said they sexually abused their own child. Hence, be aware if there are sudden negative changes in a child's behavior. Some children withdraw and others act out when there is sexual abuse.

I know a teacher whose daughter was molested by her husband, the child's biological father. This couple were together until the little girl was four, but at three years of age this child began to act very differently than before. She became quite aggressive with peers and would strike out if anyone got close to her. She had night terrors all of the sudden, began to wet the bed after having been successfully potty trained and sometimes her mother would find her sleeping in the closet. When the mother found semen in her daughter's underwear, she contacted the abuse hot line and took the underwear to a lab for testing.

Regarding abuse by biological fathers, another person I know told me her father sexually abused her for several years, until she began menstruating. Her anger at her own mother, 35 years later, was still intense as her mother did not protect her. Protect your daughters and sons. Be aware. Continue to develop your own self-respect and self-sufficiency so if you do need to protect your children by leaving, you have the strength to do so.

Because the ratio of men to women perpetrators of sexual abuse is 165 to 1 (1 out of 20 men opposed to 1 out of 3,300 women), I am giving examples of men perpetrators. This statistic is certainly validated by my professional experience. However, the important point is to be aware and keep your children safe. There are both male and female perpetrators.

Sudden changes in behavior . . .

Changes in behavior may be dramatic or subtle. I remember a young child of five whose mother was concerned about her emotionally. I was equally concerned as when her daughter came into my office, she scurried around the desk, crouching down and trying to hide from me. No child had ever acted that way with me before. Her drawings indicated sexual abuse.

Sometimes the signs may be physical, such as unexplained bruising or scratches near the sexual organs, or a change in movement, such as walking as if it is painful in the groin area. Sometimes the behavior of the child changes: the child may withdraw, seem disturbed or begin to act aggressively, fearfully or in sexual ways. If the child has had a close relationship with someone ten years of age or older and all of the sudden seems fearful of being with the person, pay attention. Do not reprimand your child for not being friendly. Respect your child's feelings. Observe. *Make sure your child is not alone with that person* while you give yourself time to watch and see what is happening. Do not assume it is a developmental stage the child is going through. If the child is fearful of a particular person, do not let that person be alone with your child.

Educate

A good relationship with your child which includes Us Time, active listening and nurturing family time is an essential part of protecting your child, as not only will your child be more secure, confident and assertive, he or she is more likely to share if anything is amiss. You are also more likely to observe sudden changes in behavior.

Educate One: Names of private parts

Educate your child when they are toddlers about the names of their private body parts: vagina and breast for girls, penis and anus for boys. Just as you begin to teach them to name their eyes, nose, mouth, ears, arms, legs, fingers, toes, tummy and hair when they are babies, use the real words for private parts when they are a little older. Begin to teach the names for their private parts *after* they can point to and name the above ten non-private body parts.

It is important to teach the names of their private parts in the same way you teach the names of eyes, arms and legs, etc., that is, without embarrassment. You may need to rehearse this in your mind if this is uncomfortable. As toddlers they will need to hear the names a number of times in order to learn them. When they are bathing is an appropriate time for them to hear the names in a natural way. For example: "Did you wash your vagina?" "Did you wash your penis and anus?" "Did you use soap?" "Great."

Educate Two: No touching . . . and an assertive response

Introduce the topic of no one touching their private parts, and an assertive response, after your child has mastered the social skill of using words to say no to hitting, biting or name calling as described in the chapter on bullying. Some toddlers may be ready to learn this social skill at two years of age, most will be able to do this at three years. Once they can say with self-respect and confidence, "Stop. No hitting," or "Stop. Be a peace star," it is much easier for them to learn to say, "No! No touching!"

Mastering the no-hitting assertive response first is recommended as then the no-touching assertive response can be learned in a way which is not fear-inducing or traumatic. You may need to practice with yourself, your partner or a friend before introducing it to your child so you can do this peacefully, especially if you have painful memories. It is best to do this naturally so the child does not feel frightened.

Begin in a peaceful, friendly yet serious voice. To girls: "Girls have private parts. Your private parts are the vagina and breasts." To boys: "Boys have private parts. Your private parts are the penis and the anus." "Your vagina and breast/penis and anus are called private parts because they're private. That means only you have the right to touch them. If someone else wants to touch them, that's not okay. If someone little tries to touch them, that's not okay. If someone big tries to touch them, that's not okay. So if someone ever tries to touch your private parts, I want you to tell me. You are my precious angel and I want you to be safe." Listen to any comments of the child and actively listen or discuss as appropriate for their age.

Then say, "If someone tries to touch your vagina/penis and anus, I want you to say in your loud voice, "No! No touching," *and walk away*. Practice with the child, as noted in the chapter on bullying, until the child can deliver the "No! No touching," in a confident manner. Practice a couple of times a week for a few weeks: "What do you say if someone little or big tries to touch your private parts?" "Yes, good saying it loudly." "And what else do you do?" "Yes, that's right, you walk away." When they are three and four years old, ask them once a month to keep the skill current. "Do you remember what to say and do if someone tries to touch your private parts?"

Do inform your children before going to the doctor that sometimes a doctor may need to look at and touch their private parts if they are sick. "But if you are sick, Mommy or Daddy will always be with you when the doctor touches your private parts. No one should ever touch your private parts if Mommy or Daddy or _____ isn't there. Add the name of another person, if an aunt, grandmother or another safe, trusted adult sometimes helps care for the child.

Educate Three: Safe and unsafe big people

When your child has mastered the last step for a couple of months, and is at least three years old, introduce the concept of safe and unsafe big people. You may be able to find appropriate children's books on this topic. Say, "There are teenagers and adults who are safe, and there are also big people who are not safe."

Ask:

♦ How do you think you can tell if a big person is safe?

Listen carefully to your child's answers. Help refine the answers so a fairly accurate list of actions describes safe teens and adults. For example, a safe big person: is kind to children, treats children with respect, only touches children in a safe way, and likes them to share about their time together with Mommy and Daddy.

Ask:

♦ How would you know a big person is not safe?

Listen carefully and help the child come up with answers. The list should include: An unsafe big person might offer children toys, candy or money if they will go with them somewhere alone where no one else can see them. Only an unsafe big person would try to touch children's private parts and ask them not to tell their Mommy and Daddy.

Say in your own words: "Most teenagers and adults are safe. But some are unsafe. Some unsafe big people want to take a child into a room or another place where no one else can see them and touch the child's private parts. And then they tell the child to never tell their Mommy or Daddy. If someone ever tries to touch your private parts, and tells you bad things will happen if you tell Mommy or Daddy, then you know that person is a very unsafe big person. Do you remember what to say if someone tries to touch your private parts?"

"Yes, that's right. Good remembering. Then what do you do?" "Yes, that's right, you walk away."

Then say, "Sometimes an unsafe big person wants the child to touch his private parts. A man's private parts are his penis and his anus. It is wrong for a big person to ask a little person to touch his penis. That is never okay. It doesn't matter who the adult is, if it's an uncle, a cousin, a neighbor or a stranger, it is *never* okay for a big person to ask a child to touch his private parts."

Ask: "What should a child say and do if that happened?"

"Yes, that's right. Say, 'No! No touching,' in your loud voice and walk away."

Listen to any comments of the child, and answer any questions in an age-appropriate manner. Tell the child to always tell you if this ever happens so you can make sure he or she is safe and it never happens again. Of course, this needs to be done in a peaceful, caring, gentle yet straight-forward manner.

Educate Four: *Explaining where babies come from and sex*

When children are between three and five years of age, they will usually ask where babies come from. Answer in an age-appropriate manner, such as "Babies grow in the Mommy's womb. Mommies have tiny, tiny eggs inside and the egg can grow into a baby when the Daddy fertilizes the egg." Give them a little more information as they ask, in a natural and positive way.

By the time the child is five or six, if the parent is open to questions and comfortable responding, most children have asked what sex is. Of course, respond in a way which is consistent with your culture and religion. It is good for children to know what sex is in a positive, healthy way before you continue to educate about sexual abuse.

One possible explanation about sex to young children is: "Remember when you were little and asked about where babies come from? And, I told you babies grow in the Mommy's womb? Mommies have tiny, tiny eggs inside. An egg can grow into a baby when the Daddy fertilizes it. Daddy fertilizes the egg during sex. During sex the man's penis goes into the woman's vagina. Semen come out of the man's penis and fertilize Mommy's egg. Parents make a baby when they love each other very much and want to have a family." You may wish to add something about your personal beliefs here, such as "Your father and I believe sex should only take place when people are married and love each other very much. Some day when you are all grown up and have a good education, you may want to have a family."

Educate Five: *Sometimes unsafe big people do very wrong things*

When children reach the age of five and a half to six years of age, many leave the protected environment of kindergarten and begin to be around more people without their parent or teacher nearby. They are hence more vulnerable. Continue to educate as they reach this age.

You might wish to say, "Do you remember what to say and do if someone wants to touch your private parts or have you touch their private parts?" ("No! No touching!" in a loud voice and then walk away.) "Good for you. I'm happy you remember so well."

Then perhaps share your feelings, saying something like, "I need to talk to you about unsafe big people because I love you very much and I want you to be safe. It's hard for me to talk about it sometimes. But, today I want to tell you that sometimes unsafe teenagers and adults do very wrong things. They have sex with young children."

If you are talking to a girl, say, "Men have sex with girls by sticking their penis into the child's vagina. It hurts little girls very much. Sometimes they put their finger into the child's vagina, too." If you are talking to a boy, say, "Men have sex with boys by sticking their penis into the boy's anus. It hurts the boy very much. Sometimes they put their finger into a boy's anus, too."

Continue: "I want you to be careful so you stay safe. If a stranger wants you to go by yourself with him, and offers you toys or money, you must never go. We've talked about that before. The problem is we don't always know who the safe teenagers and adults are and who the unsafe teenagers and adults are. It's possible that there are unsafe big people who visit us at home, or unsafe big people at school, at a relative's house or at a neighbor's house. Maybe a friend's older brother or father wants you to be alone in a room and touch your private parts or have you touch theirs. Some men show children pictures of people without their clothes having sex. Adults know it is very, very, very wrong to have sex with a child so they don't want other people to see them. It would be very, very, very wrong for an older brother to hurt a little sister or brother in this way, or for a father or uncle to hurt a little boy or girl. It's abuse.

Ask: "So, what should you say and do if anyone wants to touch your private parts or have you touch theirs?" "Yes, that's right. Say it very loudly and then walk away." Listen to their concerns and answer any questions, actively listening and validating as appropriate.

Discuss other things they can do to stay safe. For example, a child can say if asked to go into a room alone with a big person: "No. I don't want to go with you. I want to stay with my friend," or "No. I'm not comfortable. I'm leaving," and go to a room where there are more people. Practice these responses with your child until he or she can say them confidently.

Tell the child to always trust his feelings. Tell her to always tell you if someone approaches her in a way that feels unsafe so you can figure out a way to be safe together. Tell them that if the unsafe person tells them not to tell Mommy or Daddy then it is especially important to tell Mommy or Daddy.

Tell the child you can have a *secret code*. If she is in a room with someone she does not feel safe with, she can come and stand by you and whisper, "I'm not feeling safe."

Ask:

♦ Would you like to have that secret code?
♦ If not, ask: Is there another secret code you would like to have? Perhaps they would prefer to have a nonverbal code.

Tell the child: "If you tell me the secret code, I will know I need to pay special attention to keep you by me so I can make sure you are safe. We will stay together until you can tell me what is making you feel unsafe. It's important you are always safe.

Ask:

- ◆ Is it ever right for any adult to use a child to have sex? (No.)
- ◆ What do you think all unsafe big people should know?

End with something like, "Wow, that was a serious conversation! Shall we run or play or dance away these feelings for a while and get back to feeling safe again?" Perhaps choose a bedtime story with a feeling of peace, love and safety. Do a Quietly Being Exercise together before going to sleep.

If the child is thinking and talking about this in the next few days, actively listen to the emotions and conversation and continue to discuss the topic. During the next few days suggest the child draw a picture of an unsafe big person and a safe big person. Perhaps she can make up a slogan to put on the picture. A slogan might be: "Only safe big people allowed here!" Ask the child to share the picture. End by sharing how much you love him or her and that you will always help them be safe.

Educate Six: Safe-drivers list

Of course, as children grow, help them be aware of safety issues. For example, never get into a car with strangers or go anywhere with a stranger. Never walk out of sight of the people you came with if a person acts nice and asks you to come with him. Never. Let them know people can act extra nice to try to attract them. Let them know that if you are there with them, then it is okay to talk to strangers and it is always okay to talk to policemen and firemen.

Decide what your family rule is about accepting a ride with someone and inform the child. For example, "Only accept a ride from your father and me, your grandparents, Aunt Lonnie, and Susie's mother. These are the people on your safe-drivers list. That means you are *not* allowed to accept a ride from *anyone else.*" (Of course, if your own father was abusive when you were a child, then he wouldn't make the safe-drivers list.)

Be clear that this means not accepting a ride from a man who is a neighbor, a man who is a scout leader and a man whom you've known for a long time. The rule: "Only accept rides from people on the safe-drivers list. That means, don't accept a ride from any other adults you know, unless your Dad or I give you permission. If a person you know tries to convince you to accept a ride, say, 'Thanks, but no thanks. I'm not allowed.' 'Thanks, but no thanks. I'd get grounded.'" Role play with the child until he or she can deliver the responses with self-respect and confidence.

Given the statistics of men to women perpetrators of 165 to 1, you may wish to tell them that in case of an extreme emergency they may go with a woman they know, but never a man.

Other family rules might be: Always stay with friends when walking home from school. Always wait exactly where I or _____ tell you to wait. Always come home before dark.

Educate them about drugs and alcohol and encourage and reinforce abstinence as lapses in judgment are more frequent when under the influence, both on the part of the child and the perpetrator.

Educate Seven: Encourage achievement and "true love waits"

Encourage and set up opportunities for tweens and teens to engage in meaningful activities with friends, find a sport they enjoy and achieve academically. Continue with drug education and sex education, teaching self-respect and respect for others. For teens, include the varieties of sexually-transmitted diseases and the dangers of date rape. Talk about the concept of "true love waits" or a similar idea from your religion or personal belief system which encourages no sex while in high school and the advantages of celibacy while in university. Unplanned pregnancies have prematurely ended the education of many young women, while prison time for rape has prematurely ended the education of many young men. Discuss the importance of good friendships and education.

While it is not considered sexual abuse when two 13-year olds engage in sex, it is a very bad idea. They are not prepared emotionally and certainly are far too young to be parents. The girl's reputation can often be set, with a steep dive into low self-esteem as she is treated like a sexual object and used as such. In general, it is considered sexual abuse if the sexual partner is five years older and in a powerful position from which to manipulate or control, be it physically or emotionally. In the USA, statues and consequences vary for each state, but in general it is considered sexual abuse if the girl or boy is under 14 and the perpetrator is several years older.

General guidelines for safety

> Play with your child or have Us Time every day, actively listen, encourage and keep your relationship good.

> *Educate* as noted above and develop your secret code so your child can tell you when he or she feels unsafe. Actively listen if he ever tells you the secret code and then do all you can to make sure the child is not left vulnerable in that situation. If a child is unhappy about doing the dishes, that is a different matter; the dishes the child needs to do. But the secret code of "I'm not feeling safe," needs to be listened to and discussed. Don't panic, be calm, but when you can do so discreetly, take some time to be with the child

alone and listen. Ask what the person did that made her uncomfortable. Ask the child what she did. Did she remember to use an assertive response? Positively reinforce the child for using her protective assertive skills. Ask, "What else could you do to stay safe?" "Good thinking!" Positively reinforce the child for using your secret code. Protect. Do not leave him or her alone with the person with whom they feel unsafe.

If the child was simply uncomfortable with an adult, and the adult did not try anything, simply actively listen to the child. Tell him you are glad he is being sensitive to his feelings as that will help him stay safe. Do not shame the child, saying, "Why did you use the secret code and make me all scared when nothing happened?"

➤ Don't rush into a live-in relationship with a new male partner if you have children under the age of 18, and especially under the age of 14. If he is really interested in you, he will still be there in a few years. Never allow a boyfriend to have access to your children or to babysit your children. I know this sounds quite strict, but how many children have been sexually abused by seemingly trustworthy adults? Millions upon millions.

➤ Know the people at the pre-school, club or organization with which your child is involved. Do they have a child protection policy? Are their teachers and facilitators required to have a criminal background check? Is the organization comfortable with you coming in unannounced and visiting all areas of the facility? You may wish to start your child in a pre-school with a Mommy and Me class. Because of the greater number of adults in one classroom, sexual abuse is highly unlikely.

➢ Do not allow your child, girl or boy, to go alone for an outing or away for a weekend with a man alone, unless he is the biological father. Do not allow yourself to be pressured into doing so by a boyfriend or live-in partner. "But, honey, she never gets to go anywhere…" Your response: "That'll be fun. Let's all go together." If they continue to pressure, say: "I'm sorry, but that's our family rule. No exceptions." If they pressure, be extra cautious. Go on outings together as a family or as a group of friends. Make sure your child has assertive skills and is part of a group of friends or siblings if he or she goes on an outing with a male relative or another family.

➢ Be sensitive to changes in your child's behavior. If there are sudden negative changes in behavior, spend more Us Time with the child and renew your relationship. Perhaps cut down on other activities to make sure you have having more time together. Be light and receptive, play with the child and listen. Do things together that perhaps you have not done in a while. Think about who has access. Positively reinforce and build his or her protective social skills.

➢ Ask your partner to be available or be available yourself to take your child places. Make a very short list of safe adults if there is a need for another person to drive or accompany the child somewhere. The child needs to be able to easily remember the list. The list might include grandparents if they were not abusive and favorite aunts. It is safest to put women on the safe-drivers list as the odds of abuse are considerably lower with women. While many, many men are amazing with children, loving, kind, protective and terrific role models who would die for children, it is very difficult to discern who the one male perpetrator is out of 20. There have been far too many instances of sexual abuse by men who were thought to be trustworthy to allow them access to your child. Be respectful of all adults — and set family rules and boundaries.

➤ Enjoy your family and extended family and friends, but do so in a safe gathering where you are all together. Be especially aware and careful if there is drug use or excess drinking in the homes you and your children visit. Sexual abuse is frequently related to the imbibing of drugs and alcohol.

If you think there might be abuse . . .

If the child is hurt, immediately take the child in for a medical exam. If you suspect abuse, stay calm and write down exactly what the child tells you. Do not put words into the child's mouth. Actively listen and be loving and receptive. Call the abuse hot line, tell them what the child said, answer their questions and follow their suggestions. They will take the information and when appropriate will refer the case to the protective social services agency in your country or to the police. Make sure your child is safe and the perpetrator no longer has access to your child. Keep any evidence safe if investigation by the authorities is suggested.

Reassure your child of your love and provide a loving safe place for expressing emotions. Actively listen to what the child shares. Tell your child the unsafe big person is sick and very, very wrong to do such a thing. Tell your child that abuse is never the fault of the child. Ask the child how teens and adults should act. Actively listen to their responses and validate as appropriate.

As there would be extra stress for a few weeks, please make sure you and the child are eating well and getting extra rest, and you have time to share with a close friend or counselor to debrief. With your child, perhaps suggest playing an old favorite board game, card game or another of your favorite family-time activities, if you think it would be comforting. Perhaps the child would like to play with something he used to like when younger or draw his feelings. If the child chooses to withdraw … fine, be a reassuring, calm, loving presence. Perhaps put on some music or sing a few songs together. If the child wants to stay in your room to sleep, allow him or her to do so for a few nights or a week or two, until they feel less frightened. Spend quality time before going to sleep. Perhaps dust off the old rituals and do a bedtime story together and pray together.

If there has been sexual abuse, the child will need counseling. A woman therapist is recommended for a girl child. A therapist of either gender is fine for a boy child.

~ 33 ~

When There's Anger in the Family

Many things are difficult to live with — anger is high on the list. Anger is harmful to families and negatively impacts each person in the family emotionally, spiritually, physically and neurologically.

There has been some interesting research on "angry families". I took a professional development course a few years ago at which the presenter noted a study where parents were observed to respond to an angry teen 10 percent of the time when the teen first did something negative, such as throw something against the wall. However, if the parent responded with anger, the teen responded to the parent with anger 30 percent of the time. The parent then negatively responded 70 percent of the time. The teen responded to the second negativity from the parent one hundred percent of the time — and all of that happened in 17 seconds.

We all want harmonious, loving relationships. If you have anger issues and angry children, it will take effort, but you can co-create loving harmonious relationships. This is not to say everything will be "perfect," for life always has its challenges, but you will be able to enjoy each other, have peace and kindness in your home most of the time, and be able to deal with issues and conflicts when they come up.

This change will require self-reflection, love, patience, tolerance and self-control on your part as well as time to learn and practice parenting and communication skills. With persistent and positive effort, gradual positive change will happen and be there to give you hope. You will see some change within a few weeks. You may see solid change in three to four months if your child is young and the anger has not been intense; it will take longer for real change with teens. If there is a history of abuse, then it will take longer; counseling for the child is necessary. Persist. Each time you are positive, you are creating a brighter present and future for yourself and your children.

A very angry five-year old

Once I had an intern who helped design a behavior plan for a five-year old who was angry and deliberately hurt other kindergarteners. If unattended, he would put another child's hand in the door jam and then slam the door. He would throw sand in faces, kick, etc. His behavior was such a danger to the other children, he was assigned a full-time aide who was to stay at his side constantly at school. My intern told me about the child and the behavior plan. The child had a mother who had no idea of what to do and a step-father who did not like the child. The children at school wanted to stay away from him, and I imagine the teacher was already quite busy with a full kindergarten class.

I listened carefully to my intern as he told me the plan, and then told him I didn't think it would work. They had already been carrying out the plan for two weeks and there had been no positive change. I asked the intern, "Where is the child getting love? It sounds like the adults in his life are not giving him any, and the children are avoiding or rejecting him." I suggested the child's personal aide play with him during recess, and one other time for 15 to 20 minutes during each school day. I asked him to talk to the aide and tell her how important it was to enjoy the child and engage in child-led play. He did. The attempts to hurt the other children dropped dramatically in three weeks. My intern was not responsible for guidance to the parents, but I trusted the professional in charge of the case was able to help the mother and step-father look at what was happening at home and change the dynamics.

Every child needs love. If they cannot obtain love, affection and attention through normal positive behavior, they will do any number of negative things to get any kind of attention, including negative attention. There is a need to be in relationship.

So angry he smeared

I remember fondly a woman I worked with whose son had had a difficult early childhood. He had been mistreated by an older relative who had died several years earlier. I was doing counseling with the student and wanted the mother to spend time being with and enjoying the child. I encouraged her to give positive attention and affirmations appropriately, detach from the child's negative behaviors and give logical consequences in a more matter-of-fact manner. The mother had had a difficult childhood herself. She showed little control over her emotions when her son yelled at her and when he smeared his feces on the bathroom walls. We had many sessions. She would improve for a short time after a session and then revert to her former screaming behavior. I remember looking at her one afternoon, searching for a way to help her have more determination to control her own behavior.

"How do you wish your father had treated you?" I asked. When she finished replying, I asked, "What qualities would have helped him do that?" She thought for a while before replying, "I wish he had treated me with respect and love."

"Beautiful," I said. "Sometimes what we wish for is what we need to give. Do you think it would make a difference to treat your son with the kind of love and respect you wanted from your father?" She nodded yes.

I was pleased and a bit surprised at the result. She was able to maintain a much higher level of calmness, care and consistency after the conversation. The child's encopresis (smearing of feces) stopped in time and we continued to work on the elements needed for a loving safe relationship.

Dynamics

Children, teens and adults are angry for many different reasons. Some parents have had difficult childhoods, with neglect or physical, emotional or sexual abuse, many with alcoholic and/or drug-addicted parents. Others received frequent parental criticism and little nurturing, or were on the receiving end of bullying or violence from siblings or peers. Some are victims of war or street children. The list is overwhelming and endless, so I will stop here. Each of us knows to some extent the hurt, fear and feeling of being unsafe that unkindness, violence or lack of love generates. If adults have a problem with anger, those adults are likely to act in anger in front of their children. Anger harms.

Some children react to parental anger by trying to be perfect. These children usually internalize the critical nature of the parent and are hyper-critical to the self. They often become depressed, a form of internalized anger. Other children react with anger because they feel unloved and worthless with the lack of affection and positives from their parents and life in general. Others feel worthless and unlovable when abandoned by their mothers. They can act out quite aggressively. Some are angry because they have been violated through the violence and abuse of others, be it at home, or in school or the community. Some young people show their anger by yelling and with open defiance and meanness, punishing parents and other adults for not giving them what they need and want. Others punish their parents by not obeying and not doing well at school. Some punish by doing the opposite of what their parents want them to do. Some show their anger, and their need to belong, by joining gangs. All of them are angry because they are hurt, scared and/or shamed.

Some children do not have "angry parents," but act and feel angry because they are spoiled. They have been allowed to get their own way when they have tantrums. Some of them feel "entitled" and have a fit when the world does not fall at their feet. Their parents are often frustrated as they feel they are doing so much for the child. In this situation there is a need for a balance of nurturing and discipline. Children need limits, logical consequences, and thinking-time timeouts when they act inappropriately. They benefit by learning to be responsible and respectful. Kindly refer to the section on disciplining with peace and respect.

Steps toward peace, respect, love and a healthy relationship

This chapter is at the end of the book for a reason. I hope you have read the previous chapters, have thought about the content deeply, and have been experimenting with the skills and attitudes you feel are relevant to you and your family. I hope and imagine you now know some to the steps toward peace, respect, love and a healthy relationship. Knowing them is one thing … now to put them into action! I'm sure you have already started.

Step one with your child: Reread the chapter on "The Importance of Play and Us Time." Play or have time together with your child daily. If for some reason this is impossible, make it possible every day you and the child are home together. This is an essential building block of relationship — positive time together, with your full attention. This means turning off the phone and not texting or looking at a message when it comes in. Be in the present moment and enjoy time with your child, even if it is five, ten or 15 minutes. Make it longer when you can.

If you promise to spend some time together "tomorrow," *keep your promise*. Be very careful about what you promise. If you promise to take a walk with them tomorrow, play dress-up, play ball, play a board game, pick them up, read a story, sit and talk, play ping pong, go shopping or go to a practice game, do it. It is very, very, very important to keep each promise. You are creating a new beginning. Fulfilling promises builds trust and creates hope. A return to broken promises destroys hope. It is a million times better to say, "Let's see," or "Give me some time to think about it," than make and break a promise.

Step one for the parent: Please read "Taking Care of You," particularly the chapters on nourishing your spirit and transforming negative mental habits. You know what you need to do. Start gradually and be gentle with yourself. Lovingly accept your feelings and emotions. Know you are the greatest treasure in your child's life and it is your love which helps your child be safe. You are a courageous soul with the power to be positive with the self.

If you have anger issues, learn to manage your outbursts of anger at your children. Notice your physical reaction when you start to get angry. Does your chest tighten? Do your arms tense and your shoulders rise? Do you clench your hands into fists, clench your teeth or press your lips together? Notice your first physical reaction, the tensing in part of your body. What do you notice first, the physical tensing or your initial thought when you begin to get upset?

Give yourself a timeout when this happens, that is, *exit* to another room or outside. If you are still cool enough to speak calmly, you can say something, such as "Oops, I forget something," "Excuse me, I need to rest for a few minutes," "Be right back," "Need to cool down," or whatever you can think of that is not negative to the child.

Once you have exited, away from the area of the child, you may wish to take a few deep breaths. Experiment to see if counting to ten with each breath helps you calm down. Then, name and accept your emotion, take a few more deep breaths and deliberately think a positive thought you strongly believe in. Find a thought that works for you. Some possibilities: "Anger destroys, love builds." "My anger harms, my love protects. I am love." "Love and respect between us will happen." "Only my love protects." "If I can get peaceful now, I can do anything!" "I believe in peace for this family. I will be peaceful. I am peace." You may want to take a walk, stretch, exercise, play a song and dance to it, stick your head under a cold shower, grab something inspirational to read or journal. Keep repeating your positive thought until you begin to experience it. Time yourself out until you feel calm and can use the quality or value you want to use.

If your anger comes up when you are drinking or on drugs, then it is time to let go of substances. Anger harms not just you. It harms your family. If you are serious about having more peace and harmony in your family, and building trust with your children, it is *essential* to get off the drugs and alcohol so you can manage your anger. Please start a 12-step program or another effective program to deal with drug and alcohol use. Call today and commit to the next meeting. Provide the opportunity for your teenagers to go to Alanon.

I have a dear friend who used to go into a rage when he was on alcohol or drugs. I was told it was like he was a different person. He finally committed to being drug and alcohol free. He had the courage to do so as he realized he was ruining his own life and the lives of his wife and children. Their family life has changed dramatically. It is now full of love, respect and happiness.

Commit. Please start a 12-step program or another effective program to deal with drug and alcohol use — today. *Don't do step five until you have taken this one.* It is not a good idea to have your children open up to hope and then slam the door of hope shut, again and again. You are very important to your family. You are naturally good. You deserve to be in control of your emotions and create the life you wish. This would be a real gift to yourself and your children.

Step two: You guessed it, reread the chapters "Love, Affection and Attention" and "Appreciation and Building Positive Behaviors." Start with three appreciative comments or specific praises, that is, positive descriptive comments a day for your children.

If this is hard for you or you think they'll be surprised, start with a simple "Good morning," and a smile. End the day with "I love you," a hug and "Goodnight". Don't overdo it. If you have not been giving any positives, don't give more than three a day for the first few days. Make each comment genuine. If the child you are concerned about is a teen, do this in a way she can tolerate. It may need to be a whispered "I love you," and a quick shoulder squeeze if she has been closed-off for a long time. If you have three children, this means three positives for each child. It may seem artificial at first, but it will become more natural. If you wish, write down what you said to each of your children the first night and the second night. If this helps you be happy and appreciative of your own efforts, continue doing it. After one week of three positives a day, increase it to five a day during the second week. Simple comments are okay: Good job. Good thinking. Thanks. I appreciate you doing that. I'm glad you thought of that.

Do you see a thaw in the relationship by the end of week three? If not, look at your attitude. Love with no expectations. You are the parent, you are the giver. Love given freely creates a flow, love given freely creates happiness. If your child is young, 50 percent of the negative behavior is likely to have disappeared. If your child is a closed-off angry teen, you may need to be consistently positive for a longer time before there is a thaw and some of the negativity drops. If there has been a history of abuse, it may take longer. Continue to manage your anger and keep your promises. You are rebuilding the foundation of trust.

Step three: While you are implementing steps one and two, reread the first few chapters of the "Disciplining with Peace and Respect" section and peacefully and respectfully implement the ones you feel are right for you and your family. Please start with a thinking-time timeout as this tool will allow you to get away from punishing. As is suggested in the chapter, begin with a discussion about thinking time when no one is upset. Once you have established this, feel free to call thinking time for the child and yourself. If you are getting upset, it is okay to say, "I need a timeout. I'll be back in a few minutes."

Reread the first few chapters in the Discipline section several times, until you feel comfortable with the concepts and methods. Stay away from punishing, arguing and fighting. At this stage, don't stress or worry about the chores being done perfectly or focus on the main area of resistance. Chores will be done cooperatively once the flow of love and positivity is trusted; resistance will melt away once trust is re-established. This is going to take all of your patience and tolerance. Hang onto your self-respect and try a bit of humility, easiness and lightness. Tough to do? Yes. Keep your eye on the big picture. If you have had a lot of anger toward the children, it takes time for them to trust your love. It takes courage to be loving.

Step four: Reread the chapter on Active Listening. Try out an active listening response at least once daily with each child. It can be something simple, such as "You look pleased," or "You look a little worried." It will seem artificial at first, but you will get good at it with practice. Listen. Enjoy being silent sometimes. Be receptive. Stop trying to control everything. Relax and enjoy your children. You are able to influence in a positive way when you stop controling. Know each one of your children is unique. Be interested in discovering their qualities.

Step five: Download the Peace Unit on the livingvalues.net website. Under Resource Materials, go to Regular schools and choose the age level appropriate for your child. The Peace unit is taken from the *Living Values Activities* books by this author. One is for children ages three to seven, the second book is for children ages eight to fourteen, and the third is for young adults. Read the "Imagining a Peaceful World" activity (lesson one or two, depending on the age) in preparation for doing it with your child.

Think about what you would like to create at home — and how you would like to communicate about you and your relationship. You might want to say to your child something like: "I love you very much and I would like our relationship to be more peaceful and loving. I've been thinking. I've been angry a lot for many years … and I'm trying to change. The anger is not good for me and it's not good for you. I'm sorry I've been so angry with you sometimes. Can you think about forgiving me?" Listen. Cry together if that happens. Listen some more. If the child just nods with a face like stone, accept. That child has been wounded by the anger and broken promises. Don't demand a positive reaction. Create a safe space for your children to express themselves. Do not defend yourself. Do not blame. It would be good to do this with all the children and your partner, if available.

Do the "Imagining a Peaceful World" activity together. Afterwards, each person can share what she or he imagined. If your children enjoy drawing, provide colors for them to draw what they imagined and share afterwards. Then everyone, including you, can share what you think you can do to be more peaceful in the self, in relationships and in your home. Listen with respect to what each one has to share. Ask if everyone wants there to be more peace and love in the house. Talk about it. Perhaps everyone can contribute one idea of how they can increase the love.

If one of the children says something negative, simply actively listen. For example: "So you don't think peace in this house is possible." Listen with respect and give respect. If your history together has been tough, it's natural for the children to feel suspicious. Relax and know that all you need to do is listen and give respect and love. You may want to laugh and agree, "I'm afraid sometimes, too, that it's not possible, but I'm going to trust we can make it happen together."

Tell them you have been learning about peace and love and you know when we are full of peace and love, the grumpiness and anger begin to go away. Listen to what each one has to share. Sit for a few minutes together at the end of the sharing and fill yourselves with peace and love. You may wish to share several things for which you are grateful and a prayer. Ask God for help, or do what is appropriate in your faith tradition. Close with hugs if that feels right.

Step Six: Continue with the Peace Unit activities. Do at least one a week. Instead of mind-mapping peace, mind-map peace and anger, one on each side of a large piece of paper, as a family. Each person can contribute their thoughts about the effect of peace and anger, for the self, the family and the community. If you have older children, also include a branch for the world. There are no wrong answers.

After lesson four, do a Quietly Being or Relaxation/Focusing Exercise together and discuss creating a peace tent or a peace corner in your home. Do Peace Lesson 4 and make things to decorate the inside of your peace tent or peace corner. Each person can make something which helps them feel peaceful or loved.

Step Seven: Continue with the Peace Unit activities and implement the ideas in Chapter 26, "When Children Squabble and Fight", including practicing conflict resolution and doing the "Building kindness" activities at the end of the chapter.

You are now well on your way. Continue to be gentle and encouraging with yourself and your children. If you get angry, say, "I blew it — I'm sorry, I got angry and blew up." If you lash out, the children may lash out, too. If this occurs, when you are peaceful again talk together about what happened and how to stop the downward spiral. Perhaps as a family you might decide it would be okay for anyone to call a thinking time. You could all sit down together in your Peace Place, or separate. Do something which works for you all.

Reread the chapters noted above until you feel you can put the attitudes and skills into action. Reread the chapters which help you stay on track. Each time you will see something you didn't notice before or understand it more deeply. Over the next year, do a few LVE activities you like in the units on respect, love, happiness, honesty, humility and cooperation. Perhaps do one activity a week as part of your family time with the entire family. Have a good time together. Enjoy you and your child during Us Time.

All good wishes to you and your family and congratulations on your courage and determination.

Section Eight

Developing Values

~ 34 ~

Helping Children Explore and Develop Values

There are two complementary processes in helping children explore and develop values. The first is the creation of a values-based atmosphere — the second is the process of facilitating your child's exploration of values at several levels.

The short version of the chapter!

You are creating a values-based atmosphere as you live life, live your values and help your children feel *loved, respected, valued, understood and safe* through your way of being and way of interacting. It can take a lot of thought to figure out what to do sometimes. I hope the previous chapters have been helpful in learning even more about nurturing and guiding — and I hope things are more positive, healthier and happier with you and your family.

There is no short version of the second part of the chapter, "Facilitating Values Exploration." It summarizes some of the things you have been reading about and ties together different components you are already using to help your children develop and live their values. Perhaps pick up this chapter in a couple of months, after you have reread the former chapters once more and made them your own. Enjoy parenting . . . with love, peace, respect and wisdom.

The regular version of the chapter

One: A values-based atmosphere

All parents have tremendous power and influence over their children. Even if the outside world is more difficult than you would like it to be, you are the one who has the power to create a space where your children feel *loved, respected, valued, understood and safe.*

When we help children feel loved, respected, valued, understood and safe, they move toward their potential. Whatever the behavior of the child, positive or negative, it is how we respond to the behavior that affects the child. When children are treated by adults with harshness, meanness, neglect and punishment, that is, in ways which induce feelings of *inadequacy, hurt, fear, shame or feeling unsafe*, they move away from developing their potential. The more children have healthy, nurturing relationships at home, and a wide range of positive family experiences and educational activities, the more balanced they will be and the more they will easily acquire values.

The adults are in charge of creating a values-based atmosphere. In the last 18 years, I have asked many groups of women and men in different countries what they would tell the adults of the world if they were five years old and could tell them how they wanted to be treated. What would you tell the adults of the world if you were a young child? ......

The answers are always almost identical:

Listen to me.

Respect me.

Spend time with me.

Explain to me.

Show me how to do things.

Guide me.

Encourage me.

Be positive.

Be happy.

Hug me.

Play with me.

What would you add? This is an enjoyable way to start defining a values-based atmosphere. All the attitudes and skills you have been reading about in previous chapters contribute to creating a values-based atmosphere. Your particular style of optimism, your hopes and dreams, your interests, your sense of humor, and your combination of values and how you live those, make it unique.

The most important key: You already know this one … walk your talk.

"Be peaceful," she yelled. "**Now!** Are you listening?" Oops. Was that from me, you or someone else?

If you want children to communicate peacefully, communicate peacefully. If you want children to pet animals gently, pet animals gently and touch children with love. If you teach about respect, they may love respect, but they are much more likely to be respectful if you are, and much, much more likely to communicate with respect and love if you do.

The parent is the first educator in a child's life. We teach through every tone of voice, attitude, word and action. Children learn what we care about through what we do. If we use words to tell them what to do, but do the opposite, what do they do? That's right, they do what we do. Our chances of influencing a child in a positive way are a million and one times better when we walk our talk — when we live our values.

It may be a little challenging to think we are teaching values at every moment and to realize it will really help your children acquire values if you walk your talk. Please don't worry about this and feel you need to be "perfect". We all become grumpy, testy or sad sometimes. We are all human. If you give too big a consequence because you are angry, tell the child later, "I felt angry when you didn't come home on time. Because I was angry, I gave you too big of a consequence. I think a fair consequence is _____."

You may want to call a Me Time when you are frazzled. This models for the children that it is okay to know your needs and say what you need. For example, share: "Mommy needs some peace. Let's go down to the park and watch the rocks grow." You can sit and have some quiet time while they run and play.

Children nurtured with peace, love, respect and wisdom will naturally be more secure, peaceful, positive, happy and respectful than children raised without such. These children will usually appear to have similar values as their parents and caregivers ... at least in their early years.

The second process of facilitating values exploration is important so young people are better able to combat influences of negative role models, violent games and media and unhealthy messages of society as their exposure to such increases with age.

Two: Facilitating values exploration

Knowing our values is a tremendous benefit in life. When difficult decisions come up, answers come more easily when we view the situation through the lens of our values. Young people of today benefit by being able to recognize the difference between the impact of values and anti-values on their lives, the community and the world. Recognizing the impact on themselves and others — with the heart as well as the head — helps them love values, resist the powerful messages of negativity and make positive and socially-conscious choices. The choices young people make can be critically important, not only for their own happiness and wellbeing at this vulnerable time in their lives, but also for their future.

The following categories of ways to help children explore and develop values include suggestions shared in previous chapters. They are being put together so you can see, in one chapter, the many components which help children and young adults move toward living their values. Some of the information will be a bit of a review for you, but as you read about the larger picture you will also see how much you are already doing!

A) Receiving information — Share stories, songs, music, films and activities with values and about values.

Children love stories. Start when they are infants with stories about peace, love and kindness. After the age of two, slowly allow a small amount of cartoons or films into their life. Choose programs full of the values and qualities you want them to hold. Don't accept violent video games just because they are the rage. Continue with stories about kindness, courage to be honest and true and being a friend of nature. As they grow tell them about the values of your culture and the values of other cultures through stories, songs, music, art and dance.

Download the reflection points from the livingvalues.net website. Those for children ages three to fourteen can be found under Resource Materials and Free Downloads as Living Values Posters. These provide information about the meaning of the value being explored. As Thomas Lickona states: "Understanding core values is essential to teaching values if students are to develop lifelong adherence to high principles." The reflection points are universal in nature, while holding an interdependent perspective of the importance of dignity and respect for each and every one. For example, a Respect Reflection Point is: "Everyone in the world has the right to live with respect and dignity, including me." A Tolerance Reflection Point is: "Tolerance is being open and receptive to the beauty of differences." As a family, you may all wish to make up or contribute reflection points of your own.

B) Reflecting internally — Imagining and reflecting

Much of normal family life is doing the tasks necessary to function in daily life: getting up, dressed, going to school or work, making preparations for eating, creating time for eating together, keeping things clean and in some kind of order, taking the kids to activities, paying bills, shopping, keeping ourselves and the children clean and clothed, etc. Our way of being infuses these activities with love, peace and respect — or doesn't. When there is interaction time, it is often about what is needed that day or the next, homework, etc. Hopefully, there is regular play time or Us Time and a ritual at night before bed, perhaps including prayer, meditation or sharing what you are grateful for, and goodnight kisses and/or hugs. A discussion about values may rarely come up. But occasionally it does, even if only once or twice a week or once or twice a month.

You may wish to do the "Imagining a Peaceful World" activity in the Peace Unit of the *Living Values Activities* book so you have a feel for what happens when you engage your children in an imagining or reflective process, and so they know what it feels like. This can be invaluable when a real values question or dilemma comes up. At that time you may want to ask the young person to imagine or reflect.

Questions to begin the process might be: "What would you like to happen? Shall we imagine what that would look and feel like?" Or, "What value do you think is important in this situation? What do you think would happen if everyone lived that value?" Create the opportunity for them to reflect, imagine and share rather than rushing in to tell them what you think they should do or how terrible others are or the world is. Perhaps follow it up with, "Is there something you could do to help create that?"

One opens a box before putting things in it. You are creating a space for your children to open up their own minds and hearts to possibilities and come up with their own ideas. After they have done this, if you have something beautiful, wise, sensible or cautionary to add, do so. They may need help putting things in perspective. Make it personal, rather than a lecture. Starters might be something like: "I remember when …" "I sometimes feel …" "I am concerned …" "I think the value of …"

A suggestion when your children are tweens or teens: Rarely give advice. After all, who wants a constant monologue of should and should not? But when you decide it is important to educate or correct, share your perspective when they can hear it and heed it, that is, when your relationship is good and you both have some time to really think and share together.

I remember a teen I counseled. I had driven up to his school mid-day and there was a fire engine parked outside. The principal asked me to see him. I told the principal I didn't have time for another counseling case. He pleaded, saying, "This kid gets the whole school going. I don't know how he does it, but at least twice a week he gets whole groups of students in complete uproar. I have fire engines or police here at least twice a week. He never fights, but he gets everyone else to. Please see him." This was an outstanding principal who had already gone through his tools. I reluctantly agreed.

I asked this young man, let's call him "Tim," why he thought he had been asked to see me. Tim accurately told me the reason. I minimized the problem, saying, "So you don't have a problem with your hands or your feet, just with your mouth." He smiled and said, "Yeah." He didn't want to talk much, but loved to draw, so he would draw and then share. In the five months I saw Tim, I only gave him six bits of reflective sharing, commenting on what he was experiencing and sharing my perspective about the benefit of another way of looking at the situation or dealing with it. However, after a couple of months, the fire engines and the police were no longer making unscheduled visits. After five months, someone stole his skateboard and he handled it appropriately. I said to him, "Months ago this would have really gotten you going. You would have gotten different groups of kids involved and created uproar. Why didn't you?" Tim looked at me and said, "I thought about what you said." Much to my surprise, he then repeated the six bits of advice I had shared over the months.

Our relationship had become a good one. He trusted my caring and respect. With teens who are in trouble, resisting change, and not caring how many negative consequences you throw at them, work on the relationship and occasionally share in a personal way. No force. Recognize the soul. Each person has beauty deep within. Share your perspective when there is receptivity and when it is natural to do so. Sometimes less is more.

C) Exploring values in the real world

When a child feels bad about worrisome, sad, tragic or violent things she has heard about in the neighborhood, community, country or world, listen.

Perhaps there is bullying, a suicide or violence. Our receptivity and ability to listen consistently is one of the things which allows children to continue sharing. When the child shares, actively listen. When the upset settles, explore values. Perhaps ask: "Why do you think this happened?" Listen. "What value do you think would have helped prevent this?" Listen and positively acknowledge.

After listening, perhaps help give meaning to the situation so it becomes more understandable. For example: "Some people act hatefully because their hope and love has dried up inside. No matter how someone feels, it is wrong to be hateful and harm others."

Sometimes you may be feeling a little concerned yourself about an event in the world. While it is not good to share these events with young children, occasionally an event offers an appropriate opportunity to engage in a values discussion with older teens. They may come home from school with concerns about larger social issues. If so, share or listen as appropriate, and then look at the values and anti-values. For example: What do you think the factors are that contribute to this problem? What are the anti-values which create those factors? What values are needed? What actions would living those values result in? Perhaps take up her questions for one factor.

You may wish to share your view of which value or values would help the situation and perhaps help the child see the situation in a larger context, perhaps a historical or spiritual context. However, if the teen is really interested in the concern, enjoy the conversation and encourage her to learn more about it. Your teen may be interested in researching the subject or contributing to a solution. Getting involved in a values-based concern cements the value as part of their self-identity.

D) Discuss

Create an open, respectful space for discussing and sharing. Talking about feelings in relation to values questions can clarify viewpoints and develop empathy. Discussions in a supportive environment can be healing. When there is caring receptivity and openness, negativity can be accepted and gently questioned. "Why do you think _____?" Actively listen to their response. When this is done with genuine respect, young people who are resentful begin to drop the defenses which necessitate their negativity. When the positive values under the negativity are understood and validated, children feel valued, gradually allowing them to experience the freedom to act differently.

E) Exploration of ideas

When children show interest in a values-based problem or project, be receptive to their interest and concern or excitement. Ask: "Why do you think that happens?" "What is the relationship between _____ and _____?" "What would you like to happen?" "What are different ways to do that?" It can be helpful to mind-map a value and its anti-value. For example, it is much easier to understand the importance of honesty, and its effects, when it is contrasted with corruption and its long-term effects. There are unlimited ways to explore, so step back and enjoy the ride, supporting their interest in learning more, research and/or doing something positive. Perhaps there is a club or a group of youth interested in the same topic. Be receptive to their creative ideas and offer a bit of direction if needed. When there is passion about something, real learning takes place naturally. Perhaps they are concerned about the toxic plastic soup in the ocean gyres, pollution in rivers or the lack of potable water. Be supportive of their effort to make a positive difference.

F) *Skill development — Personal social and emotional skills*

It is wonderful to care about peace, but children also need the social and emotional skills to be able to live their values. If you have been sharing stories about peace, love, kindness, respect, honesty and compassion, and modeling those values, they will have love for those values. As you play with them, engage in Us Time and actively listen to them, they will feel loved and valued and be better able to tune into their own feelings and intuition. They will become resilient. As you engage them in Peace Tent or Peace Place activities and create the opportunity for them to fill themselves up with peace, love and respect, they will improve their ability to self-regulate and concentrate. As you communicate positively, encourage, give choices, and use I-messages well, they are learning positive communication skills. Notice if your child needs to learn a communication skill. If so, find a good time to model it and reinforce the use.

As we learn to not blame and shame, they will learn not to blame and shame. As we learn to manage our anger, we can help them manage their anger. As we use logical consequences in a kind and fair manner and allow them responsibilities, they will become more responsible and think about the consequences of their actions. As we encourage, they will learn to encourage others. Your optimism and guidance are invaluable and help them work through challenges. Your passion about values helps them explore the meaning of life.

There are many personal social and emotional skills in the *Living Values Activities* books, such as learning to set goals and use empowering thoughts instead of discouraging thoughts. Your family may wish to choose a value of focus — for a month or two or three. Glance through a values unit if you wish and choose a few activities which appeal to you or you think will appeal to your children. Have fun exploring — and let them build on the activities with their own ideas.

G) Skill development — Interpersonal communication skills

As we deal with children squabbling and teach them conflict resolution skills, we are teaching them how to get along with others and solve problems. Experiment doing this with the values of peace, respect and love. This helps them emotionally and cognitively understand the benefits of creating positive solutions. Simultaneously, they develop alternative thinking skills so they can think on their feet in difficult situations.

If family projects are a struggle, you may wish to do a few cooperation activities, including one of cooperative communication. Have a good time with it and let your creativity flow. Perhaps make up songs or create colorful slogans. Perhaps the kids might like to video a skit/sketch on lack-of-cooperation versus cooperation.

If you choose to have family time every night around the bed of the youngest child or do bedtime rituals which include building kindness and gratitude, you will be teaching them about the importance of family and embedding in them the interpersonal skills of closeness. Our way of being teaches them a way to be. Quietly observe their interpersonal communication skills as they grow. If something seems lacking, think of a positive way to introduce and nurture the new skill or perspective.

H) Society, environment and the world

As I look at the world, I see many people who use their values only in their family and with their circle of friends. They do not use them for those outside their circle. This is clearly seen in the history of slavery. The modern-day version is seen in far too many companies and corporations in both developed and developing countries. Is it logical or even remotely just for a CEO to earn 30 million while the workers earn so little that providing adequate food and shelter for the family is a struggle? One of the LVE activities in the young adult book asks students to design a company at which the owner has love for the employees and another company at which the owner does not have love for the employees. Please imagine this in your mind…. Now imagine this with the values of respect and appreciation…. Is there a difference in relationships, work conditions and wages? Is there a difference in availability of child care and health care? Is there a difference in the food and shelter the workers can afford? Is there a difference in the workers in happiness, productivity and absenteeism? Is there a difference in the safety of the workplace and the community? Yes.

I asked one of my favorite wise women, Dadi Janki, a question about the difference between a virtue and a value and liked her answer very much. She said, "A virtue is a quality you naturally have. A value is using that virtue all the time." If every parent decided to live their values at home, in their circle of friends and in the workplace and community, and taught their children to do the same, what do you think would happen within ten years? And twenty? Wonderful possibilities. Each one of us can create beauty in the world.

If you would like to explore values and the environment with your children, you may wish to download the *Living Green Values* stories and activities. They are available on the livingvalues.net website free of charge in honor of the Earth and her oceans. You may wish to do a practical project or two as your contribution to the Earth.

If your children are older, you may already be discussing news and world problems seen through the media. Include two branches for the community and the world if you mind-map a relevant value and its opposite anti-value. Values are a wonderful way to introduce systems thinking: how one thing can affect many things. Indeed there are innumerable applications of respect, honesty, love and cooperation.

I) Creative expression

Create the opportunity for your children to artistically express their thoughts about values and values projects they love. Perhaps they've already drawn a peaceful world, painted the feeling of peace and created a poem about peace, love or respect. Would they like to paint a mural, make up songs about simplicity, happiness or unity, and create skits about the effect of violence, drugs or bullying? Perhaps teens would like to create skits or videos about a problem in the community and values-based solutions. Perhaps they can find songs about values in their culture or create new songs. Let them creatively display their positive solutions, dance values applications and act out alternatives. The creative process can bring new understanding and insights; the value becomes more meaningful as it becomes their own. When children express their ideas about values artistically, it helps the value become a firmer part of their self-identity.

J) Integrating values in life

Allow your children to apply values-based behaviors in their lives — with the family, society and the environment. Create the opportunity for them to do special projects which exemplify different values. For example, if they are interested in helping the Earth and her animals they may wish to have an organic garden, help clean up a stream or volunteer at an animal rescue center. They may be interested in the values of love and responsibility and want to help children learn to read or collect books for children who have few in the home. Let them create dramas and music about the importance of being kind to all others. Help them post positive messages. Allow them to express their concerns and make a positive difference. The ability to make a difference builds their commitment to values, their skills and confidence — and helps the world be a kinder, more caring place for us all.

~ Cited Materials ~

Bowden, J. (2007). *The 150 Healthiest Foods on Earth.* Gloucester, MA: Fair Winds Press.

Bowes, L., Maughan, B., Caspi, A., Moffitt, T. E., & Arseneault, L. (2010). *Families promote emotional and behavioural resilience to bullying: Evidence of an environmental effect.* Journal of Child Psychology and Psychiatry 51 (7), 809–817.

Eimers, R. and Aitchison, R. (1977). *Effective Parents, Responsible Children.* McGraw-Hill.

Everyday Challenges: Children and Bullying. www.surrey.ca/Parent_bully_tools. pdf. (Accessed April 2014.)

Gordon, S. *6 Types of Bullying.* http://bullying.about.com/od/Basics/a/6-Types-Of-Bullying.htm. (Accessed April 2014.)

Italie, L. (2010). *Parents may not recognize bullies: Many fail to see aggressive behavior in their own children.* Children's Health. http://www.nbcnews. com/id/36460872/ns/health-childrens_health/t/parents-may-not-recognize-bullies/#.Uz2dsPldX14 (Accessed April 2014.)

Jameson, M. (2008, September 8). *C'mon, get happy.* Los Angeles Times, Health.

Lickona, T. (1993). "The Return of Character Education." *Educational Leadership* 51(3). Available online: www.ascd.org/readingroom/edlead/9311 /lickona.html.

Lyubomirsky, S. (2008). *The How of Happiness: A Scientific Approach to Getting the Life You Want.* New York: The Penguin Press.

Page, L. (2004). *Healthy Healing: A Guide to Self-Healing for Everyone (12th Edition)*. Healthy Healing, Inc.

Stopbullying.gov. A website of the U.S. Department of Health and Human Services. *Bullying Definition*. http://www.stopbullying.gov/what-is-bullying/definition. (Accessed April 2014.)

The Children's Assessment Center. *Child Sexual Abuse Facts*. http://cachouston.org/child-sexual-abuse-facts. (Accessed April 2014.)

The Gottman Institute. *The Positive Perspective*. http://www.gottmanblog.com/2012/12/the-positive-perspective-dr-ottmans.html. (Accessed April 2014.)

Tillman, D. (2000). *Living Values Activities for Children Ages 8–14*. Deerfield, FL: HCI.

Tillman, D. (2003). *Living Values Activities for Street Children Ages 7–10*. Restricted access; LVE training required.

Tillman, D. (2003). *Living Values Activities for Street Children Ages 11–14*. Restricted access; LVE training required.

Tillman, D. (2000). *Living Values Activities for Young Adults*. Deerfield, FL: HCI.

Tillman, D. (2000). *Living Values Parent Groups: A Facilitator Guide*. Deerfield, FL: HCI.

Tillman, D. and Hsu, D. (2000). *Living Values Activities for Children Ages 3–7*. Deerfield, FL: HCI.

Tillman, D. and Quera Colomina, P. (2000). *LVEP Educator Training Guide*. Deerfield, FL: HCI.

~ Acknowledgements ~

I would like to thank my Living Values Education colleagues, family, friends and the many parents around the world who encouraged me to write this book. Special thanks to Caroline Druiff, Susan Hustad, Kurt Krueger and Peter Williams, who read the book as the chapters were still unfolding, for their comments, enthusiasm, love and encouragement. Loving thanks to Diane Holden and Kevin Helms for their gracious editing help, David Warrick Jones for his wonderful assistance with the cover, Ary Woodbridge for her laughter and photographic skill, and Joanne Corcoran for her instant cooperation and the three illustrations. Loving appreciation to the LVEP, Inc., board of directors and my yogi family in California and England for their interest, enthusiasm, love and support.

A special thank you to Health Communications, Inc. (HCI), the publisher of the Living Values Education series of books, for their belief in values education, their support over the years, and permission to use excerpts from several of the books I wrote previously. Loving gratitude to the Brahma Kumaris for planting the seed of Living Values many years ago and asking me to help create Living Values Education for children and educators around the world. I rarely thought about values previously and have learned so much thinking about this powerful tool in relation to children, education, parenting and the state of our world. I appreciate immensely the educators and parents who have had the willingness and courage to live their values, giving children the gift of moving toward their potential.

All love and good wishes to the children, parents, educators, friends and family members who starred in the stories of this book! I enjoyed being with each one of you and very much appreciate the experiences we shared. Thank you for being an important part of my life.

And, thank you to the parents, caregivers, aunts, uncles and grandparents reading this. I know many of us share the hope that someday all the children in the world will be loved, respected, valued, understood and safe. Enjoy being mindful … as you help create a difference by bringing more peace, love, respect and wisdom into your home, neighborhood, society and the world.

~ About the Author ~

Diane G. Tillman brings together in this book her expertise as a Licensed Educational Psychologist, School Psychologist, Marriage and Family Therapist, international values-education authority, and meditator.

Diane worked with thousands of parents during more than 20 years as a School Psychologist in a public school district in southern California. She was involved in the diagnosis and treatment of regular students and students with special needs, consultation with teachers and parents regarding academic, behavioral and emotional disorders, and direct counseling with children and families. She also provided guidance services and facilitated parent groups.

Diane helped create a global values-education initiative in 1996. She is the primary author of 15 resource books on values education. The five books published by Health Communications, Inc., as the Living Values Education series won the Teachers' Choice 2002 award and are published in 12 languages. The LVE at-risk resource books help educators engage in a values development and healing process for children affected by war, street children, youth in need of drug rehabilitation, at-risk youth and young offenders. Her latest educational resource book, in cooperation with educators from Brazil and China, contains stories and activities for living green values.

Diane circled the globe numerous times to conduct seminars on personal development and values education in more than 30 countries. In her personal development seminars, she integrates the knowledge of psychology with spirituality and meditative tools, drawn from her practice of raja yoga meditation for 33 years. She has enjoyed facilitating Living Values Education seminars for UNESCO, ministries of education, educators, parent facilitators and street children agencies, at universities, schools and retreat centers, and in refugee camps.

Diane served two terms on the board of directors of the Association for Living Values Education International (ALIVE), the parenting body for ALIVE Associates and Focal Points for LVE in more than 60 countries. She is currently a member of the International Advisory Committee of ALIVE and on the Living Values: An Educational Program, Inc., board of directors, the non-profit ALIVE Associate in the USA.